COURSE TECHNOLOGY
CENGAGE Learning™
Professional • Technical • Reference

The Art of
STOP-MOTION ANIMATION

INCLUDES CD-

* 000255921 *

D1340343

riebe

word by

ohnson

Co-director, *Corpse Bride*

COURSE TECHNOLOGY
CENGAGE Learning™

The Art of Stop-Motion Animation
Ken A. Priebe

Publisher and General Manager, Thomson Course Technology PTR:
Stacy L. Hiquet

Associate Director of Marketing:
Sarah O'Donnell

Manager of Editorial Services:
Heather Talbot

Marketing Manager:
Heather Hurley

Acquisitions Editor:
Megan Belanger

Marketing Coordinator:
Meg Dunkerly

Project Editor:
Dan Foster, Scribe Tribe

Technical Reviewer:
Lionel Ivan Orozco

PTR Editorial Services Coordinator:
Elizabeth Furbish

Interior Layout Tech:
Bill Hartman

Cover Designer:
Mike Tanamachi

CD-ROM Producer:
Brandon Penticuff

Indexer:
Katherine Stimson

Proofreader:
Karen Gill

For product information and technology assistance, contact us at
Cengage Learning Customer & Sales Support, 1-800-354-9706

For permission to use material from this text or product, submit all requests online at **cengage.com/permissions**. Further permissions questions can be e-mailed to **permissionrequest@cengage.com**.

Cover credits: *The Nightmare Before Christmas* cover images courtesy of Touchstone/Burton/Di Novi/The Kobal Collection. Puppet cover images by Ken Priebe, Stephanie Mahoney, and Jason Vanderhill. Ken Priebe photo courtesy of Frozen Reflections.

All other trademarks are the property of their respective owners.

Library of Congress Catalog Card Number: 2006923481

ISBN-10: 1-59863-244-2

ISBN-13: 978-1-59863-244-6

Course Technology, a part of Cengage Learning
20 Channel Center Street
Boston, MA 02210
USA

Cengage Learning is a leading provider of customized learning solutions with office locations around the globe, including Singapore, the United Kingdom, Australia, Mexico, Brazil, and Japan. Locate your local office at: **international.cengage.com/region**.

Cengage Learning products are represented in Canada by Nelson Education, Ltd.

For your lifelong learning solutions, visit **courseptr.com**.

Visit our corporate Web site at **cengage.com**.

Printed in the United States of America
2 3 4 5 6 7 8 12 11 10 09

*This book is dedicated to my amazing
wife Janet and daughter Ariel.
I love you both and thank you for
your never-ending inspiration.*

Foreword

If you are holding this book, you have a passionate (perhaps unhealthy) interest in stop-motion. Maybe you're a fan. Perhaps you're a teacher. You might be a professional animator, or maybe you're thinking about pursuing a career in stop-motion, and you're searching for useful information that will guide you along your chosen path.

Well, you've hit the mother lode, because within these pages you'll find top-secret tricks of the trade, insightful interviews, and practical instruction on every aspect of stop-motion animation. This book is an invaluable resource for the seasoned professional and the budding young student alike.

But there is one piece of practical information that should not be overlooked: *Most animators work on computers now. And it makes things a hell of a lot easier.*

Gone are the days of standing for hours on end, feet aching, squinting against the hot lights as sweat runs into your eyes, hunched over, hands cramping, babbling, begging, cursing in isolation like a deranged witch doctor performing some unholy ritual as, by sheer force of will, you wrestle life into a foam-rubber puppet or a greasy lump of clay.

All that seems a bit unnecessary when you consider the technologically advanced animators of today, cradled in ergonomic comfort, computers humming softly from the womb-like darkness of air-conditioned offices, while their clean, delicate fingers lightly pat the keyboard and gently prod the mouse.

Pity the poor, old-fashioned stop-mo animator slaving away at his one-man puppet show, head throbbing, teeth grinding, as he mentally dissects his performance into tiny slivers of time that must then be reassembled, frame by frame, like a fragile house of cards, to be left behind like a trail of breadcrumbs dropped in the forest as evidence of his lonely passage.

That sounds like a lot of effort when today's enlightened frame-farmers work by committee, pooling their talents as efficiently as bees in a hive, creating polished performances that can be endlessly refined through a democratic process of approvals. No more pressure to deliver a shot in one take, to improvise in the moment, to forge straight ahead guided only by your instinct, experience, and skill.

Who needs that kind of stress? Why, dear reader, in these modern times, would an animator choose to forego these technological triumphs in favor of the outmoded and archaic medium of stop-motion?

If you're still holding this book, you know why.

So read on, and meet some kindred spirits....

Mike Johnson
Co-director of Tim Burton's *Corpse Bride* and founder of Fat Cactus Films.

Acknowledgments

Through the long hours and late nights writing and animating for this book, it would not have been possible without the generous support and contributions of many others: Thanks first and foremost to my Lord Jesus Christ, the ultimate animator who makes all things new. Thanks to my wife, best friend, and creative companion Janet, who endured the slings and arrows of her first pregnancy during the whole process, sharing her talents and advice, helping with photos and graphics, and ultimately keeping me focused. To our little animator on the way, we can't wait to meet you!

Thanks to my parents for supporting me and giving me wings, and to my brother Jonathan and my brother Dan who helped me with my first clay animation experiments many years ago. Thanks to my father-in-law John Worth for lending his skills and tools, to my entire extended family in the US and Canada for their support and inspiration, and to my church family at Cedar Park for their prayers and enthusiasm. And to Lucas for being a good dog. Rest in peace my friend!

Thanks to Frank Beaver and Alan Young at the University of Michigan for helping me get started with my first student films, to Jim Pinard for his inspiring work and contribution, and to my friend Brandon Moses for acting in my film. Extra special thanks to my animation "Obi-Wan," Steve Stanchfield, for kick-starting my career and passion for animation, and for providing many of the history images for this book.

Thanks to the incredible students and staff at VanArts, to Lee Mishkin for laying the foundation, to Charles Phillips and Marcos Gonzalez for their help, and a big thanks to Mike Brown for the technical advice and assistance! To all of the students who have taken my stop-motion course over the years, I have learned so much from you and your creativity. Thanks to my former students who contributed their work: Anthony Silverston, Andy Simpson, Jason Vanderhill, Matt Hooker, Stephanie Mahoney, Nicole Tremblay, Luke Wareing, Darren Lee, Junko Ogawa, José Torrico, Yatindranath Shinde, Dharmali Patel, and to Katie Nielsen for her wonderful sculptures. Thanks to Margaret McCollough and the wonderful staff at Glen Lyon Norfolk School, and to Riley, Julian, and Renee for their enthusiasm in keeping stop-motion alive. Thanks also to Ken Southworth for his wisdom and to Bob Godfrey for his voice and inspiration.

Extra special thanks to my interview subjects David Bowes, Dave Thomas, Nick Hilligoss, Anthony Scott, Larry Larson, and Lynne Pritchard for the generous gift of their time and advice and for the contribution of images. To others who contributed their support, time, comments, and/or permission and assistance for images and content: Paul Moldovanos, Ann Marie Fleming, Tim Hittle, Serge Bromberg, Will Vinton, Quintin Rice, Ray Harryhausen, Jerry Beck, L.B. Martin-Starewitch, Mike Brent, Marc Spess, Rick Goldschmidt, Arnold Leibovit, Michael Stennick, Milewski Ragnhild at the National Film Board of Canada, Premavision Studios, Kathi Zung, Kevin Harte, Bruno Moreira, Pat Matthews at Grace & Wild Studios, Tom Perzanowski and Megan Harris at CCS, and Cole Campbell, Russell Papp, Chris Calvi, Rob Ronning, Jim Pescitelli with Bowes Productions.

Special thanks to my project editor Dan Foster, and to technical editor Lionel Ivan Orozco for images and fine tuning of my manuscript, and to the entire staff at Thomson Course Technology for making this book a reality.

And last but not least, my acquisitions editor Megan Belanger, who initially e-mailed me out of the blue and asked if I would be interested in writing this book, who has been a guiding light throughout the whole process. This has been a life-changing experience for me and my family, and I cannot thank you enough.

This book is for all of you, for the community of stop-motion artists who frequent StopMotionAnimation.com, and for all who love this challenging, rewarding art form.

Happy Animating!

About the Author

Ken Priebe earned a BFA from the University of Michigan School of Art & Design, majoring in film & animation. He has worked as a 2D animator for several children's games and short films for Thunderbean Animation and Bigfott Studios. He has developed curriculum and taught stop-motion animation at Vancouver Institute of Media Arts (VanArts) and for the Academy of Art University Cybercampus. He is also an independent filmmaker, writer, puppeteer, animation history fanatic and movie reviewer for HollywoodJesus.com. Ken lives near Vancouver, BC with his graphic artist wife Janet and daughter Ariel.

Contents

Introduction xiii

Part I
Overview 1

Chapter 1
Appeal and History of Stop-Motion Animation...3
Appeal of the Medium 3
The Beginnings of Stop-Motion Animation 8
Cut-Out Animation 12
Dinosaurs to Dinosaurs: The Life and Death of Creature Effects 13
Miniature Worlds on the Big Screen 19
Stop-Motion on the Small Screen 26
Feature Presentations 31

Chapter 2
The Stop-Motion Industry 35
The Production Pipeline 35
    Step 1: The Idea 35
    Step 2: Concept Art and Design 36
    Step 3: Storyboarding 37
    Step 4: Sound Recording and Exposure Sheets 37
    Step 5: Story Reel 38
    Step 6: Designing and Building Puppets and Sets ..38
    Step 7: Animation 40
    Step 8: Post-Production 43
Opportunities 43

Chapter 3
An Interview with David Bowes 51

Part II
Creating Animation..........61

Chapter 4
What You Need 63
Cameras 63
    Film 64
    Video 66
    Digital SLR Cameras 68
    Webcams 69
    Tripod 69
Computer and Capture Card 70
Software 71
Set 75
Lights 77
Supplies 80

Chapter 5
Basic Animation..................83
Timing and Spacing 84
The Problem of Gravity 89
The Bouncing Ball 92

Overlapping Action and Follow-Through 97
    The Animated Vine 98
    Bouncing Ball with Pigtails 104
Anticipation, Action, Reaction 108
The 80-Frame Morph 113
Basic Performance 118

Chapter 6
An Interview with Dave Thomas 121

Chapter 7
Building Puppets 129
Character Design 130
Evolution of a Character: Hamish McFlea 135
Other Characters with Doll Armatures 141
Ball-and-Socket Armatures 146
Wire Armatures 149
Building a Simple Wire Puppet 150
Molds and Foam Latex Methods 158
Latex Build-Up Puppets 166
Clay Puppets 173
Other Techniques 177

Chapter 8
An Interview with Anthony Scott................181

Chapter 9
Puppet Animation.......................................187
Posing 187
Walking 191
Action Analysis 197
Facial Expressions 199
    Blinks 204
Dialogue 205
Motion Blur 214

Chapter 10
An Interview with Larry Larson.................215

Chapter 11
Sets and Props...223
Setting the Stage 223
    Securing the Set 226
Interior Sets 226
Exterior Sets 228
Alternative Set Methods 232
    Chroma-Key Compositing 233
Props 241

Chapter 12
An Interview with Nick Hilligoss 245

Part III
Showing Your Stuff 253

Chapter 13
Making a Film 255
Ideas and Film Types 256
    Narrative Films 259
    Objects with Personality 260
    Characterization Films 262
    Abstract Films 262
Storyboarding and Editing 263
    Shots 263
    Angles 267
    Camera Moves 269
    Composition 269
    Lighting 273
    Editing 275
Getting It Made 282
    Format 282
    Sound 283
    Titles 283
    Schedules 283

Chapter 14
An Interview with Lynne Pritchard 285

Chapter 15
Distribution..297
Demo Reels 297
Personal Web Sites 299
Internet 299
    www.stopmoshorts.com 299
    www.atomfilms.com 299
    www.ifilm.com 300
Festivals 300
    Spike and Mike's Animation Festival 301
    The Animation Show 301

Chapter 16
Conclusion 303

Appendix A
Suggested Supplies for Stop-Motion
Animation...305

Appendix B
Stop-Motion Animation Studios................309

Appendix C
Stop-Motion Animation Courses................311

Appendix D
Timeline of Important Events in the
History of Stop-Motion Animation.............315

Glossary 319

Bibliography and Further Reading............325

Index..329

Introduction

Stop-motion animation is a filmmaking technique that works like this: you take a picture of a puppet or object, then move it a little bit and take another picture. Then you move it again, and take another picture. By repeating this process hundreds of times and playing the individual pictures back in sequence, the illusion is created that the puppet or object moves by itself and comes to life! Believe it or not, there are people who devote much of their lives to doing this very thing, in order to tell stories and entertain an audience. It is likely you have seen a stop-motion film somewhere and been inspired by it, which may have led you to pick up this book and learn more about it. If stop-motion animation excites you so much that you might want to try it yourself, welcome to the club! You are now part of a community of artists who lurk in dark corners, contributing to this amazing underground art form. Compared to other forms of filmmaking, stop-motion animation has always had an under-appreciated existence, very much on the cutting-edge, which is part of what attracts many of us to it in the first place.

For me, stop-motion animation is something that I felt was always sneaking up on me and then finally grabbed me at the right time. As a child growing up in Grosse Pointe, a suburb of Detroit, Michigan, I loved animated films, and I would see the odd stop-motion film here and there without really knowing what I was looking at. The first glimpse I ever saw into how it was done was a behind-the-scenes television special for *The Empire Strikes Back*, when I saw Phil Tippett bringing a Tauntaun to life frame by frame. In later years, Will Vinton's *Meet the Raisins* special really caught my attention in regards to how expressive and lifelike his clay characters were. One day, while watching an episode of *Ren & Stimpy* on Nickelodeon, the show was interrupted unexpectedly by a film called *Creature Comforts*, which blew me away and piqued my interest even further. Upon attending the University of Michigan School of Art, *The Nightmare Before Christmas* and Wallace and Gromit in *The Wrong Trousers* were both released, and by that point I was so inspired that I decided I had to try this technique myself. Animation was not really taught formally where I was, so I managed to combine my art courses with as many filmmaking courses as possible and start teaching myself. I started making 16mm films with Monty Python-style cut-outs and then tried my hand at animating clay and was fascinated when I got to see the results projected. My first experiments led to an independent study in my final year, where I created a live-action/clay animation silent film called *Snot Living*. During this time I also got to work in 2D animation with a local animator named Steve Stanchfield, who taught me how to improve my animation and gave me a real passion for the films of the past. Having now been consumed by the animation bug, I discovered a one-year program in Vancouver, Canada, at a school called VanArts, and moved there in 1998 to further my training in Classical Animation under the master animator Lee Mishkin. The school offered me the opportunity to stay a second year and make a film, so I decided to try and return to my stop-motion roots. Once again, I created my own opportunities to shoot my film using a new software that had just come out called Stop Motion Pro. While working on my student project, someone suggested I should offer a workshop for some students at VanArts who were interested in trying stop-motion. I started teaching workshops, and they soon grew into a 12-week part-time weekend course which I have taught there ever since. My student film, *Bad News*, was never completed, but the trade-off was full-time work at VanArts as an admissions advisor and meeting a cute animation student named Janet, who I eventually married in 2001. Having established roots in Vancouver, I later started another film that is still in progress, *Storytime with Nigel*, combining stop-motion with 2D animation. Alongside my own projects, the main thing that has kept me going with stop-motion animation has been my students from all over the world with whom I have shared in pursuing this wonderful craft (see Figure I.1).

Figure I.1 Student José Osorio Torrico hard at work.

In the art world, there has been and always will be a "clash of the titans," you could say, between artists with a vision for art and businessmen with a vision for money. Stop-motion animation is often referred to as a medium for artists rather than for producers. Right now, due to the monumental success of computer-generated (CG) animation by Pixar and other filmmakers, there is what some would call an over-saturation of this brand of digital animation. Mainstream Hollywood has seen the dollar signs racked in by these CG films and has concluded that this is the best way to make money…and, oh yes, movies too. Producers, directors, and animators alike also like CG because it's easy to change things and go over the animation repeatedly until they get it right. Stop-motion does not typically allow for going back to make changes to please a client or producer; once a scene is animated after long hours of hard work, it is finished. Ultimately, as technology grows and computers get faster, production for CG animation also gets faster, and cheaper. When faced with the budget for a CG production versus the vast amount of expensive studio space, materials, equipment, and specialized talent required for a stop-motion production, investors and producers will most likely go for the cheaper CG route, especially in our fast-food culture that wants everything *now*. To be green-lit, stop-motion productions have always relied on the dedication of talented craftsmen who love to create these miniature worlds from scratch, combined with creative management who believe in the project.

So long as there are good stories to back them up, there is nothing inherently wrong with the CG films and effects being made today. I quite enjoy some of them, and every medium has its place in the animation industry. The main concern that I have, which I already get glimpses of from working in an animation school, is that young people today growing up with CG films and video games are looking only at the final product. They see that it is made with a computer, so they think that if they learn everything about computers, they can be animators. However, animation is an art form that for most of its history has been created with pencil and paper, or a lump of clay, perhaps. The computer can mimic the same effects created with these materials, but what will happen to these original art forms if they are not learned first, or at all? Luckily, today's major studios still recognize the value of measuring an animator's skill by their artistic ability rather than their technical knowledge, but what happens if there are no longer any young artists who know how to create art without plugging something in? My friend Ken Southworth, who worked at Disney, MGM, and Hanna-Barbera studios from the 1940s through the 1970s, describes an animator as being "one-third artist, one-third actor, and one-third engineer." There should always be a balance between all of these skills: the ability to draw and create art, to create a performance, and to understand the technical side of how to put it all together. The technology behind animation is always changing, but art and performance are the heart and soul that never change, regardless of the medium used.

Sometimes I hear common people complain about a stiff, lifeless quality to some of the CG films being made, and this is simply what happens when the traditional skills are ignored in any medium. It is also why most people perk up when a good stop-motion film is released every now and then. It is a medium that people love to watch! They love watching real physical objects move on the screen with a life of their own, bathed in real lights on real sets. It truly is a fantastic magic trick that people really respond to. I think part of this fascination deals with the subconscious mind, in that we all have memories of playing with dolls, action figures or Play-Doh from our childhood, and the tactile senses that come with it. So to see these kinds of materials come to life on screen is a kind of surreal nostalgia trip that harkens us back to old pastimes and imagining the life we would give to our toys. All observation of animation involves the senses of sight and sound, but for the one creating it, stop-motion also combines this with the senses of smell (although not all of them pleasant) and more importantly, of touch. Like King Midas turning all he touched into gold, the sensation of touching a puppet and feeling the life inside it is another discipline that takes us back to simpler times and a world of magic. There is also something strangely satisfying about seeing a puppet made of clay have its own life on screen, while at the same time seeing fingerprints of the animator dance around on its clay surface. It is much like leaning in close to a painting to see all of the brushstrokes and canvas texture leaking through, and then stepping back to see the wonderful illusion it creates. The mark of the creator is evident in the work itself, which is why we still travel miles to see the pyramids or an original Leonardo or Picasso. It is all part of the same human impulse for staying connected to our past by exposing ourselves to great art. Stop-motion animation satisfies this hunger within us in a way that no other medium can, and that is why it must and will continue, whether it is through the occasional million-dollar studio production or the lonely artist living on noodles in their basement.

As much as computer technology has dominated the practice of creating animation, the irony is that the same technology has made stop-motion more accessible and better looking than ever before. What used to be only possible with expensive film equipment can now be done with a webcam on the same machine you use to check your e-mail. The Internet has also opened a whole new world of possibilities for showcasing films for all to enjoy and for artists to share ideas. The technical tools of the present and future are allowing people of all ages to enhance and improve the quality of this unique art form. The purpose of this book is to serve as a launching pad for you to get started with creating your own stop-motion animation. It is not meant to be an exhaustive document of every single skill or technique required to master all aspects of the craft, because there are so many: drawing, sculpting, lighting, storytelling, acting, molding, casting, welding, brazing, designing, woodworking, and the list goes on. You would need an entire encyclopedia of books to cover the multifaceted disciplines of stop-motion, and ultimately, the best way to learn the medium is to just do it! This book will help you understand the history of past stop-motion films, what the animation industry is like, how to set up your own studio space, how to build puppets and animate them, and how to plan your own films, so you can carry on with your own experimentation. The exercises and lessons are based on the animation and film training I have received and the lessons I have learned in my own experience creating and teaching stop-motion, passing them along from one artist to another. The book also contains interviews with six other stop-motion artists who share their knowledge and experience working in different corners of the industry, from feature films to independent productions. If you are a beginner and have never animated before, the basic exercises in this book will help you get started learning the principles that make animation work best. If you are a CG or traditional animator, these exercises may also help you get back to the basics and enjoy the experience of getting your hands dirty, and hopefully they'll help you improve your animation skills.

In one of my favorite stop-motion films, *Closed Mondays* by Will Vinton and Bob Gardiner, the central character looks at the camera and says, "I wonder what makes it work!" After reading through this book and using it to create your own animation, you will know what makes it work, but make sure you keep wondering.

PART I

Overview

Chapter 1
Appeal and History of Stop-Motion Animation

Appeal of the Medium

In addition to stop-motion, there are two other major animation mediums that exist today and that are mentioned in this book for comparative purposes: 2D animation (also referred to as classical or traditional) and CG (computer-generated) animation (also referred to as 3D or digital). The 2D medium was first made famous in the U.S. by Winsor McCay, who amazed audiences with this novel idea of "drawings that move." Since then, some of the artists responsible for animation's success include Walt Disney, Tex Avery, Chuck Jones, and Hayao Miyazaki, to name only a few. The animator creates 12 to 24 separate drawings on individual sheets of paper and then photographs them in sequence. When the photographs are played back in rapid succession, the illusion of movement is given. Today's most popular 2D productions include *The Simpsons, Family Guy, SpongeBob SquarePants*, as well as classic Disney features and the growing cult following of Japanese Anime.

The CG medium began coming to the forefront in the 1980s through special effects for live-action films such as *Tron* and *The Last Starfighter*, which led to the breakthroughs by people like John Lasseter, who directed the first computer animation feature *Toy Story* at Pixar. Animators work with 3D character models that exist inside the virtual reality of a software program. The process is similar to stop-motion in that the models can be moved into positions like a real puppet, and the computer moves the model from one position to the next. All of the lighting and textures are artificially created by the computer, striving to duplicate reality. The medium has become today's most popular, used to create fully CG films like *Shrek, Madagascar*, and *The Incredibles*, as well as more realistic characters that share the screen with live actors in films like *Lord of the Rings*. Video games have also become a groundbreaking vehicle for CG effects and animation.

If you visit any Web forum where animators or animation fans post messages about their craft, you are bound to find a few threads that start with a discussion about 2D versus CG, or CG versus stop-motion, and many pages of heated responses ensue. Few things get some classically trained animators riled up more than how much they believe CG animation pales in comparison to the "old-school" ways of doing things. The reality is that no technique is better than any other. All mediums shine in their own way, and, if done right, they can all be an incredible experience to watch. What it all really comes down to is the story, design, and characters, and how well they are complemented by the medium in which they are created. A film's success does not ride on what medium is used, but rather the effectiveness of the story and the relationships between the characters.

Stop-motion animation has many differences and quirks compared to other mediums that give it its special charm, as well as a few advantages and disadvantages. One example is that in 2D animation, anything can happen because it can simply be drawn. Characters' faces can be more expressive, and anything can squash, stretch, or change shape. Think of the outrageous gags in a Tex Avery cartoon, such as *Red Hot Riding Hood* (1943), or the exaggerated surrealism of shows like *Ren & Stimpy*. These effects would be extremely difficult to achieve in stop-motion, although some slightly successful attempts have been made. CG animation is starting to move more in this direction as the software develops, but it still lacks the linear quality given to the complete freedom that 2D offers. Anything the mind can conceive is simply put on paper, and the most impossible gags can happen. Stop-motion has more limitations in terms of what kinds of movements can be created, and there is also the issue of gravity, which other mediums do not contend with at all. A puppet cannot float in midair on-screen unless something holds it up, but a character on paper or in virtual reality simply needs to be drawn or rendered that way. One major advantage that stop-motion has over other mediums, however, is the fact that issues of perspective and lighting are automatically solved, in that they already exist in real life and don't have to be replicated. Stop-motion uses real lights and real depth of field, with puppets creating their own shadows. In other mediums, especially 2D, this effect must be painstakingly created by the artists who are importing the real world into their work.

In 2D animation, there are two methods that can be used in terms of the order of drawings that are created: pose-to-pose and straight-ahead. In pose-to-pose, the animator determines which poses of the action are most important and draws only those poses first.

For example, if you are animating a baseball pitcher throwing a ball, the main elements of the action would be the first initial pose (see Figure 1.1), the windup, or anticipation (see Figure 1.2), and the pitch (see Figure 1.3). These poses are called the *key* drawings and are drawn first. Then, once the timing of these keys has been determined, the drawings that smooth out the action need to be created to fill in the frames between them. These secondary drawings are called "in-betweens" (see Figure 1.4).

Figure 1.1 The initial pose.

Then all of the keys and in-between drawings are put together in sequence. Computer animators will simply position their character models into the key positions they desire, and the computer will create the in-betweens for them.

Figure 1.2 The windup.

Figure 1.3 The pitch.

Key   In-between   In-between   Key

Figure 1.4 In-between poses create movement between key poses.

1. Appeal and History of Stop-Motion Animation

5

Straight-ahead animation is achieved by starting with the first drawing and then creating each sequential drawing in the order it will be projected to the viewer. This method is rarely used for animating an entire character in 2D. Since the character must appear to be a solid, three-dimensional being, it is extremely difficult to keep the volumes consistent when animating straight-ahead. It is far easier to plan out the keys and go back to fill in the in-betweens. However, in stop-motion, it is exactly the opposite. In fact, straight-ahead is the only way stop-motion can be animated. There are no "keys" or "in-betweens"; each position leads to another, in the proper sequence. Many stop-motion animators like working this way, because it can sometimes leave room for spontaneity and last-minute inspirations for the scene that may pop into their heads while immersed in this slow-motion acting process, whether it be moving a puppet, prop, or vehicle (as in Figure 1.5).

Figure 1.5 Animator Jim Pescitelli on *Twisteeria*. (Copyright Bowes Productions 1998.)

In a 2D animation studio, most often the in-betweens will be created by a different artist than the animator who creates the keys. An in-betweener is a typical entry-level position that most key animators start off in before working their way up. So, generally, in this method, the sequential drawings are created out of order by different artists and put into the proper order for shooting. If you watch the credits of a 2D animation feature, such as *The Lion King*, you will notice that there is an entire team of artists assigned to each character. These studio employees, whether they be key animators or in-betweeners, will draw only one particular character for the entire duration of production. There are no key animators or in-betweeners in a stop-motion studio, because each frame is created by a single animator working on each sequence. When watching a 2D animation sequence, you are watching a performance guided by one supervising animator but created collectively by a team, with each frame initially drawn by a different hand. A stop-motion sequence is a performance created individually by a lone actor baring his or her soul through the puppet (as in Figure 1.6). It's also more common for a stop-motion animator to work on several characters at different points in the film, rather than sticking to only one character.

One of the biggest advantages of stop-motion over the other mediums is the fact that in stop-motion, after the puppets and sets are built and the animation is shot, it's done! Other than editing, adding music and sound effects, and possibly compositing, no more procedures are required. In 2D animation, there are many more steps to the final process. The initial animation is usually done with very rough drawings, which then need to be cleaned up with finer line quality. Then the drawings need to be scanned, colored in with the computer, have lighting effects and shadows added, and composited into the background. The process can take much longer and require more manpower to complete. CG animation has a similar process of an animated scene going through subsequent departments for lighting, texturing, and final rendering. Despite this advantage of stop-motion, the other side of the coin is that because a stop-motion sequence is a

Figure 1.6 Animator Nick Hilligoss at work. (Courtesy of Nick Hilligoss.)

one-time performance, everything has to be planned in advance that much more carefully. In 2D animation, if any changes to the timing or drawings are needed, the animator can simply add or remove drawings or erase any mistakes and redraw them. CG animation can also be tweaked over and over again until it's perfect, and the animator has exhausted every pushed pose and nuance he can dream of to strengthen the animation. That's where CG works as sort of a bridge technique; it has the appearance of stop-motion with the control factor of 2D. It's really an extension of traditional stop-motion, with the ability to do things that stop-motion can't do as easily in terms of flexible expressions and effects.

All of these comparisons really boil down to the fact that *all* animation, regardless of the medium, is time consuming, and each medium has its own pros and cons. Stop-motion in particular is a very specialized technique, and part of the reason it's not seen as much is because of the disadvantages it has in comparison to 2D or CG. It probably requires more patience and perseverance than any other medium, and it may not be a technique that every animator can master. It takes a certain kind of eccentricity to totally pursue it, because it's also the most physically taxing method. But it's always been around and will never go away, because, as I mentioned in the Introduction, people still love it!

The Beginnings of Stop-Motion Animation

If any topic deserves an entire volume of books unto itself, the history of stop-motion animation is definitely one of them. So many different artists have contributed to the stop-motion medium, and many of them are obscure and overlooked. While some have six degrees of separation between them, others have no historical connections to each other. It's a difficult task to condense the entire story of stop-motion animation into a few pages, so I will just focus on some of the artists, films, and trends that have had the most impact, been overlooked by most historians, or serve as the best reference material for this book. The main reason I believe the history of stop-motion needs to be mentioned here is that nobody can expect to move forward in any art form or trade without understanding what has come before him. The past 100 years have created many amazing ideas that should serve as the ultimate inspiration for any stop-motion animator, not only in watching the films, but in knowing about the artists who created them. Knowing your history is so important, because it prevents you from repeating some of the trials and misfortunes of artists past, enhances your own stop-motion work, and should encourage you to try new techniques. Once you become a stop-motion animator, you are then part of its history. Plus, you get to impress your animation colleagues because you know who artists like Starewitch and Svankmeyer are.

Figure 1.7 A zoetrope.

Animation existed before movies were invented. In the late 1800s, there was a renaissance of attempts to create the illusion of movement with inventions that would rapidly display a sequence of drawings before the viewer's eye. The zoetrope (see Figure 1.7) was one such example, where sequential animation drawings were placed inside a drum with equally spaced slits along the outside of the drum. By your spinning the drum and looking directly through it, the drawings would appear to move.

The whole concept behind animation relies on a phenomenon called the "persistence of vision," which basically means that the retina of the eye will retain any image for a brief moment of time until replaced by another image, thus creating an illusion of movement, rather than individual static images. Edward Muybridge started applying this discovery to still photographs by photographing human and animal movements with a row of cameras that each took one successive picture to create a series of separate "frames." Before long, other inventors developed ways to package this process into one camera. In 1882, Etienne Jules Marey of France developed a camera that could take 12 successive pictures per second. Thomas Edison went a step further and developed the first Kinetograph movie camera in 1890. These earliest cameras were operated by a crank that would run the film through while the shutter opened and closed once for each turn of the crank, creating a series of static images that would appear to move when developed and projected.

The discovery of stop-motion animation happened primarily by accident. Accounts differ as to the first actual person to create the "mistake" that led to this art form. According to legend, French stage magician and amateur filmmaker George Melies was shooting a street scene when the film got stuck in the camera gate. During the process of fixing the problem, life continued on as normal on the street and, once the camera was fixed, Melies continued filming where he left off. In the final film, he was amazed to find that pedestrians and vehicles had instantly transformed, or jumped, from one side of the street to another. This experiment led to the idea of deliberately stopping the camera, changing elements of the scene, and starting it up again to create illusions of transformation: people vanishing into thin air, turning into mannequins, or men turning into women and vice versa. The "stopping" of the camera to manipulate objects between captured frames apparently inspired the actual term *stop-motion* still used today. Melies continued experimenting with this technique and incorporating his "trick films" into his magic stage shows. His most famous film using the technique was 1902's *A Trip to the Moon*, the first science-fiction effects picture in film history. Meanwhile, in America, Thomas Edison was making similar film experiments such as *Execution of Mary, Queen of Scots* (1895), in which a real actress was filmed in a guillotine and replaced with a dummy while the camera was not rolling, giving the final illusion of being decapitated. In an age before the Internet or any other kind of instant global communication, it is interesting that similar trick film experiments were happening almost simultaneously in different corners of the world.

The first known American film to use animated puppets was *The Humpty Dumpty Circus* (1898) by Albert E. Smith and J. Stuart Blackton (see Figure 1.8). Blackton continued experimenting with stop-motion puppets, objects, and clay animation techniques in *Fun in a Bakery Shop* (1902), *The Haunted Hotel* (1907), and *Princess Nicotine* (1909), and he also created the first animated film involving sequential drawings on a chalkboard, *Humorous Phases of Funny Faces* (1906). Other stop-motion films were created by filmmakers who remain mysteriously anonymous today, such as the delightful *Automatic Moving Company* (1912), which featured pieces of furniture sliding out of a moving truck, up a set of apartment stairs, and magically setting themselves up inside. The extensive use of clay as an animation medium made its debut in a series of shorts called *Miracles in Mud* from a series entitled *Reel of Knowledge* (see Figure 1.9) Back in France, inspired by the French premieres of Blackton's films, filmmaker Emile Cohl made similar films with animated objects, creating shapes on a tabletop, such as *The Bewitched Matches* (1906; see Figure 1.10).

These early forays into the stop-motion technique amazed audiences during the time they were made, but by the late 1920s, their novelty was overshadowed in America by the animated 2D cartoons of Winsor McCay, Earl Hurd, and Walt Disney. The Fleischer brothers in New York were more experimental in a few early attempts to combine 2D animation with clay animation. The Koko the Clown short *Modeling* (1921) featured the title character escaping from his drawing board and throwing clay at the artists in the studio.

Figure 1.9 *Swat the Fly* (1917) from the *Miracles in Mud* series, by Willie Hopkins.

Figure 1.8 J. Stuart Blackton, one of stop-motion animation's founding fathers.

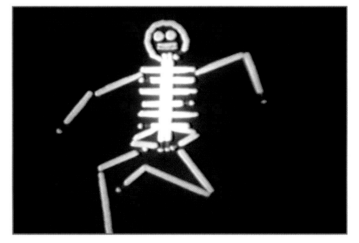

Figure 1.10 Emile Cohl's Bewitched Matches (circa 1906).

Sadly, many of these early films do not exist today, because early film stock was a perishable material unless preserved with the proper care. Early films made before the advent of celluloid were also printed on nitrate, which is highly flammable and was known to burn down entire movie theaters by getting stuck in the projector! Thanks to the efforts of film collectors and preservation societies, a precious few of the earliest stop-motion films remain intact. Occasionally, lost films continue to turn up in the most unusual ways. In the 1960s, one such body of stop-motion work was discovered unexpectedly in the projection room of an old French movie theater. After much investigation, these short films were found to be made by Charley Bowers, an American filmmaker who had since been all but forgotten. Bowers had worked as a 2D animator, writer, and director on the famous *Mutt and Jeff* cartoons in the 19-teens and '20s, and had also created a series of slapstick live-action shorts, often starring himself, in the tradition of his contemporaries Buster Keaton and Harold Lloyd. The difference was that his films also contained inspired sequences of surreal stop-motion animation effects involving wacky inventions and repeated gags of cars and animals hatching out of eggs.

Later films produced on into the 1930s include the bizarre cult favorite *It's a Bird* (1930; see Figure 1.11) and the strange promotional film *Pete Roleum and his Cousins* (1939), which was commissioned and directed by Joseph Losey. The rediscovery of these lost gems of surrealistic filmmaking led to screenings at the Annecy Festival in the 1970s and a DVD release by Lobster Films in 2004. To watch these films and ponder the fact that Bowers had been neglected by the history books until now, one has to wonder if they had an influence on the works of Tex Avery or Dr. Seuss, as there are many striking similarities in designs, ideas, and weird humor. Bowers' films are full of ingenious techniques that could make for some fantastic stop-motion effects using today's updated technology.

Figure 1.11 *It's a Bird* (1930) by Charley Bowers. (Copyright Lobster Film Collection.)

Cut-Out Animation

Another technique that is a close cousin of three-dimensional stop-motion animation is that of 2D cut-out animation, which also had its genesis during the early 1900s. In this method, flat 2D "puppets" would be manipulated under a rostrum camera pointing down on a tabletop. The cut-outs could be jointed with strings or tiny paper fasteners so that they could be moved frame by frame in the same method as traditional stop-motion. The technique originated largely in France by Emile Cohl with short experimental films such as *The Neo-Impressionist Painter* (1910; see Figure 1.12), and, in Germany, Lotte Reiniger used the technique to bring the traditional Asian art of shadow puppets to the movie screen. Due to the limited scope of movement that cut-out animation provides, it never caught on as an extremely widely used medium. Most of the cut-out films made through the years have an offbeat surreal quality to them, where part of their charm is in the stiff graphic style they exude.

In the 1940s, the Ottawa Film Board in Canada made several cut-out films, including a strange promotional spot called *Three Blind Mice* (1945) where cut-out mice demonstrate the hazards of the average workplace by going through a series of repeated injuries. Through the 1960s and '70s, cut-out animation really came to the forefront in the UK with the surreal anarchy of Bob Godfrey's *Do-It-Yourself Cartoon Kit* (1961) and Terry Gilliam's cartoons from *Monty Python's Flying Circus* (1969–1983). The original films that would become Trey Parker and Matt Stone's *South Park* series were made in cut-out animation, but the series itself is done on the computer, which is now carrying on the cut-out look with other similar series. The current trend of Flash animation for Web and television is very much a modern extension of the 2D stop-motion techniques that have been around since the very beginning.

Figure 1.12 *The Neo-Impressionist Painter (Le Peintre Neo-Impressionniste) by Emile Cohl.*

Dinosaurs to Dinosaurs: The Life and Death of Creature Effects

From an early point in stop-motion's history, there are two timelines that represent two major uses for the medium. One of these timelines came to an abrupt end in the mid-'90s, and the other timeline is still moving into the future. The former timeline has its origins in the U.S., where stop-motion began being used as a special effect for movie sequences that involved scenes where an animated creature or vehicle needed to be merged with live action. Many of the early stop-motion films used this technique, but the effect was usually with puppets or objects that were either the same size or smaller than the actors. In the genre of what I like to call "creature effects" using stop-motion, the puppets would be approximately 12–18 inches tall, but on the screen they would appear to be towering over the live actors with whom they shared the screen. The director's vision of giant creatures or spaceships attacking cities or battling heroes could be realized in this method.

Several different film techniques were employed to create this illusion. One way was to create a matte shot. By masking out certain portions of the set in front of the camera with a black card, filmmakers could shoot live action footage that fit outside the masked-out area. The black card allowed no light to be exposed onto the film. The film was then wound back to the exact starting frame of the scene, and the black matte was reversed so that the previously unexposed area was now visible and the previously filmed area was masked out. Then the animator could move his puppets within this area, and when the film was developed, everything would blend together into the final image. The only limitation offered by this method was that the live-action and animated elements were not allowed to cross the line of the matte; otherwise, they would be cut off. Other methods included small screens built into miniature sets with live-action images projected into them, and using an optical printer to marry certain elements together to create a seamless composite.

Another popular method was that of front or rear projection. This technique was often used in live-action films to create the illusion of actors driving a car down the road. A stationary car sits in front of a screen with a projector behind it, projecting previously shot footage of a moving road. This technique was invented to avoid the expensive process of shooting the actors in a moving car.

To use this method in stop-motion (see Figure 1.13), a miniature set would be placed in front of a projection screen. The rear projector

Figure 1.13 An illustration of a rear-projection set for stop-motion film effects.

would then project one frame at a time of the previously shot live-action footage, and the puppets animated on the set to match it. If the shot required any foreground elements that the puppet must move behind, these elements would also be matted into the shot with black cards on a glass plate. Careful attention had to be paid to the lighting to make sure the puppet blended in seamlessly with the projected background and foreground.

The pioneer for this genre of stop-motion filmmaking in the U.S. was San Francisco native Willis O'Brien, who first experimented with stop-motion while working in a decorator's shop. O'Brien developed intricate armatures that could form the skeleton for his puppet figures and hold each position they were moved into. His further experiments led him to begin making puppets with a foam rubber skin covering a metal ball-and-socket armature. It was around this time that many of the first dinosaur skeletons were being dug up and displayed in museums, awakening the public's imagination to these giant beasts of the past. O'Brien picked up on this trend and created short films with miniature dinosaur puppets. His first films, though crude by today's standards, were authentic enough to convince audiences that they were "lost footage" of real dinosaurs!

His short dinosaur film *Ghost of Slumber Mountain* (see Figure 1.14) in 1919 led to his groundbreaking work on *The Lost World* feature film, released in 1925. The film had a modest success due to O'Brien's masterful work, not only animating the puppets but supervising the construction of miniature sets and camera tricks. In 1931, O'Brien started an ambitious project called *Creation*, which was never completed but served as a test reel for the effects that could be done for an upcoming project by RKO. That project was Merian C. Cooper's *King Kong*, finally released in 1933 (see Figure 1.15).

Figure 1.14 *The Ghost of Slumber Mountain* (1919). Stop-motion effects by Willis O'Brien.

Figure 1.15 A poster for the original *King Kong*.

King Kong was about a band of American filmmakers who find a giant gorilla named Kong on a native island and bring it back to New York with them. Kong was masterfully animated by O'Brien and composited into each shot to blend with the live actors. The impact that *King Kong* would have on the movie-going public and the medium of stop-motion animation can hardly be put into words. Today, hundreds of films are released every year with mind-blowing effects, so it's hard for us to imagine what a big deal this film really was. Released during the Great Depression, it was pure escapist entertainment in the tradition of the best adventure film and radio serials of its day, and it gave its audience a welcome respite from their daily trials. One classic scene after another kept viewers riveted, from the violent duel between Kong and a Tyrannosaurus Rex (probably included due to O'Brien being a boxing fan) to the climactic face-off on top of the Empire State Building. But even more than the action scenes, *King Kong's* true breakthrough in America for the medium of stop-motion was the raw emotion that O'Brien displayed through the character of Kong. For the first time, puppet animation for American audiences was not just a novelty of moving objects but a true form of acting. In the final moments before his death, Kong's facial expressions and body language are just as tragic and powerful as any human performance on stage or screen.

One of the many audience members *King Kong* changed forever was Ray Harryhausen. After seeing the film at age 13, he immediately began learning how to make stop-motion films of his own, and one of his first jobs was at George Pal's studio working on the *Puppetoon* shorts. Harryhausen eventually got to work with his mentor O'Brien on the 1949 film *Mighty Joe Young*. Already in those days, he proved himself as an excellent animator and innovator. He is now rightfully credited as a legend in the stop-motion field and has been the inspiration for practically everyone working in the industry ever since.

I had the rare privilege to meet Ray Harryhausen briefly in 2001 at the Vancouver Effects & Animation Festival (see Figure 1.16). When I told him I was a stop-motion animator and instructor, he remarked, "Ah, you're still young! You haven't pulled your hair out yet!" I found him to be an extremely friendly and generous man.

Harryhausen carried O'Brien's techniques to even greater heights. Although his early films featured cartoon-style fairy tales and fables, Harryhausen is most famous for the creature effects he created for a series of live-action adventure films from the 1950s to 1980s, marketed as a film technique called Dynamation. He also created his own puppets (see Figure 1.17). Harryhausen worked closely with the directors, writers, and designers, and his films started in the genre of monsters attacking big cities (such as 1953's *Beast from 20,000 Fathoms*) but eventually came to be based on hero myths and legends of

Figure 1.16 The author with Ray Harryhausen in 2001.

ancient civilizations. His first color film was 1958's *7th Voyage of Sinbad*, the first in an eventual Sinbad trilogy, which featured fantastic creatures such as the Cyclops and a sword-wielding skeleton. The skeleton returned, along with six others, in the climactic battle scene from 1963's *Jason and the Argonauts*. That scene is among Harryhausen's most famous work, and it is still studied by filmmakers and animators today. (If you have never seen this sequence, go find it and prepare to be amazed!) Each skeleton engaging in a sword fight with the live-action Argonauts had to be animated at the same time to ensure that each frame matched up perfectly with the choreographed live-action footage. Harryhausen had to keep track of which puppets were moving forward and backward, using only his own memory and notes on paper, without the use of frame grabbers or video monitors. The results are unbelievably stunning, not only in the smooth animation, but in the editing as well. What is most interesting about Harryhausen's work today is that the sequences are like a kind of fanciful cinematic theater in the way they are staged. Since the technology did not allow the camera to move much, the action relied more on the editing and the relationships between the puppets and actors, versus today's films, which tend to stress too much jarring camera movement. And again, it's important to remember the impact these films had in a time when there was less competition for entertainment than there is today.

Harryhausen's last film before his retirement was *Clash of the Titans* (1981), which included his *tour de force* sequence of Medusa the Gorgon stalking the Greek hero Perseus. Assisting Harryhausen in creating some of the other animation shots were some of the rising stop-motion animators and effects artists of the industry, such as Jim Danforth. Danforth had started his career in stop-motion at a young age on the TV series *Davey and Goliath* and moved on to animate on feature films such as *7 Faces of Dr. Lao* (1964), *When Dinosaurs Ruled the Earth* (1970), and dozens more. On some of these films, he

Figure 1.17 Some of Ray Harryhausen's puppet creations. From left to right: Skeleton from *Jason and the Argonauts,* Medusa from *Clash of the Titans,* and the Bowhead Statue from *The Golden Voyage of Sinbad.*

had worked with another talented animator named Dave Allen, who went on to become another of the industry's most dedicated stop-motion professionals. In addition to being on the crew of several films through the '70s and '80s, Allen spent 20 years working on an ambitious live-action/stop-motion feature called *The Primevals*, which unfortunately remains unfinished due to his death from cancer in 1999. Other stop-motion animators who had worked with Danforth and Allen who continued to make their mark on the industry included folks like Randall William Cook and Jim Aupperle, who have now successfully transitioned into today's CG visual effects field.

Another influential stop-motion artist is Phil Tippett. Tippett first began animating on his own homemade films and a few B movies before joining the effects team on *Star Wars* in 1977. The phenomenal success of that film paved the way for more groundbreaking work with George Lucas' Industrial Light & Magic (ILM) studio well into the new decade of the 1980s. While creating stop-motion effects for *The Empire Strikes Back* (1980), Tippett came up with a technique that would attempt to reduce the jerky movement of previous works. In studying live-action film frame by frame, animators noticed that in some frames, the motion would be blurred as a result of a slightly longer shutter exposure. Tippett devised a way in which his puppets could be rigged with a computerized armature that would move the puppet slightly while certain frames were being exposed, resulting in a motion blur that would have a closer resemblance to real live movement. The full results were utilized for the 1981 fantasy picture *Dragonslayer*, in Tippett's animation of the dragon Vermithrax. In several amazing shots of Vermithrax crawling through her cave, the fluid movement created by the motion blur has a similar appearance to today's CGI effects, which didn't exist at that time. This motion blur technique was coined "go-motion," and it was improved upon at ILM in subsequent features such as *Return of the Jedi* (1983) and *Willow* (1988). The continued influence of O'Brien, Harryhausen, and Tippett on Hollywood gave us a great variety of stop-motion effects on through the '80s, appearing in films such as *Caveman* (1981), *Ghostbusters* (1984), *Evil Dead II, The Gate,* and *Nightmare on Elm Street 3* (all 1987), to name only a few. It is because of this era of filmmaking, and the eras that had come before, that we now have the CG effects being created today. Tippett himself was involved with one of the films that ultimately started this digital transition.

In the early '90s, preproduction began on Steven Spielberg's *Jurassic Park*. With Tippett on his effects team, early tests were created to animate realistic dinosaurs using the traditional go-motion technique. However, there was much experimentation going on at ILM with computer animation and the possibilities offered to them by continually advanced technology. James Cameron's films *The Abyss* (1989) and *Terminator 2* (1991) were among the first films to begin using this new technology to its fullest potential. A team led by effects artist Dennis Muren began a series of tests to prove to Spielberg that computer animation could be used to achieve better results than go-motion. The final test results were so authentic that Tippett's verbal reaction was "I think I'm extinct." Impressed by the fluid realism offered by this new technology, Spielberg made the decision to replace the go-motion dinosaurs with CGI throughout the entire film. Tippett's team of puppet animators, who were so used to creating their effects by hand, were beginning to feel the pinch of this new technology that was threatening to pull the plug on their craft. But Tippett, due to his expertise in animal behavior and movement, was still able to use his skills to aid the computer animators. His shop actually devised a special armature that was encoded with wires extending from its joints into the computer. Nicknamed the D.I.D. (Dinosaur Input Device), it allowed the animators to move a physical puppet into position as they were accustomed to, and have their movements translated into a 3D computer model. This model could then be mapped with the proper lighting and textures needed to blend it into the live-action footage. The sequences with the T-Rex first emerging from its pen, and the Velociraptors in the kitchen, were actually stop-motion animation that had been fed into the computer. The stop-motion dinosaur movie genre that started with *The Lost World* in 1925 had come full circle in 1993 with the release of *Jurassic Park*, and continued into its 1998 sequel, also ironically titled *The Lost World*.

The success of *Jurassic Park* and its groundbreaking effects heralded the end of traditional stop-motion puppets as filmed by O'Brien and his protégés for the use of realistic creature effects in mainstream Hollywood movies. Today traditional stop-motion is used only for independent projects or B-movies intended to hark back to these old films. The photo-realism created by CGI has enhanced the expectations of modern audiences to the point that any attempt to animate foam rubber puppets on miniature sets would look crude by comparison. It's rather ironic that today's "realism" has proven to be better achieved through computer models, which lack the realism of an actual physical puppet. Some purists may argue that there is a coldness to CGI that does not warrant the same sense of texture derived from actual materials. Perhaps the improvements made in digital compositing and the technical smoothness of stop-motion animation will warrant a renaissance for creature effects in the future, but only time and the right people, story, and budget will tell. The important thing to remember is that today's films owe their very existence to the special effects of the past, and much can still be learned from them. While *Jurassic Park* may have faded out this timeline of stop-motion's history in 1993 (not to mention *Army of Darkness* adding a coda of final B-movie tribute to the medium), that very same year saw the release of two films that would carry the medium forward in a huge transcendent leap: Tim Burton's *The Nightmare Before Christmas* and Nick Park's *The Wrong Trousers*. In both of these films, the animated puppets did not share the screen with live actors, but rather existed in their own world, representing the latter of the two timelines I mentioned previously. The genre of stop-motion in films that are exclusively animated is still alive and well today and has had a vibrant history of its own.

Miniature Worlds on the Big Screen

While Willis O'Brien was busy pioneering the American method of using stop-motion for creature effects, on the other side of the globe another style of the medium was being developed. Ladislas Starewitch, born 1882 in Moscow to Polish–Lithuanian parents, was responsible for changing stop-motion from a technical novelty to a storytelling art form, much like Walt Disney did for 2D cartoon animation. Starewitch grew up with a keen interest in art and entomology, collecting and studying all varieties of insects. While working as a filmmaker at the Khanzhonkov Studio in Russia, he began making experimental documentaries about live beetles. His early attempts at making the beetles do anything he wanted under hot lights proved to be frustrating, so, inspired by Emile Cohl's film *Bewitched Matchsticks*, he rigged some embalmed beetles with wires and animated them. The stop-motion technique applied to real insects had never been seen in Russia, and many audiences thought that the beetles had been trained to "act" by some odd form of science. In one of his most humorous films, *Revenge of the Cameraman* (1912; see Figure 1.18), Starewitch told a silent tale of adultery between a group of suburban insects. This was one of the earliest known attempts to actually tell a real story exclusively with stop-motion puppets.

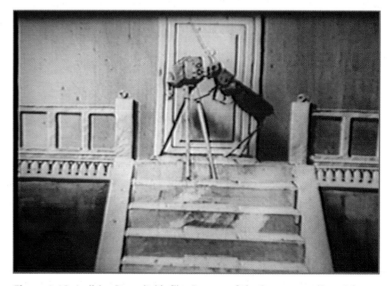

Figure 1.18 Ladislas Starewitch's film *Revenge of the Cameraman*. (Copyright L.B. Martin-Starewitch.)

The success of these insect films led Starewitch to move on to more detailed puppets made of metal armatures, wood, felt, and chamois leather. Due to the growth of the Communist regime after World War I, he moved to Paris in 1920 and began producing two to three films a year. His stories were inspired by Eastern European folklore and fairy tales, ranging from gentle children's stories like *Voice of the Nightingale* (1923; Hugo Rosenfield Prize winner 1925) to bizarre horror/fantasy films like *Fern Flowers* (1950). The level of detail and emotion that Starewitch was able to inject into his characters was outstanding for the time the films were made, especially those with several different puppet characters, such as *The Old Lion* (1932). This film featured a flying elephant nine years before Disney created *Dumbo* (1941), and his 1928 film *The Magic Clock* featured his own daughter escaping the hand of a giant, similar to scenes from *King Kong*. These scenes are just a few examples of how Starewitch was very much ahead of his time and had an impact on other filmmakers. Many of his films also featured a motion blur technique for certain quick puppet movements, which may have been created by smearing Vaseline on a plate of glass in front of the camera, or by using wires.

One of Starewitch's most famous and elaborate films was *The Mascot* (see Figure 1.19), which was released in 1933, the same year as *King Kong*. Framed by live-action sequences, *The Mascot* tells the story of a small dog toy that goes on a quest to find an orange for a hungry little girl and ends up at a party thrown by the devil and his guest list of grotesque characters. The macabre imagery of *The Nightmare Before Christmas* and modern tales of toys coming to life (such as *Raggedy Ann* or *Toy Story*) could certainly have been influenced by *The Mascot* and other films by this creative storyteller. Many of Starewitch's films are lost in the annals of history, but enough of them remain to inspire us today.

Figure 1.19 Ladislas Starewitch's film *The Mascot*. (Copyright L.B. Martin-Starewitch.)

While Starewitch's filmmaking career flourished in France, there began another renaissance in stop-motion that originated in Czechoslovakia. Czechoslovakia has always had a long tradition of storytelling through live puppetry, which carried over into film once the stop-motion technique had gotten around. The Czech style of puppet film differs from the more naturalistic styles chosen by Starewitch and O'Brien, with one example being the use of the face. Since Czech films were in many ways an extension of traditional puppet theater, faces would remain static throughout, with the acting dependent on the movement of the body. It is the way the puppet moves that tells us how he is feeling, despite the unchanging nature of his face. Live puppet theater relied on this technique for centuries, as large audiences would need to be able to read the puppets' emotions even from the farthest seat. Cinema brought the puppets closer to the audience, so more intricate ways to depict realistic facial expressions could now be explored by puppet filmmakers. Nevertheless, most Czech puppet films put more emphasis on a lyrical quality based on body language combined with music and story.

One of the Czech movement's earliest pioneers was female animator Hermina Tyrlova, who made a series of films at Ziln Studios. Starting with commercials and trick films in the 1920s, she became known for fairy-tale fables such as *Ferda the Ant* (1944) and the anti-Nazi propaganda short *Revolt of the Toys* (1945, released in 1947, well after the war; see Figure 1.20), and continued to make films aimed at children well into the 1970s. Tyrlova collaborated on a film called *Christmas Dream* in 1946 with another influential Czech animator, Karel Zeman, who went on to create fanciful films combining puppets with live-action and other special effects, including *The Fabulous World of Jules Verne* (1958).

While Tyrlova's career in puppet films was just beginning, an illustrator named Jiri Trnka was creating 2D cel animation and would eventually transition into puppet films himself. Trnka became one of the most prolific Czech animators and had a major influence on the stop-motion medium. In 1946, he opened his own puppet film studio, which became a training ground for a whole legion of Czech animators. Trnka's own

Figure 1.20 *Revolt of the Toys* by Czech animator Hermina Tyrlova.

films were based largely on local folktales and Czech customs. Many of them had a paradoxical reaction from the Communist government, who appreciated the films and supported them financially, but at the same time tried to dictate their subject matter and banned those they didn't agree with. Several films, such as *Archangel Gabriel and Lady Goose* (1964), were rejected as church propaganda. Trnka wanted not only to explore religious imagery, but expand the subjects of his films beyond Czech legend and history, adapting tales from Spain and Shakespeare. His attempts to do so were met with mixed reactions from the public, as was his insistence on creating beautiful works of art while neglecting to appeal to the common interests of most audiences. The frustrations that Trnka endured throughout his career are important to study further, as there will always be a conflict in the animation industry, not necessarily between art and government in most societies now, but between art and business. Artists working in a large studio environment will often find themselves succumbing to the pressures of a corporate authority who doesn't know anything about art yet will praise the artists when the product makes money. Trnka's last film, *The Hand* (1965), was a metaphorical summary of his career and struggle to create art within a dictatorship government. The central puppet character is an artist who is constantly forced by a giant intruding hand to make sculptures of only the hand. The artist stubbornly refuses until the hand imprisons him and ultimately causes his death, only to then honor him with a state funeral.

The Hand is a fitting tribute to one of stop-motion's great artists, as is the influence that Trnka passed on to many other filmmakers who studied with him, among them Jiri Barta, Vlasta Pospisilova, Bretislav Pojar, and Jan Svankmeyer. Svankmeyer is one of the most well-known animators from the Trnka tradition, and his films go beyond the traditional Czech puppet style into some of the most bizarre imagery ever put on screen. Many of his films are based on nightmares and dream states, often combining live action with puppets and animated found objects: toy dolls, dead animals, meat, food. Anything is possible in a Svankmeyer film, usually exploring dark topics and political commentaries very common to Czech art. His most well-known work is probably his 1988 live-action/stop-motion feature *Alice*, based on Lewis Carroll's legendary story but decidedly much different and more disturbing than any other version. The influence of his films is most prominent in the films by two brothers from Philadelphia known as the Brothers Quay (Stephen and Timothy), who started their career in 1979. They produced their most famous works in London, creating nonlinear dream-state films using found objects, dolls, and puppets in decayed antique sets. The dark imagery of the Brothers Quay has had a profound influence on many contemporary rock videos by Tool, Nine Inch Nails, and other groups, so even though most Czech films of this genre may be unknown to modern American audiences, their mark has certainly found their way into unexpected areas of pop culture.

The Trnka studio has also been a haven for stop-motion filmmakers from other countries, such as Kihachiro Kawamoto from Japan, who combined the traditional Czech style with the popular Japanese Bunraku puppet techniques. Co Hoedeman, an animator from the Netherlands, immigrated to Canada and studied briefly with Trnka in Czechoslovakia in 1970. He then returned to Canada to make puppet films for the National Film Board and made many films based on Inuit legends, such as *The Owl and the Lemming* (1971). In 1977, Hoedeman made the Oscar-winning short *The Sand Castle* (see Figure 1.21) and since then has had a successful career making films about societal and environmental issues, as well as series for children.

Hoedeman is a rare modern example of a kind of filmmaker who has taken inspiration from European traditions of filmmaking and brought them to be produced in North America. Through the National Film Board, Canada has had a more similar history to Europe in regards to government sponsorship for experimental filmmaking for the sake of artistic exploration through film. Historically, the idea of stop-motion films intended for theatrical distribution has mostly thrived in Europe. Part of the reason for this is the strong tradition of puppet theater dating back to even the Middle Ages, including the popular Punch and Judy traveling shows. In America, the early experimental days of trick films developed into an industry, once the medium began being used for storytelling and entertainment. Film distribution became a contractual obligation to produce series of regular film packages in a method called block-booking. Theaters would purchase films from studios in a specific packaged format, which included newsreels, live-action short subjects, and animated shorts along with a feature film. The quick turnaround for these film packages meant that the animated content had to be delivered at a faster and cheaper rate, and cel animation proved to be a more convenient medium for this assembly-line approach to distribution. Thus, stop-motion films created by Americans took a different route into the realm of special effects for films like *King Kong*. Europe did not have this block-booking method for film distribution, so there the focus was more on creating films for the sake of creating art, telling stories, and often making societal or political statements for public enlightenment.

An influential stop-motion pioneer who took this filmmaking tradition from Europe to America was Hungarian-born George Pal. Pal set up his first cartoon studio in Prague in 1933, and he started making films with puppets because he couldn't find any cameras that were designed for shooting 2D cartoon animation. His early commercial projects eventually led him to set up shop in Holland, where he continued to make animated ads and short subjects. Pal's breakthrough technique was the use of "replacement animation." With this method, instead of building one puppet and manipulating it, several different versions of a puppet would be produced, each one slightly different from the next. The animation, in a sense, was created by the individual puppets them-

Figure 1.21 *The Sand Castle*. (Copyright 1977 National Film Board of Canada.)

selves, and they would simply be replaced one at a time in front of the camera. Oftentimes, the animation would be done on paper and then 3D wooden pieces would be carved to match the drawings, which allowed for fluid 2D-style squash and stretch effects impossible to achieve with just a single puppet. Up to 100 different replacement pieces would often be needed to create the wide range of movements for some characters. The unique visual style was appealing to the audience, and when Philips Radio in the Netherlands saw them, they began sponsoring Pal's films. In 1939, when the Nazis invaded Poland, George Pal took that as his cue to move to America, sign a deal with Paramount Studios, and set up the first puppet film studio in Hollywood, creating a series of theatrical shorts called *Puppetoons* (see Figure 1.22).

Figure 1.22 From *The Puppetoon*® *Movie*. (Courtesy Arnold Leibovit Entertainment.)

One of Pal's best films, *Tulips Shall Grow* (1942), was an autobiographical sketch of the European Nazi attacks. World War II inspired many propaganda shorts made by animators, including Lou Bunin's *Bury the Axis*, featuring puppet versions of Hitler, Mussolini, and Hirohito. Amidst the many films made in this style, Pal's film stands out as very unique. A frolicking Dutch couple dance in front of a windmill, only to be invaded by an army of soldiers called "Screwballs." The couple is separated during the chaos, and the male character seeks shelter in a nearby church. He prays for rain, which comes down and causes the metal soldiers to rust. The young lovers are reunited and continue to dance, leaving on a note of hope that "tulips shall always grow." The optimistic nature of this film during a time of war was a signature style of Pal's work. Another historically significant film of his was 1946's *John Henry and the Inky Poo*, based on the American folktale of the legendary railroad worker. Most animated films of this period, including Pal's own popular series about a young African-American boy named Jasper, depicted black characters as stereotypes and are considered politically incorrect by today's standards. *John Henry* was one of the first animated films to portray African-American characters with dignity and respect and helped to move us away from the racist caricatures that were more common back then. As the costs for *Puppetoons* rose, their profits fell, as they were charming but unable to compete with the antics of 2D stars like Tom & Jerry. The best lesson from George Pal's career for today's filmmakers is that he picked up on upcoming trends and knew that theatrical short subjects would not always continue to be popular. Feature films were the best way for him to continue his film career, so he took the experience he gained from his *Puppetoons* and used it to create miniature models and special effects work for features. His work on films such as *Destination Moon* (1950), *War of the Worlds* (1953), and *The Time Machine* (1960) paved the way for miniature model effects used in films like *Star Wars*, so George Pal's influence has extended even beyond the realm of the puppet film.

After World War II, as theatrical short films in America slowly became a rarity as part of feature film packages, they began being produced for television, schools, or the limited venues of specialized film or animation festivals around the world. Today, thanks to the popularity of film festivals, making short films exclusively in stop-motion is rather commonplace worldwide. The Academy Awards continued to honor animated short subjects with a special Oscar each year for "Best Animated Cartoon," until the winning film in 1975 changed the award title to "Best Animated Short Film." This was because the film was not a "cartoon" in the traditional sense, but the first stop-motion clay animation film to win the Oscar. The film was *Closed Mondays* by Will Vinton and Bob Gardiner (see Figure 1.23), made entirely in clay, about a drunk man who wanders into a closed art museum and watches the art come to life in surreal ways. In one scene, the man accidentally turns on a

Figure 1.23 *Closed Mondays*. (Courtesy of Will Vinton, www.willvinton.net.)

talking robot that proceeds to morph into random objects and then melt, to which the drunk man remarks "Blabbermouth computer!" (A hilarious and rather prophetic comment about modern technology!)

The breakthrough technique of *Closed Mondays* was the use of clay to achieve a realistic method for dialogue and detailed facial expressions never previously attempted in stop-motion. Riding on the success of his Oscar win, Vinton started his own studio in Portland, Oregon (Will Vinton Studios) and continued making short films with this technique, which he trademarked specifically as *Claymation*. The popularity of Vinton's work is proven by the fact that the term "Claymation" has become so commonplace that it is often used to refer to stop-motion animation as a whole, including puppet films that do not use clay at all. Vinton assembled a team of talented artists and animators, including Barry Bruce, and perfected his clay craft with beautiful works such as *Martin the Cobbler* (1977), *A Christmas Gift* (1980), and *The Great Cognito* (1982).

Meanwhile, in the UK, a couple of schoolboys named Peter Lord and David Sproxton made some clay animation films that led to the founding of Aardman Animation Studios. Because the clay medium lent itself so well to subtlety in puppet dialogue, they started a series of films called *Conversation Pieces* in the 1970s, which were based on improvised interviews and recorded conversations. Several animators, such as Barry Purves and Richard Golezsowski, would eventually lend their talents to the Aardman studio to create a diversified range of styles for films made for BBC television and film festivals. The most significant recruit for Aardman was Nick Park, who was making a clay animation film at the National Film and Television School called *A Grand Day Out*, about a man named Wallace and his dog Gromit, and their trip to the moon. Aardman hired Park part-time to work on commercials while helping him finish his 30-minute film, which took 6 years to complete. Shortly afterward, in 1989, Park created his own version of the *Conversation Pieces* series, *Creature Comforts*, which took improvised dialogue about living conditions in England and put it in the mouths of zoo animals. The brilliant results made the 5-minute film a huge success and won Nick Park his first Oscar. Riding on the success of both *Creature Comforts* and *A Grand Day Out*, which also won several awards, Park began another half-hour film at Aardman starring Wallace & Gromit called *The Wrong Trousers*. It was a suspenseful tale involving a mysterious penguin, a jewel heist, and a pair of mechanical pants. It was another smash hit in its 1993 release, eventually making its rounds in festivals and public television screenings around the world. *The Wrong Trousers* and its 1995 follow-up *A Close Shave* both won Oscars again for Nick Park, putting him and his colleagues at Aardman on the map as one of the most successful stop-motion studios in the world.

Stop-Motion on the Small Screen

Before the advent of television, there was a very little known method in the U.S. for watching films in the comfort of one's own home. Kinex Studios in Hollywood produced a series of stop-motion shorts in the 1920s and '30s for the Kodak Cinegraph company (see Figures 1.24 and 1.25). These films were not distributed to theaters, but rather to camera shops where customers could buy or rent them on 16mm film for home projection, much like video and DVD rental stores of today. Some of the known artists who worked on these bizarre Kinex shorts include John Burton and Orville Goldner.

Eventually the television became a standard in the average home, and the 1950s were the golden era of the television age. Broadcasters began showing theatrical animated films from the war era, and cheaply produced new cartoons using limited animation began a new trend for this new method of distribution. Suddenly there was a whole new venue for animated content, and stop-motion productions, though still few and far between compared to 2D cartoon shows, began making their mark on the popular culture. Before stop-motion puppets became popular on American television, they were preceded by close

Figure 1.24 *The Witch's Cat* starring Snap the Gingerbread Man (1928), Kinex Studios.

Figure 1.25 *The Doodlebugs' Circus* (1929), Kinex Studios.

cousins of the puppet variety. Productions with hand puppets and marionettes, created by artists such as Bil Baird and Burr Tillstrom, started making their way from live stages to the TV screen. Muppet creator Jim Henson got his start in the 1950s as well, with his first TV series, *Sam and Friends*. It was then on the *Howdy Doody Show*, a popular children's puppet program, that TV's first stop-motion star Gumby emerged in 1956.

The genesis of Gumby started with an experimental theatrical short by Art Clokey in 1955 called *Gumbasia*, which featured animated clay moving to jazz music. The film was seen by 20th Century Fox producer Sam Engel, who hired Clokey to develop a wholesome clay-animation series for television. Gumby, his faithful horse Pokey, and a whole cast of characters became household names once they had their own series, which continued a successful worldwide run well into the 1960s. This was the first time that clay, as a medium for stop-motion, had finally been used to full effect to create a mainstream pop icon. The creators' studio, founded as Clokey Productions, was also commissioned by the Lutheran Church in 1959 to produce a show that could teach religious values to children, and the result was the *Davey and Goliath* series about a boy and his dog. This show used molded puppets dressed in real clothing, in a style more similar to European puppets, except that their stories involved much more dialogue. Their dialogue was achieved with paper stick-on mouths that would be replaced for each frame—one of the methods used in limited animation for TV, and which is still used in a digital fashion today (even for *South Park*!)

Gumby and *Davey and Goliath* had both faded into syndication and cult status by the 1970s and early '80s, but each had their own rebirth as well. *The New Adventures of Gumby* brought the clay icon back in 1987, and was the first job for many animators who would later work on *Nightmare Before Christmas*, including Anthony Scott, who also got involved with *Davey and Goliath*'s comeback in 2004 (see Chapter 8, "An Interview with Anthony Scott").

During the early days of Clokey Productions, another American studio that successfully brought stop-motion to television was Rankin-Bass, founded by Arthur Rankin Jr. and Jules Bass (see Figure 1.26). The studio started as an advertising company that was introduced to animation through a partnership with a Japanese animation studio. This deal led to the 1960 series *New Adventures of Pinocchio*, produced in their syndicated term for the stop-motion medium "Animagic." The modest success of their first series gave them the resources to put 100 animators to work for 18 months creating their first television special, *Rudolph the Red-Nosed Reindeer*, which first aired on NBC in 1964. *Rudolph* (see Figure 1.27) became the longest-running special in the history of stop-motion, repeating every Christmas and becoming a wonderful holiday tradition.

More Animagic specials followed throughout the '60s and '70s, often with holiday themes, such as *Santa Claus Is Coming to Town, Here Comes Peter Cottontail,* and *Rudolph's Shiny New Year*. Since then, Rankin-Bass has segued more into 2D production, but their stop-motion series are still popular today and have been very influential to the medium. The fact that the animation was done in Japan makes their productions a unique cross-cultural phenomenon. While the stories and designs originated in America, the style of the animation is very much Japanese, in that the characters' movements are expressed through a pantomime-like style with limited lip sync. The characters' lip movements are not always fluid and exact, which could be because of

Figure 1.26 Arthur Rankin Jr. and Jules Bass. (Courtesy of Rick Goldschmidt Archives/www.rankinbass.com.)

Figure 1.27 Rudolph and Santa as they appear today. (Courtesy of Rick Goldschmidt Archives/www.rankinbass.com.)

language barriers in translating the dialogue. The most important thing to the animators was not the mouth positions, but more that you knew which character was speaking, which is a stylistic choice that is also common in 2D Anime films.

Elsewhere in the world, stop-motion had found its way onto television with series such as the German cold-war propaganda children's show *Sandmannchen* (*Little Sandman*), the French/Polish series *Coragol* (about a globe-trotting bear, known as *Jeremy* in Canada), and Aardman's *Morph*. The French series *The Magic Roundabout*, by Serge Danot, became even more popular in the UK and has more recently been resurrected through the CG feature film *Dougal* (2006). The design of *Magic Roundabout* was influenced by animator Ivor Wood, who went on to produce shows like *Paddington Bear* and *Postman Pat* for the BBC. The Nickelodeon network, which began in the U.S. in 1979, slowly began introducing some of these foreign stop-motion works to North America, partly through shows like *Pinwheel*. The 1980s introduced a wide variety of stop-motion to television, on shows such as *Pee-Wee's Playhouse*, a Saturday morning show starring comedian Pee-Wee Herman. Each episode featured clay animation sequences with a girl named Penny, a family of dinosaurs, and occasionally a brief segment from George Pal's *Puppetoons*. Several noted animators such as Peter Lord, Craig Bartlett, Steve Oakes, and David Daniels contributed their talents to the show. Another popular venue for stop-motion during this period was music videos, most notably in Peter Gabriel's *Sledgehammer* and *Big Time* (1986). The animation in *Sledgehammer* was created by Aardman Studios, and the Brothers Quay made their contributions as well.

Will Vinton Studios became very famous for commercials and television work in addition to their short films. Vinton created his most famous Claymation characters, the California Raisins (see Figure 1.28), for an advertising campaign that spawned a series of entertaining TV specials, including the Emmy-winning Christmas special *A Claymation Christmas Celebration*. Years later, in the late 1990s, he produced the first prime-time stop-motion series, *The PJs*, featuring Eddie Murphy as the voice of the lead character Thurgood Stubbs. *The PJs* was created with another trademarked technique called *Foamation*, in which the puppets were made of foam latex and rubber so that they could be easily duplicated for use on different sets at the same time—something that would be much more difficult with clay on a short production schedule. Another short-lived stop-motion series, *Gary & Mike*, was created by Vinton Studios before the company was taken over by Phil Knight in 2002, and Will Vinton was laid off from the studio he had founded. Vinton has now started a new studio in Portland, called Freewill Entertainment, and is continuing to create new shows in stop-motion and CGI.

Stop-motion has appeared on television in other various forms well into the '90s and the new millennium. San Francisco studio Danger Productions made a Saturday morning series *Bump in the Night* in 1994, about a monster named Mr. Bumpy and his various adventures. MTV started their own animation studio in New York and created a popular show called *Celebrity Deathmatch*, where puppet caricatures of celebrities would duke it out in a stadium wrestling ring. Independent animator Corky Quackenbush made a series of animated segments for the *MAD TV* comedy show, where classic stop-motion characters like Rudolph and Gumby were parodied in various violent situations. Many of these recent stop-motion sequences for television were not meant to be remembered for intricate flowing animation, but more for adult entertainment value and satire with a more crude style.

Today, stop-motion on television is very popular for children's series such as *Bob the Builder*, *The Koala Brothers*, and *Jojo's Circus*. On the other end of the age scale, adult audiences enjoy shows like *Robot Chicken* and *The Wrong Coast*. The stop-motion medium has had a rich history on the small screen and should continue to do so as long as there are good ideas for various audiences. To this day, there still has not been a CG television series that has rivaled the cultural impact of 2D shows like *The Simpsons* or stop-motion shows like *Gumby*, so in this arena, both mediums are still dominant.

1. Appeal and History of Stop-Motion Animation

Figure 1.28 Will Vinton's California Raisins. (Courtesy of Will Vinton, www.willvinton.net.)

Feature Presentations

When Walt Disney set out to make his first animated feature, *Snow White and the Seven Dwarfs*, the production was cursed with the name of "Disney's folly" by much of Hollywood, because nobody believed that audiences could sit through a cartoon that long. The phenomenal success of that picture proved everyone wrong, of course. It took much longer for stop-motion animation to reach the same pinnacle of success in a feature-length format. In America, it was more common for the technique to be used for brief sequences or special effects inside live-action features, such as the Harryhausen pictures and more offbeat stuff like animator Bruce Bickford's trippy clay animation sequences from Frank Zappa's concert film *Baby Snakes* (1979). Stop-motion amazed audiences when used for short sequences like this, but the crudeness of early attempts made it an even riskier venture to hold an audience's atten-

tion by itself for 75 to 90 minutes of screen time. Also, due to the time-consuming nature of stop-motion, making a feature-length motion picture with the technique has been a historical rarity compared to the number of shorter pieces in the past century.

What is believed to be the world's first feature-length animated film is German animator Lotte Reiniger's *The Adventures of Prince Achmed* from 1926 (see Figure 1.29). The film was created with cut-out figures entirely in silhouette, acting as a frame-by-frame extension of traditional shadow puppet theater, and it took three years to make.

Soon afterward, Ladislas Starewich created the first feature-length puppet film, *The Tale of the Fox*, which was finally released in France in 1941. Years later, Jiri Trnka made several stop-motion feature films, including *The Emperor's Nightingale* and *A Midsummer's Nights Dream*, which had limited releases in the United States as well as in Europe.

Figure 1.29 *The Adventures of Prince Achmed* (1926), by Lotte Reiniger.

A stop-motion/live-action version of *Alice in Wonderland* was produced by animator Lou Bunin in 1948, but Disney's version overshadowed it, and the film slipped into cult status over the years. The first American stop-motion feature was *Hansel and Gretel: An Opera Fantasy*, directed by John Paul and Michael Myerburg in 1954. The film's score, based on an 1892 opera, was nominated for a Grammy and saw a few theatrical rereleases for years afterward. In addition to their popular TV specials, Rankin-Bass made some features in their Animagic stop-motion technique, starting with *Willy McBean and His Magic Machine* in 1965, followed by *Mad Monster Party* in 1967, and *Rudolph and Frosty's Christmas* in July 1979. Clay animation found its way to limited screen releases in the 1980s with *Pogo for President* (1980, based on Walt Kelly's famous comic strip) and Will Vinton's *Adventures of Mark Twain* (1985). Vinton also used Claymation for the "Speed Demon" sequence in Michael Jackson's feature film *Moonwalker* (1988).

In 1983, UK studio Cosgrove Hall made a foam puppet adaptation of *Wind in the Willows,* and George Lucas produced the film *Twice Upon a Time*, which was created in a technique called "Lumage." This method employed flat textured cutouts that were lit from underneath to give a translucent quality. The result was a graphic 2D appearance, although the procedure was done with stop-motion cutout and replacement animation. Like most of these former stop-motion features, *Twice Upon a Time* was not marketed well enough to generate much of an audience. Many of these films found enough circulation in the early days of cable TV to gain cult followings among animation fans. Today, most of them remain lost treasures awaiting possible resurrection on DVD.

The biggest turning point for the sporadic, dismal performance of stop-motion features began in the early '80s, when Disney animators Tim Burton and Henry Selick struck up a friendship while working together on *The Fox and the Hound*. In 1982, Burton was given the opportunity to direct a stop-motion short called *Vincent*, and while wrapping up the film, created some sketches for a poem entitled *The Nightmare Before Christmas*. Meanwhile, Selick left for San Francisco to focus on stop-motion commercials and short films of his own. Tim Burton left Disney and quickly became a successful feature film director, starting with *Pee-Wee's Big Adventure* and *Beetlejuice*, both of which had some brilliant stop-motion effects weaved in (such as the classic Pee-Wee "Large Marge" scene!). As the '80s segued into the '90s, the industry saw the beginning of a renaissance for the animated feature film, partially inspired by Jeffrey Katzenberg's involvement at Disney and brought on by the amazing success of *Who Framed Roger Rabbit, The Little Mermaid*, and *Beauty and the Beast*. The time was right for Burton and Selick to join forces and approach Disney, who still owned the rights to Burton's poem and concept designs for *The Nightmare Before Christmas* (see Figure 1.30). Production began in 1990 for turning Burton's vision into a big-budget feature film in stop-motion, which would be the first of its kind to receive worldwide distribution. Brilliantly executed, the film was a success in its initial 1993 release and continues to get better with age. *Nightmare* is one of the most significant films in the history of stop-motion animation, for the fact that it came out at exactly the right time, when the validity of using the technique for creature effects was challenged. It also captured the surrealism and charm of classic puppet films by Starewich and Trnka, and it used George Pal's replacement technique for some of the characters' dialogue. The film combined elements of these films with nostalgic nods to the Rankin-Bass holiday specials and brought them to a higher level of technical smoothness and artistry, all the while creating something fresh and new.

The success of *Nightmare* led director Henry Selick to create a follow-up feature, *James and the Giant Peach*, in 1996, which also featured live-action, CG, and cutout animation. Having now made two films aimed at children yet universal in their appeal, Selick's next project was meant to be darker and more adult-oriented. He began production on a feature film based on the graphic novel *Dark Town*, which went through many changes until it was finally released under the title *MonkeyBone* in 2001. It was primarily a live-action film but featured a stop-motion monkey as a primary character along with many other surreal puppet effects. The film was not very successful at the box office, but the animation was inspired and blended well with the live actors.

Figure 1.30 Jack Skellington and Sally from Tim Burton's *The Nightmare Before Christmas.* (Touchstone/Burton/Di Novi/The Kobal Collection.)

More recently, Selick has created stop-motion effects for feature films like *The Life Aquatic with Steve Zissou,* and he has joined forces with Laika Entertainment to continue making films in CG and stop-motion.

1993 also brought another stop-motion feature from the UK, *The Secret Adventures of Tom Thumb,* directed by Dave Borthwick, which combined puppets with pixilated live actors to tell a dark tale similar in style to Svankmeyer and the Brothers Quay. The years since have also produced a Gumby feature film and a Russian production called *The Miracle Maker,* which tells the story of Jesus Christ using very realistic stop-motion puppets. Nick Park's Oscar-winning *Wallace & Gromit* had also caught the world's attention and led to a multipicture deal between DreamWorks and Aardman Animation Studios. DreamWorks, founded by Jeffrey Katzenberg, Steven Spielberg, and David Geffen, had ventured into animation with their 1998 releases of *Antz* and *The Prince of Egypt,* and wanted to continue supporting stop-motion animation. The first feature to result from this partnership was the release of *Chicken Run* in 2000, directed by Nick Park and Peter Lord. Described as "*The Great Escape* with chickens," the film was one of the biggest hits of the year and took the medium of clay animation to new heights never before achieved on the big screen. The DreamWorks/Aardman team continued with preproduction on more features. The idea for a Wallace & Gromit feature had always been on their minds as part of the multipicture contract, so before long it became the next project to go into production. At the same time, Tim Burton started realizing a project based on a Russian folk tale called *Corpse Bride*, and production soon began on it as a stop-motion feature. Shortly before shooting began, the decision was made to shoot the film digitally, making it the first stop-motion feature in history to be shot without film. Both films became notorious for being top secret among industry insiders, and both were produced in the UK. Finally, after years of anticipation, *Corpse Bride* and *Wallace & Gromit: Curse of the Were-Rabbit* were released within weeks of each other in the Fall of 2005. Both were nominated for "Best Animated Feature" at the 2006 Oscars, and *Wallace & Gromit* took home the award yet again. Their simultaneous releases, nominations, and win were a historical first for the genre of the stop-motion animation feature. Both films featured outstanding animation that raised the bar to a whole new level of technical artistry. They were also groundbreaking in the way they combined classic stop-motion with the latest in digital compositing technology. What does this mainstream success mean for the medium of stop-motion animation today and in the future? Time will tell....

The history of this wonderful art form is vast and varied, and there are hundreds of other artists who have contributed to its exploration who I have regrettably not mentioned. There are also mysterious works that have been lost or forgotten, just waiting to be rediscovered and made new again. In that sense, the history of stop-motion is never antiquated but forever being discovered by those who dare to look back in hopes of finding inspiration for the future. I would encourage you to hunt for as many of these rare gems as you can, through the Internet or your local independent video store. Compared to other art forms, we've only scratched the surface of stop-motion animation, and there is still a long way to go.

Chapter 2
The Stop-Motion Industry

L ife in a stop-motion studio is very exciting. Most studios are very unassuming from the outside, usually tucked away in a warehouse district or downtown corner. Inside, the typical studio is a business like any other, often with a reception desk, offices, computers, and a little kitchen area, but also with intricate tiny stages, a maze of lights and cables, and strange beings called "animators" hunched over miniature puppets and pushing them around. It may sound like a playground, but this is hard work. The employees of these companies, large or small, put in long hours and toil under tight deadlines. A feature film made in stop-motion takes an average of 3 to 5 years from start to finish. The meticulous quality of the work involved is no easy feat, but it is all worth it in the end for creative teams of artists doing what they love. Some of the interview subjects in this book provide their own detailed stories about how studio productions are run, but first I will provide a basic overview of the whole process.

The Production Pipeline

In an animation studio, one of the most common terms used to describe any particular production is a "show." Whether it is a feature film, TV series episode, or commercial, industry insiders still use this word. The procedure for creating the show is executed by a team of people working in different departments, each with his own set of skills, talents, and experience. Following is an overview of the production workflow.

Step 1: The Idea

Every show has to start with an idea. Ideas can come from anywhere, sometimes from the strangest places. From the age of 16, author C.S. Lewis had an image in his head of a faun carrying an umbrella, standing in a snowy wood. Many years later, this picture would provide the inspiration for his book, *The Lion, The Witch, and The Wardrobe*. Where this picture came from is a mystery, but we all have images like this that often make their way into our creative work. Many of the best ideas also come from personal experiences we've had or people we know. Part of Nick Park's inspiration for the character of Wallace came from his own father. Other story ideas trace their roots back to ancient myths and religions. George Lucas derived many of the themes in his *Star Wars* films by incorporating similar patterns from myths in all different cultures throughout history.

Wherever the inspiration comes from, in a studio environment these ideas are discussed among a team of writers and artists all working toward a common vision. The idea may originate from the person who directs the show, or the studio may decide to hire a director whose personal style matches the idea perfectly. If the production is a commercial, the idea may come from company executives who want to sell their product. The company becomes a client of the animation studio team, who are hired to use their creative skills to find the best way to grab the public's attention. Ultimately, there must be some kind of motivation behind the idea that is being discussed. Is it to sell a product, educate children, teach a moral lesson, or just simply entertain the audience? Once these agendas are agreed upon, a story treatment or script may be written to flesh out the ideas on paper and provide a framework for the show.

Step 2: Concept Art and Design

Once an idea has been brainstormed, the next step is to translate that idea into visuals. Often, the idea itself will come from a drawing or design (for example, the drawing in Figure 2.1), and this design merely needs to be developed further. Concept artists and illustrators create a series of drawings and paintings to find a look for their idea.

Characters, backgrounds, props, and vehicles go through a series of different variations until they finally arrive at a design that works perfectly. Much attention is paid to color schemes and the mood of the show. In some productions, like *The Nightmare Before Christmas*, there are different worlds that have their own design sense: the dark, expressionistic look of Halloween Town is a totally different design from the colorful softness of Christmas Town, yet both worlds had to be used in the same film and fit in with the overall vision of the director. Much of the concept art created in these early stages will not likely be used for the final look of the show, but it is necessary to go

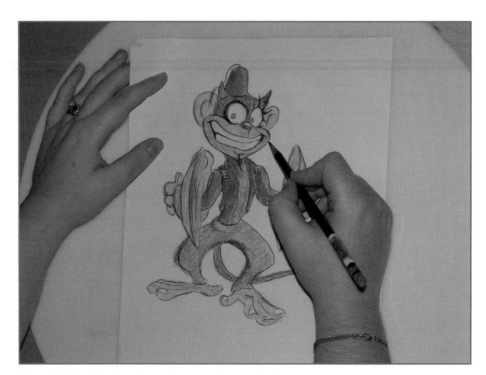

Figure 2.1 An idea for a show often comes from a drawing.

through this evolutionary process to arrive at the best design possible. The concept art can be shown to the studio's clients to give them a sense of what the finished product will look like and to give them the opportunity to offer their opinion. The concept artists must be willing to compromise their own creative ideas to please the client or the director.

Step 3: Storyboarding

The script and final concept design for the show is translated into a series of static drawings called a *storyboard*. A storyboard is similar to a comic book, consisting of square panels that tell the story visually rather than using only words. Storyboard artists draw each of the scenes and post them up in sequence on a huge bulletin board, which often takes up the entire wall of a room (see Figure 2.2). In this room, the writers and artists have story meetings with the director, where they describe the action taking place in the storyboard. A commercial client can sit in on story meetings so that they can be taken through the entire show and get a real sense of how it will look, and suggest any changes of their own. The concept of storyboards and story meetings is one of the many innovations of the Walt Disney studio in animation's Golden Age, and it has since been used even for live-action productions.

The storyboard phase is the most important part of any animated production. Any changes to the story must be decided upon and confirmed before production begins. This ensures that no time or money will be wasted on animating any scenes that eventually may end up slowing down the story. Because the individual storyboard panels are small, they do not take much time to draw, so changes can be made quickly. The end goal of the storyboard is to provide a visual blueprint for all of the production stages to follow.

Step 4: Sound Recording and Exposure Sheets

While characters are being designed and storyboards created, dialogue is also recorded by professional actors or voice artists (see Figure 2.3).

There is often a strong correlation between the design and voice of a character. The voice of a particular actor may provide the inspiration for how the character is designed, or the opposite may occur, where the actor creates a voice based on the design. After going through several takes to find the right inflection and acting for each scene, the best takes are edited together to create the final soundtrack. Any musical numbers in the show are also written and recorded at this stage.

Figure 2.2 Storyboard artists plan out how the story will be told on screen.

Figure 2.3 A voice artist records dialogue. (Courtesy of Bowes Productions Inc.)

The soundtrack is broken down frame by frame onto exposure sheets (also referred to as "dope sheets"), which will serve as a kind of road map for the animator during production. Every syllable or musical beat is broken down so that the animator will know the exact frame in which to place a particular mouth position or to plan movements to synchronize with a musical number.

Step 5: Story Reel

The storyboard drawings can then be synced up with the soundtrack to create a *story reel*. This is the earliest version of the actual show, and it provides a blueprint for the timing of each scene, the camera movement, and editing. Story reels have traditionally been created with static storyboard drawings that change in sync with the soundtrack, but in more recent years, new developments for storyboarding have become an industry standard. Many studios now embellish their static storyboard drawings by scanning in different levels of artwork to create simple character movements that more closely imitate the actual animation to be created later. Studios are also using 3D computer animation software to create simple low-resolution versions of their scenes. Simple models or stickmen are moved around to give a sense of how the scene will look. Different camera angles or movements can be explored and changed to achieve the best possible dramatic effect for the action. The results are crude and not meant to be anything more than that, for their goal is to provide a guide for the animator as to how each shot should look. This kind of "moving storyboard" is also referred to as an *animatic*.

Step 6: Designing and Building Puppets and Sets

While storyboards are being finalized and sound is being recorded, the approved concept designs are given to craftsmen who now have to translate 2D sketches and paintings into three dimensions (see Figure 2.4). Sets need to be built so that the animators have easy access to the puppets they are animating. Oftentimes, a miniature mock-up version of the set will be built out of cardboard or foam so that the director can evaluate it before the actual set is built. Most stop-motion sets are built on steady wooden platforms to prevent them from being moved.

Figure 2.4 Cole Campbell paints a set piece for *Twisteeria*, 1998. (Courtesy of Bowes Productions Inc.)

If the set needs to be large enough to accommodate several puppets in a group shot, trapdoors may need to be hidden within the set so that the animator can enter the set from underneath and reach the puppets. Everything is planned out very carefully based on the shots dictated in the animatic and the actions of the characters. Backgrounds may be painted on giant backdrops behind the set, or the sets may be shot in front of a green screen so that a live-action or computer-generated background can be composited in later.

Puppets are created by an entire team of artists working on different stages of production (see Figure 2.5). Puppet armatures and materials are created based on the movements that need to be performed by the puppet. Decisions are made as to which materials will allow the best freedom of movement for the animator, whether they be plasticine or foam latex materials. Most studio productions build their puppets using foam latex around a metal ball-and-socket armature, because this process allows for several different copies of a character to be created. This is useful, since the puppets go through a lot of abuse by the animator. It also makes it possible for several different animators to be working on scenes with the same character on different sets at the same time. If the show's design calls for a clay animation look, as for shows such as *Gumby* or the *Creature Comforts* series, molds may be created from which to shape the characters so that artists can duplicate the characters and still have them made out of clay. Oftentimes, the only part of the puppet that will be replicated in clay will be the hands and faces, since these are the most expressive parts of the character. Their bodies, or any other parts of the set that do not have to be manipulated, can be made out of Sculpey or other hardened clay material, so that the whole character still has a clay "look." Or, foam latex over an armature may be used, with the head and hands remaining clay.

Figure 2.5 Puppet supervisor Rob Ronning paints a puppet for MTV/Insight Films' *Monster Island*, 2004. (Courtesy of Bowes Productions Inc.)

2. The Stop-Motion Industry

39

Whatever materials are used, the puppet-making process has an assembly-line procedure, starting with the armature and sculpture departments. Armatures are assembled by machinists based on the design and movement requirements of the character. Meanwhile, the sculptor creates a clay model of the character that will fit exactly over the armature. A mold of the clay model is cast by the molding department, and the armature is laid inside and filled with latex to create the final puppet. The puppet is then sent to the fabrication department for painting and application of any textures such as hair, fur, or clothing that are needed.

Step 7: Animation

With the sets and puppets ready to go, cameras and lights are set up for each shot. The puppets are placed into position on stage, and the animators begin bringing them to life (see Figure 2.6). If time and budget allow, they can go through a series of test shots with the puppet, simply moving them into the key positions of the scene. This allows the animator to discuss the shot with the director to make sure that the acting and posing are exactly the way they want them. This process is accomplished in a daily screening routine called "dailies," where the team gathers to watch the previous day's shots. Once a shot has been approved, the animator can move on to the "hero shot," which will be used in the final show. Most stop-motion animators in a studio setting will create only 3 to 4 seconds of animation in a single

Figure 2.6 Key animator Chris Calvi at work on MTV/Insight Films' *Monster Island*, 2004. (Courtesy of Bowes Productions Inc.)

day's work. By the end of the day, after hunching over puppets under hot lights for hours on end, the toll it can take on the animator's body can be painful (as depicted in Figure 2.7). It's common for some major productions to hire a massage therapist for this reason.

Depending on the production, the animation may be shot in several different ways. Throughout history, most professional stop-motion has been shot on 16mm or 35mm film. The animator checks his animation by looking through the viewfinder of the camera and visualizing the movement with his mind's eye. A device called a *surface gauge* is often used by the animator to keep track of the movements. A surface gauge is simply a metal pointer on a stand that is lined up with the appendage of the puppet being animated (see Figure 2.8). By moving the puppet away from the gauge into its next position (see Figure 2.9), the animator has a reference point for the last position it was in and can measure this distance to make sure the movements are properly registered.

Until the hard work is done and the film is sent to the lab to be developed, the animator has no idea what the shot looks like until the film is sent back from the lab and projected in dailies. If the shot is not usable, it must be completely redone, which can often disrupt the production schedule and budget. A great deal of concentration is needed for every frame, and the entire crew must be very careful not to disturb elements of the set or equipment. One little mistake, like bumping the camera, knocking over a light, or breaking a puppet, can destroy hours of hard work, which is very stressful.

Figure 2.7 Hunching over puppets all day can wreak havoc on an animator's body.

Figure 2.8 A surface gauge is lined up with the puppet's position.

Figure 2.9 After the puppet's position is changed, the gauge provides a reference for how far it has moved.

2. The Stop-Motion Industry

In more recent years, technology has changed the face of stop-motion animation, making it much less unpredictable and easier on production. One of the first innovations was placing a video camera next to the film camera so that the animator could see his puppet on a TV monitor rather than needing to look through the viewfinder. The animator could make marks directly on the monitor screen with a grease pencil or dry-erase marker to plan out the movements and register them (see Figure 2.10).

This method led to a video-assist device that actually fed a video image directly from the viewfinder of the film camera, which allowed the animator to see on a monitor exactly what the camera would record on film. An even further aid to the animator began with the use of a frame-grabbing system. This allowed animators to store a captured image of each frame, which they could then compare to the frame they were currently working on. With the touch of a button or flick of a switch, they could "flip" their movements in the same way that a 2D animator flips two sequential drawings.

Figure 2.10 Drawing on a TV monitor is one way to plan the animation. (Courtesy of Nick Hilligoss.)

Eventually, computer technology and specialized software allowed several frames to be stored so that the animator could play back more than just the previous frame, and see the animation develop without needing to wait until the whole thing was finished and then hope it worked. This innovation allowed for more accurate registration of movements and smoother results.

All of these breakthrough methods have now been combined with other handy tools into dozens of computer applications developed specifically for stop-motion animation (which I will talk about in more detail in Chapter 4, "What You Need"). These stop-motion frame-grabbing applications are allowing some industry productions to be shot digitally with high-definition video or still cameras, storing all the frames inside the computer with no need for film. The footage can always be transferred to film later on for theater distribution. The medium used to shoot the animation ultimately depends on the final output of the show, and sometimes the budget.

Step 8: Post-Production

As animation shots are completed, they can be placed into their proper sequence in the animatic, and the final look of the film gradually unfolds until all shots are completed. If each shot has been created with the exact number of frames as indicated by the exposure sheets, very little editing will need to be done. At this post-production stage, digital effects can be composited into the shot if needed. In a recording studio, sound effects are created by special technicians called *Foley artists*. Background music is composed, recorded, and edited into the footage. Once all of these procedures are complete, the final show is finished and ready for marketing and distribution.

Opportunities

Now that you have a sense of how these productions are made, you may be wondering, "How can I get a job doing stop-motion animation?"

First of all, there is no cookie-cutter way of breaking into the animation world. Every artist is unique. We all come from different backgrounds and have had different experiences that have shaped us into who we are. We all have different skills, tastes, and beliefs. Every single person working in animation today has a different story of how he got there, even though many have taken the same steps. So the best thing to do is to evaluate which of these steps are the most important, embrace them, and then see where life takes you. Often it's just a matter of being in the right place at the right time.

There are probably more studios doing stop-motion today than in most of its history, but compared to those in exclusively 2D or CG production, they are still few and far-between. Depending on the state of the industry, the few studios that do stop-motion today will not always have a steady flow of projects. Some of them do not actually have a permanent studio space, but rather rent a space when working on a show and then move out when it's over. The competition is growing all the time, and many stop-motion studios are still feeling the pinch from the CG revolution. Many studios have succumbed to the pressure to add CG production to their repertoire just to keep the doors open. The current boom for computer-generated effects and animation is part of the reason why stop-motion remains the black sheep of the animation community. Many stop-motion animators have been forced to learn computer animation just to keep their careers going and their families fed. Plus, the practical realities of stop-motion—extreme costs, shortage of skilled artists who know the medium well, and the time-consuming nature of the medium—make it a very difficult area to establish a full-time career. Many animators have been lucky

2. The Stop-Motion Industry

enough to have a prolific career doing stop-motion professionally, but many more simply make it a hobby or produce independent films. They are much like superheroes, with a day job as their secret identity and making films by night.

History has shown us that the animation industry in general, which includes 2D and CG, goes through ups and downs just like any other business. At one moment, everyone seems to be hiring, and then a few months later, studios are closing, productions are shut down, and employees are laid off. Much of the work is contract based, so if a studio hires you for a project, your employment may last only as long as that production does, and unless the studio has another project in the pipeline, you're left looking for your next job. Working in animation can be a gypsy lifestyle for most, moving back and forth between different studios, cities, and even countries. You never really know where you will end up, because things are always changing. So, in many ways, the unpredictability of the industry can be exciting, and it's a good business to be in if you like to travel, but it can also be nerve-wracking not always having a strong sense of job security. Despite the cyclical nature of the industry, there is still an incredible demand right now for artists and animators, especially with the massive explosion of video games, visual effects, and computer-animation feature films. Video games are raking in billions of dollars every year, and films are ramping up to compete with them. We are currently in one of those "up" phases for the industry as a whole, and stop-motion will continue as part of this high demand for animated content.

With the competition being what it is, anyone wanting to work professionally as an animator should consider some formal art or animation training. I often like to describe the process of learning animation as becoming a Jedi. You need to find an opportunity to apprentice at the feet of a master who knows the craft and can guide you. Sometimes you must "unlearn what you have learned" from working in other art forms, and establishing the patience required to finish a scene takes discipline. Before today's hundreds of animation schools existed, animators generally were hired by a studio based on their artistic abilities and were then trained on the job. Now, with so many more studios and more artists wanting to break in, this rarely happens. It has become more important to find a specialized full-time program or a mentor who will train you to learn the craft and business of animation (see Figure 2.11).

Figure 2.11 Finding an instructor to guide you through the animation process is very helpful.

For stop-motion specifically, there are not many options in the area of schooling. Some art colleges do have a dedicated space for stop-motion production, complete with sets and cameras, and will offer workshops or part-time courses in puppet building or animation. However, it's very difficult to find a full-time program for stop-motion, and those that do exist are mostly experimental in nature or border on independent study. The issue of space and equipment is a challenge for most schools, especially when compared to the practicality of offering programs for 2D or CG animation. It's far easier to fill a lab with 20 drawing tables or 20 computer stations than to set up that many individual sets, each with its own camera and light kit. In Chapter 10, "An Interview with Larry Larson," and Chapter 14, "An Interview with Lynne Pritchard," instructors Larson and Pritchard describe the challenges of teaching stop-motion to a class full of students.

Stop-motion is a very individualistic and self-taught craft, and the way it is taught in schools reflects this fact. The finer points of the medium will be learned through trial and error and your own practical experimentation, whether it's in a school or in your own homemade studio space. If your school provides the space and equipment to create student projects in stop-motion animation and good instructors to mentor you, that is a rare find and an excellent way to get started. The best way to get the most out of a program like this is to complement it with other subjects as well, because stop-motion is a combination of many different skills.

If you pursue a formal education with the intention of applying it toward stop-motion production, I would recommend studying 2D animation, drawing, sculpture, film production and theory, photography, art history, acting, and computer graphics. 2D animation is one of the easiest and fastest ways to learn the principles of animation, because the only tools at your disposal are a pencil and paper, and space and time (see Figure 2.12). Learning how to animate on a computer puts a technical barrier between yourself and the animation, in that you have to wrap your head around the software to get anywhere. Sitting down and drawing your

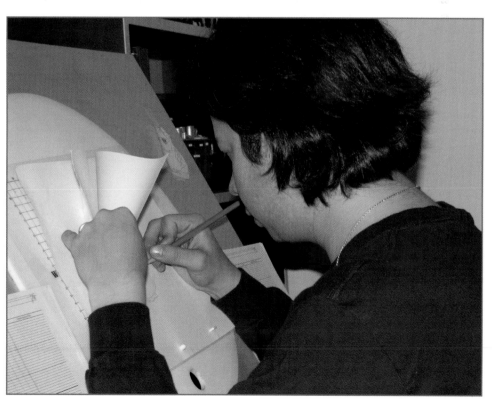

Figure 2.12 The 2D medium is a useful way to learn the basic principles of animation.

animation by hand allows you not only to develop a sense of volume and timing, but also to fix mistakes easily by simply changing, removing, or adding drawings.

Learning to animate in 2D is a great benefit to animating in stop-motion. For my stop-motion student project *Bad News*, I animated my entire dialogue scene in rough 2D drawings so that I could work out all of my posing and facial expressions beforehand. Then I simply referred to my drawings while animating my puppet, making the puppet match what I had animated previously.

Learning 2D animation obviously means knowing how to draw, and this is always a great skill to have, especially in a studio environment. The stop-motion animation process itself may not involve drawing, but as you have seen, the preproduction steps that happen before the animation do. Plus, in a studio, if you're communicating with a director about ideas or concepts, knowing how to express your idea with a simple quick sketch will get your idea across much quicker than creating it any other way. Drawing is the most basic method of communication there is, and it is usually the first thing studio recruiters want to see. Life drawing (drawing objects, landscapes, or people from real-life observation) is the key skill that every animator should have. Drawing the human figure (see Figure 2.13) allows you to analyze movement, anatomy, posing, and how the body is designed for movement. The more you understand real life, the more believable your fantasy characters will be. Understanding real anatomy and how a body moves will help when you are building and animating your puppets.

Sculpture is also an obvious subject to pay attention to, because it teaches you how to realize anatomy and structure in 3D dimensions. In a sculpture class, you can also get formal training in creating molds, which can be applied to puppet-building. If you want to create elaborate puppets and sets, you should consider taking courses in woodworking, metalworking, or mechanics.

The other subjects mentioned are important too, as they all relate to stop-motion animation. Film production and photography will both introduce you to camera operation: how to set your exposure properly, load the film, create zooms and tracking shots, and so on. You also learn about how to properly light a scene for different conditions and moods. Film production teaches you how to write, plan, shoot, and edit a film in a team setting, which is very important for getting into studio production. Courses in film theory and the "art of the film" teach you how different directors in different film genres reach their audiences on an emotional level by the way they use the language of cinema: lighting, editing, music, and composition. Studying and analyzing films shows you that there is much more under the surface than just moving images on-screen, and this knowledge will inspire you to make your film projects into true works of art. Learning art history is beneficial for the same reasons, since it broadens your knowledge of the techniques, styles, and inspiration behind centuries of past artists.

Acting is another great skill to master if you want to work in animation. The essence of animation is creating a performance with your character and making the audience believe that your puppet has a life of its own. Your character should be able to express a wide range of emotions through its body language, facial expressions, and speech. Every animator is an actor who creates a performance through his character. Animators are sometimes referred to as "shy actors" who would rather let their animation do the acting for them. The animators I know who create the most outrageous performances are often very quiet and introverted in real life. They would never act silly or violent themselves, but their characters do the craziest things, and you wonder where it all comes from! But if you are willing to break out of your shell momentarily, acting classes will help you become aware of the way your body moves and the real-time thought processes that go into becoming a different person.

Figure 2.13 Life drawing helps you understand the human form in movement.

Finally, in this day and age, it's becoming more crucial to have a good knowledge of computer graphics or computer animation. Computers, despite all of their frustrations and hard-drive crashes, are the reason that stop-motion animation has been allowed to flourish, due to the advancement of stop-motion software, so it's important for the animator to become friends with the virtual world. For editing, compositing, and post-production, the most common software in the animation industry is Photoshop, After Effects, Shake, Combustion, Flame, Premiere, and Final Cut Pro. Popular packages for computer animation include Maya, 3ds Max, LightWave, and SOFTIMAGE XSI. The main thing to remember is that the computer is just a tool that is still dependent on the discipline of a skilled artist. In the realm of CG character animation, the best animators are typically those who have first learned how to animate in the 2D or stop-motion mediums. While the technology for computer animation is rapidly changing, the principles of believable movement and acting do not change. Other foundations of color theory, anatomy, storytelling, and design never change either. Only the methods through which these principles are used will continue to change and grow into the future. So it's important to be able to adapt to the technology of the future while having a firm grasp on the past foundations of animation.

The other big advantage to going to school to learn anything related to animation is the opportunity to meet other students who have the same interests and passions as you. Keeping in touch with your classmates is the most valuable resource for your career, as they might be the ones who will hire you some day. When looking to expand their crew, most studios will seek internal references before they release job postings. They ask the people who already work for them if they know anyone they would recommend to join the team. One of the things you learn about the industry right away is that everybody knows everybody, whether they know them from working at studios or going to school together. So it's important to establish a good reputation while you're in school, because you want people to remember you as someone who not only has talent, but is also a team player, and reliable and generous. There are lots of artists out there who cannot advance in their careers because nobody will recommend them, despite their talent. Making enemies in a creative environment will haunt you for a lifetime, so play nice!

In addition to meeting people at school, for any field you choose to pursue as a hobby or career, the most valuable way to get ahead is to network. Seek out people who have that dream job you want, and talk to them. Ask them how they got started, and ask them for feedback on your own work, but realize also that these people often have busy schedules, so respect them enough not to become a pest. As you become interested in any subject and start experimenting with it, life has a way of putting the right people in your path to give you further advice or, ideally, offer you a job. Other ways to find people who do stop-motion are by looking for organizations, events, and Web sites. There are no official clubs or organizations for stop-motion exclusively, but the animation industry has the ASIFA (International Animated Film Association), Women in Animation, and many other organizations for connecting with animators, some of which are professionals in stop-motion.

ACM SIGGRAPH (Association for Computing Machinery's Special Interest Group on Graphics and Interactive Techniques)is an annual event in the U.S. that focuses mainly on computer graphics, but many schools and studios are represented there, and it's a great way to meet industry people. It's also useful to attend film festivals, most of which have an animation category, and the animators themselves will often be present for you to chat with. There are even festivals for animation only, where the opportunity to network is the best you can get: Studio reps and independent filmmakers alike gather to watch films, attend seminars, offer workshops, and party! The three biggest festivals for animation are the Zagreb, Annecy, and Ottawa festivals (see Figure 2.14), and many other smaller ones are spread out all over the world.

Figure 2.14 The Animarket at the Ottawa International Animation Festival.

The biggest and best online resource for the animation industry is the Animation World Network (www.awn.com). There you will find articles, job postings, school listings, a studio database, and many other resources for keeping your finger on the pulse of the industry. For stop-motion specifically, Anthony Scott's Web site, www.stopmotionanimation.com (see Chapter 8), has the ultimate online community for newbies and professionals to share ideas on an extensive message board that covers all topics related to the stop-motion craft. There is also a long list of links to practically every other stop-motion site on the Web. The Internet is fast becoming an incredible showcase for stop-motion and the close-knit group of artists who love it. You'll find more details on festivals and the Internet in Chapter 15, "Distribution."

With all of these resources at your fingertips, the way to get into stop-motion is just to get your hands dirty and go for it! Making your own stop-motion, and going through its trials and errors, will tell you pretty quickly whether you want to continue it as a hobby or attempt to make it into a career. Once you learn the craft, either on your own or in a school, you can make a demo reel or a short film, show it off on the Internet or at a festival, and see what happens. The opportunities are there, and they're changing all the time. So if you're still game, let's get started....

Chapter 3
An Interview with David Bowes

Figure 3.1
David Bowes.
(Copyright
2006 Bowes
Productions
Inc.)

David Bowes (pictured in Figure 3.1) is the founder, producer, director, and president of Bowes Productions, Inc., an award-winning stop-motion animation studio in Vancouver, BC, Canada. Since 1988, his company has produced a wide variety of animated productions, from television specials, commercials, and animated feature film elements, to production design, props, puppets, miniatures, and sets. Over the years, he has assembled a strong freelance team, Bowes & Associates, which continues to expand into new areas of stop-motion and CG productions. The company's Web site is www.bowesproductions.com. I first met David by contacting him for advice on my stop-motion project *Bad News* back in 1999.

KEN: *How did you get started with stop-motion animation?*

DAVID: It was actually the furthest thing from my mind when I decided in 1985 to attend Camosun College's Visual Arts program in Victoria, BC. My intention was to learn gas-firing kilns and formulate glazes for sculpture. In the second year, we were required to take a basic animation course, where we had to incorporate six forms of animation—from line drawn, rear projection, pencil crayon, cut-out, cel, and (puppet) clay animation—into a one-minute piece. I created a short entitled *At Half Past Midnight* (see Figure 3.2) and incorporated the clay sequence at the end of the short with a clay character playing a pipe organ in a haunted house miniature attic. I wanted ghosts to fly out of the pipes while the character played, so I screwed the set to my living room floor, took a window frame with glass and screwed that down against the edge of the set, and then locked down a Super 8 camera another 4 feet from the window frame. I then took a long piece of wooden dowel with a felt pen taped to the end, and by looking through the viewfinder of the camera, I was able to mark the tops of the pipes of the model organ to register where the ghost would fly out. I then animated the ghost sequence separately on cels. When the time came to actually animate the clay character playing the organ, I simply replaced each cel on an animation peg bar every time I double framed the character movement. Two weeks later when the film came back to the college, I asked everybody to leave the room so I could project it alone (a practice which became a ritual). Lo and behold, it worked! The end result was magic. The ghosts were slightly out of focus, which added to the effect of them flying around the room while this crazy little psychotic character played Bach's "Toccata and Fugue in D Minor." I was totally mesmerized, as it was one of those perfect moments where I knew exactly what I wanted to do as a career.

Figure 3.2 *At Half Past Midnight*. (Copyright 1986 Bowes Productions Inc.)

KEN: *So then how did this moment lead to starting your own studio?*

DAVID: After I graduated from the 2-year program, I decided to take a 1-year independent study to further my animation skills and ended up creating four films using the college's 16mm Bolex, which I taught myself how to use. The first time I used the camera, I left the exposure in the timed exposure (T) position, and my entire 2-minute animated short entitled *Canadian Express* was overexposed. With a lesson learned, I immediately successfully reshot. My fourth film, *The Mad Potter*, I screened at the University of Victoria as it had one of the few 16mm projectors in town that could play a magnetic sound stripe. While I was screening my film, Gresham Bradley from the Knowledge Network just happened to walk by and very excitedly asked me if he could air my piece. They paid for an original music score and editing, and while I was in the edit suite late one night in Vancouver, the editor commented that the short was pretty cool and stated, "You should start a business." This comment influenced me, and before I knew it I was sitting with a corporate lawyer. In the end, as his fee was beyond my budget, I purchased a book, *How to Incorporate Your Own Business*. I registered the company using my last name for two reasons. First, in college it was a standard, and second, and most importantly, I felt it would give me the drive to stay focused and succeed. Next, I purchased my own 16mm Bolex camera. I remember waking up the next morning and saying to myself, "Well, you're a company with a Bolex camera. Now what?" That morning I started making phone calls, and over the next several weeks found that most companies and agencies wanted to see a commercial demo tape, which I didn't have. At that time, the Carmanah Valley Rainforest, located on the west coast of Vancouver Island, was big in the media, so I decided to make a commercial about it called *The Talking Rainforest* (see Figure 3.3). I approached the National Film Board of Canada for assistance, and they recommended that I contact the

Figure 3.3 *The Talking Rainforest.* (Copyright 1989 Bowes Productions Inc.)

magazine publisher of *Adbusters* in Vancouver, who helped me produce a 30-second spot making people aware of our vanishing rainforests. When it finally aired 8 months after conception on BCTV, now Global TV, it was tough to watch it go by so quickly after spending so much time and money on it. In the end, however, it was extremely positive for the Carmanah Valley, and it became the flagship of my company.

With the *Mad Potter* now on the air with the Knowledge Network, and the media hype with *The Talking Rainforest,* a production company, May Street Productions, based in Victoria, took notice. They wanted a clay character called "Morf" to interact with live action throughout their children's series entitled *Take Off.* Basically this was our first paying contract. During this production, my then business partner and I attended the Banff Television Festival and walked away with a contract with Calico Pix/CBC for the one-hour special entitled *Alligator Pie.* We produced two clay animated segments. Clay was very popular in the late '80s and early '90s, with credit to Will Vinton's *California Raisins* series of commercials. As a result, our work became fairly steady. We secured a contract with Fuji Television of Japan, producing clay segments for its ongoing children's series *Hirake Ponkiki,* teaching children English.

Various service contracts continued coming in from station IDs, including elements for commercials, magazines, and a few 2D animated contracts. In 1996, we made the decision to move from Victoria to Vancouver with the award of a new commercial for General Mills. This was a very effective business decision, as it made it easier to meet with clients and secure additional contracts. The next big turning point was our first half-hour Halloween special for YTV of Canada entitled *Twisteeria* (see Figure 3.4), which won the 1999 Leo Award for Best Animated Program and was nominated for four Gemini Awards. Since then, we have focused on commercials, creating elements for series and features mostly, and more recently we have started transitioning into computer animation with our latest television series. I feel we've picked a good time for this transition, based on the fact that there are various software programs out now that can replicate the look of stop-motion. I don't think it will ever be the same, but it's pretty scary when you look at how close it is. We don't intend to break away from stop-motion completely, but rather develop projects that combine the two.

Figure 3.4 *Twisteeria* sharks on mopeds. (Copyright 1998 Bowes Productions Inc.)

KEN: *Do you have a particular favorite project from the past 17 years?*

DAVID: Yes, the animation sequence we did for Paramount Pictures' Nickelodeon on the feature film *Snow Day* was not only a favorite of mine, but also a favorite of the team who worked on it. The phone call came in, they flew us to Calgary for a production meeting, we returned to assemble our gear, and then flew back to Calgary for the shoot. It ended up being one of our favorites based on the fact that the overall production went off without a hitch and in the end we were treated the way you should be treated in the industry. Another highlight was a Christmas commercial we did for the ad agency Linguis for their client Western Wireless Communications—*Cellular One* in the United States (see Figure 3.5). You always have to expect hiccups during jobs in production, but this was another memorable one that was on time and on budget, and the client loved it. In the end, however, one of my personal visual favorites was the clay sequence we produced for *Alligator Pie* with Dennis Lee's poem *The sitter and the butter and the better batter fritter.*

KEN: *Can you explain a bit about the bidding process and how projects get approved for production?*

DAVID: For service work, it usually starts with a phone call or e-mail from a production company or ad agency requesting a demo. Also, we receive inquires on our Web site, from an advertisement in a trade magazine or, most often, by word of mouth. Your demo is reviewed based on the quality of past productions, or anything on the reel that might relate to what the client or director is looking for. If they like what they see, you're placed into their "A" list, which then follows through with a conference call with the producer and director. You need to understand their script and/or storyboard and be extremely creative and original with your approach. One has to be well prepared prior to this call and have reviewed all aspects with the heads of your company's department, from character or set designers, puppet or set supervisors, key animation supervisor, post supervisor, etc.

Figure 3.5 "Missy" from *Cellular One*, Linguis. (Copyright 2002 Bowes Productions Inc.)

It boils down to whoever does [his] homework and presents the best presentation to the client will get the job. Of course, one of the most important aspects of the bid is the budget. Generally, whoever is approaching you with a project already has a budget in mind, so I generally ask [him] what that figure is and then work backward and detail what we can do for that price. The bidding can be very straightforward at times, and other times there's a lot of number crunching with much patience involved. Sometimes the budget may not be as high as we would like to see it, but we consider the gig anyways, based on the fact that we like the creative and it would be a nice addition to our reel. There's actually a lot of work involved in preparing your bid, with no guarantees. There may be six other companies bidding on the same job, and they are all very capable, so as a team you have to come up with an approach that has an edge. It can be pretty nerve-racking waiting for the phone call to see who has been awarded the contract, but in the end, I love the hunt for the job. If you do not get the job, you need to move forward and not take it to heart. If, on the other hand, the job is awarded to you, you really need to hit the ground running. There might be only 6 to 12 weeks to produce a spot, and you need to have a full production team working within days. The complete stop-motion animation and effects we produced for MTV and Insight Films' *Monster Island* went into production September 5 to December 23, which was an intense effort for our team. Keep in mind there were 4 months of bidding and number crunching for the contract prior to starting.

There is a different approach altogether with your own in-house production concepts, such as shorts, specials, and series being approved for development. It all starts with a well-thought-out idea, which can take weeks, months, or even longer to get to concept. Again, I can't stress how important it is that your idea be as strong as possible. Ask yourself if your story concept can sustain 26 to 52 episodes and avoid adding holiday themes as springboards such as Christmas, Halloween, etc. Once you feel confident with your proposal, you need to get a Canadian broadcaster on board in order to trigger funding within Canada. This stage boils down to the "pitch." I always keep in mind that the pitch should be no longer than 1 minute or one paragraph. If it takes 5 minutes to get your idea across, consider going back to the drawing board. Remember, you may only have one shot at it.

Here's an eye opener: Up to a thousand proposals a year on average are submitted to a children's broadcaster, so your idea must stand out. If your idea is good and it's what they're looking for, you'll know right away. If you've peeked their interest, then the second phase takes place, which means you'll then elaborate with more detail on the concept and possibly some visual creative. Keep in mind that a visual presentation may work against you. I've pitched with full character and set designs and sadly found that it was not what a particular broadcaster liked. It's important to know your broadcaster well. Teletoon, for example, may have a different format from YTV of Canada, Cartoon Network, or Nickelodeon, in terms of what kinds of shows they are airing. Therefore, you need to watch what is on TV, what kids are watching, what's new and exciting.

It's ironic because adults make cartoons and children watch them, excluding primetime animation, so you have to know your audience. You may think you have a great show, but if two kids sitting on the couch watching it decide they don't like it, multiply that a thousand times over, and the ratings won't be there. The bottom line is to create or find a good idea, know your broadcaster and age demographics, and be passionate about your idea.

On a final note, getting picked up by a broadcaster to develop your concept is a major accomplishment. After this, your next hurdle is raising the capital. It takes a dedicated group of experienced and knowledgeable executive producers to secure the financing, which may take years. One could write an entire book on this subject alone.

KEN: *What else is important to know for someone running his own studio?*

DAVID: Starting your own studio is not as simple as one might dream. You have to be a risk taker. It takes a lot of time, money, investment, and responsibility. Capital is always the most important aspect of any business. One must be prepared to commit to long hours, perseverance, and be prepared for a lot of sacrifices. It's very rare that one becomes a success overnight. Having said this, if you choose to consider your own studio, focus on building a reel first; if you don't have a product people want, you won't have any revenue. Build a reel and learn to promote yourself; what better person than yourself? A publicist will eventually come into the picture once you're established. The Internet is a relatively fast and cheap way to promote your work and especially feature some of your animated shorts; however, keep in mind: You can't promote what you don't have. It may take years to obtain a great visual resume; however, sometimes in this ecliptic market, it's not all about the polished look. Lesser quality of puppets and even movement in some cases can be well received with a good idea and good storytelling. In the end, however, it may be more rewarding and your best option to work for a studio that is already established and gain experience through the creative, leaving the business headaches to the CEO. The film industry can be a tough business at times, and it's true what they say: "You're only as good as your last gig." If you're not prepared for the down times, well, the rest is left unsaid.

KEN: *Which materials have you found work best for building puppets in a stop-motion production?*

DAVID: Partly it depends on your budget. We always say, your animation is only as good as your armature. In the past, we've worked with lead armatures with brass fittings, but moved away from them due to the toxic component of the lead. We all like to use ball-and-sockets, but if our budget is limited, then aluminum wire is usually the way to go, and you can obtain some very nice movements. This again is governed by the skill and experience of the animator. You really need a ball and socket armature if the puppet(s) requires endurance with many scenes, you're looking for precise movements, or the puppet is large with weight, but even ball and sockets can break. For *Monster Island*, our team of extremely experienced puppet fabricators created one praying mantis and several ants out of polyurethane and foam covering ball-and-socket armatures (see Figure 3.6). This was the only way to go based on the weight. Designing the puppets out of clay would have been impossible. For us, foam rubber latex is such a joy to work with because for years while using clay the characters would need constant cleanup after every shot, and during the shoot the animator had to spend more time cleaning between frames. Moving to foam allowed the animators to focus on their animation instead of worrying about cleanup. As a bonus, the foam puppets can last for years, as long as you keep them in a controlled environment.

I still like clay, as it has a certain look to it, and the process is rather therapeutic, working with this organic material in front of you. In the mid to late '90s, clay appeared to be less common in North America compared to England, and many were concerned with the rise of CGI that clay was going to disappear altogether. But certain companies stayed true to the medium and were able to place clay into the "here to stay" category. The most obvious being Aardman Studios in Bristol with the huge success of *Wallace and Gromit,* and the list goes on.

Now there are many children's series being shot in clay throughout the international markets. If you look at the preschool lineup for the BBC, it's either clay or stop-motion. Over the years, there has been this rival battle between CGI and stop-motion, but no matter what medium is used, it all boils down to a good idea and good storytelling. In my opinion, all the various forms of animation have found their place. Every once in a while, you'll hear someone say 2D classical is a dying art. I simply point out *The Simpson's, Family Guy*, etc.

3. An Interview with David Bowes

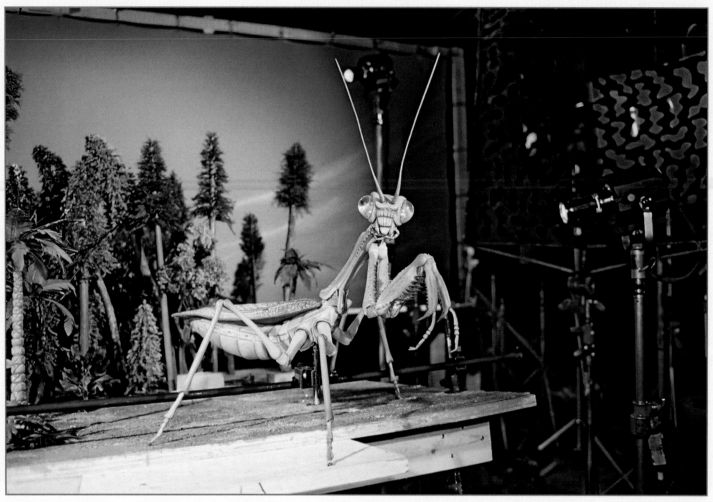

Figure 3.6 Insight Films/MTV's *Monster Island* praying mantis. (Copyright 2003 Bowes Productions Inc.)

KEN: *Do you think there are any untapped markets or trends that stop-motion is starting to cross into?*

DAVID: Well, that's a tough question. It's like asking where you think the next real-estate boom will be. Just when you think everything possible has been done in animation, someone comes along with an alternate approach. I don't think anything is truly new, only revisited by utilizing the ever-changing computer technology. In order to be more effective with limited budgets, some stop-motion companies have turned to streamlining the lip sync with their puppets by compositing CGI mouths, which have proven to be quite effective. Those same studios have successfully composited clay heads and faces on live-action bodies or vice versa. In the end, it's creative people who recognize the computer as a tool and effectively explore the combination of stop-motion and CGI that will find new trends.

Other studios are focusing on the ideas and not worrying so much with the quality of movement or puppets, which in (some) cases, works. Some label it as "guerilla animation" or "the collage look." Again, with the right idea, the wacky stuff is funny to watch, if you don't really concern yourself with the quality. My feeling is that *Beavis & Butthead* paved the way to the acceptance of crude animation with the viewer. On one side of the fence, you had the creators who threw caution to the wind without a concern for exquisite animation, and on the other side of the fence, you had the purists who cringed at it. But in the end, it was the viewer who ultimately accepted this and started this trend.

KEN: *What advice do you have for aspiring stop-motion animators?*

DAVID: First off, in any form of animation, it can take years of practice, patience, dedication, and experience on many productions to perfect your skill to become a professional. Some individuals can become a "star" (as we say in the industry) overnight, but this still requires hundreds and hundreds of committed hours in front of the camera. But, like everyone who eventually became a professional, they had to start somewhere.

Taking into account that you have the necessary equipment for filming, find out if you really have a passion for it by animating some simple objects found around the house, or a plastic action doll or something with simple armature. Don't worry too much about trying to make a perfect sculptured puppet; this will come down the road and, again, to reach a professional level of a puppet fabricator can take years. Learn your skill and gain experience. I recommend in the beginning to concentrate on short little lessons by using a small clay ball. Teach yourself about constants, tempo, timing, movement, weight, and holds. An excellent series for learning animation was produced by the renowned animator Norman McLaren for the National Film Board of Canada, entitled "Animated Motion" (NFB 1976-8). This series visually explains the basics and more advanced techniques of traditional animation, but most importantly, can be translated to stop-motion. This series can still be ordered through the NFB and is a great addition to your library.

Watch and study as many stop-motion animated productions as possible, and if you can freeze frame and then advance frame by frame, all the better. Study movement by watching people, animals, and moving objects around you. Act out movements based on 24 frames a second in front of a mirror, and time yourself with a stopwatch. In the end, animation is replicating the reality of movement with everyday life and transferring it into a character, car, tree, dog, etc.

Learn your skill and gain confidence before you set out to create an elaborate short or tell a story to avoid frustration. Having said this, it all depends on the individual; many skills are learned by working through the challenges presented while working on your short. This, of course, was the direction I took.

If you truly have passion for becoming an animator, you should consider enrolling in a classical animation course to further your training. This will help immensely with all forms of animation and may even help you land a job. Most studios, especially CGI studios, are now leaning toward hiring individuals with this form of training over those without it. There are many graduates out there, and everyone is searching for the one job.

Once you have become a good animator, you need to be persistent and continue to better yourself with every gig. You should realize that a career in animation, especially stop-motion, might require you to become a freelancer, and you must be willing to travel where the productions are. One moment you might be in Vancouver, then Toronto…next you might be in England.

In the end, learn your trade extremely well to ensure this rewarding career will continue to give you the satisfaction creatively and financially. Most important, the passion from each individual learning stop-motion will keep this age-old form of animation alive and continue to hold its place within the world of animation.

PART II

Creating
Animation

Chapter 4
What You Need

This chapter describes the basic elements necessary to create your own stop-motion animation: camera, tripod, computer, software, set, lights, and some basic supplies. Mainly I will focus on how to get equipped for a very simple setup that can be placed in the average home or classroom. With this setup, you should be able to complete the animation exercises described in later chapters and continue on with your own experimentation. If you have the time, space, money, and energy, you can move on from there to high-end equipment that would match that of a major commercial studio. But first, learn to crawl before you get to walking.

"A film is never really good unless the camera is an eye in the head of a poet."

—*Orson Welles*

Cameras

The camera is your most important piece of equipment for shooting stop-motion animation. Cameras able to shoot moving pictures have been around since the late 1800s. They started as an extension of still photography and evolved to the point where they were used to capture the images necessary to create unique entertainment, and the movie industry was born. Standard film used for movies is 35 millimeters in width, thus being referred to as 35mm film. This is the kind of film projected at your local movie theater. As early as 1923, the Eastman Kodak company began searching for a way to make film that was less expensive and cumbersome to use. The results were film stocks in 16mm, and even smaller 8mm, including a special brand called Super 8mm. By the 1950s, movie cameras moved from Hollywood into the hands of families everywhere for shooting their own home movies. This invention allowed anyone to become a filmmaker, and if this person's camera had a single-frame capability, he could be an animator, too! The movie film inside the camera would then be developed at a film processing lab, and then you would thread it into an 8mm or 16mm movie film projector for viewing (see Figure 4.1).

Figure 4.1 16mm film and projector.

Home movie cameras, mostly Super 8mm, continued their popularity until the development of video, which hit its stride in the late 1970s. By the time the 1980s arrived, families were now shooting with video "camcorders" onto standard VHS tapes. I remember the first video camera my family bought, which was connected to a separate VCR that would hang off a shoulder strap! Luckily, this antiquated, painful method soon evolved into smaller Hi-8 and Mini DV tape formats using cameras that fit into the palm of your hand. For shooting animation, video cameras have never proved to be useful at all by themselves, for none of them were capable of capturing single frames. (At the most, some modern models have a built-in feature for capturing six frames at a time, and then those frames can be loaded into a computer and the extra frames deleted. It's a very laborious process that doesn't have a great deal of flexibility for easy animating.) Eventually there came some useful devices for storing individual video frames. The Perception Video Recorder (computer system for rendering real-time playback) and Lunchbox systems (hardware for capturing video images) began being used by studios for doing simple frame grabbing, which allowed animators to see their animation evolve in real time. This equipment could be purchased for home use, but not for most animators' average budgets. With the advent of every home having its own personal computer, affordable video cards began being developed that could capture images digitally from a camcorder directly into the computer. This breakthrough led to the development of software that was specifically catered for capturing single images from a video camera to create stop-motion animation. In this setup, the camera itself does not store images but serves only as an eye for providing the images captured digitally inside the computer. This method is the most common now for shooting animation at home or in school, and it has also made its way into commercial production. To get the most out of this book and to complete the exercises later on, you will need a video camera, capture card, and software for your computer. However, film is not entirely obsolete yet, so I will discuss it briefly as well.

Film

Film has been used for a long time to shoot stop-motion animation, and most people working in the medium today, including myself, started off using film, so I do have a bit of a nostalgic soft spot for it. The best part about film is how it looks when it's finally projected; I love watching animation on film and relishing the stark, crisp quality of image you can achieve with it. There is something quite fantastic about seeing those images projected with real light behind them, and I even enjoy the aesthetic quality of dancing dust and film scratches. However, the actual process of shooting on film does have some disadvantages that are only made more significant by today's digital age. Shooting your animation on film means that all of your frames are stored inside the camera, and there is no way to know how your animation looks until you've spent a great deal of money getting it processed at a film lab. There is also the added step of setting the exposure to capture the right amount of light entering the lens. Speaking from personal experience, it's very frustrating spending hours on an animation piece, only to get the film back with the image too light (overexposed) or too dark (underexposed) as a result of improper exposure. Despite these facts, there are purists who continue to use film and professionals who still use it for commercial productions. The best compromise is to use film for capturing the final animation images along with a digital method for storing frames and checking the animation in progress. This can be accomplished with a video assist attached to the viewfinder of the camera that is fed to a computer monitor. If you are a beginner in shooting stop-motion animation, I wouldn't personally recommend starting with film, because it just gives you more technical things to think about and slows down the learning curve. The best place to learn all of the technical skills required for shooting on film is probably in film school, which is where I learned them. All the same, following are some tips and basic information about film cameras should you decide to experiment with them. If you don't mind the challenges involved in getting there, there's nothing quite like watching your animation projected onto your living room wall or against a bed sheet in your backyard on a warm summer night.

The cheapest method of shooting film is with Super 8mm. The older, regular 8mm is hard to find, and it's even harder to find a film lab that will process it for you nowadays. For even better quality and availability, use 16mm film. Affordable cameras can be found in some antique camera shops, or more likely at second-hand resellers. A good place to shop might be on eBay, as long as you bid on equipment from a reliable seller with good feedback. The best kind of 16mm camera for shooting animation is a Bolex (see Figure 4.2).

Any kind of camera you use must have single-frame capability, meaning that you can capture one frame of film at a time with the touch of a button. It's vital to have a cable release mechanism that can be attached to the camera so that the camera does not have to be touched, thereby avoiding the risk of its shifting during shooting. Hitting the button at the end of the cable will expose each frame you shoot. Most Bolex cameras run on a spring device that must be cranked before shooting. When you shoot live-action footage, the crank will unwind until its cycle is through, and it will need to be wound up again, much like a wind-up toy. For animation, a wind-up device has some drawbacks, in that you run the risk of the crank unwinding in the middle of your shot, and also it can create exposure fluctuation. So it's best to rig your Bolex with an electric single-frame motor. When shooting on film, you will also need a light meter to determine how to set your exposure. By holding the white dome of the light meter in front of the object you are shooting and pushing a button, a metered dial will indicate to you which f-stop to set your exposure to. A zoom lens is recommended for any kind of film camera, as it will give you a wide range of shots and allows you to keep your camera a good distance away from your subject and still create close-ups. To make sure your image is in focus, zoom all the way in for an extreme close-up on any part of your subject. Turn the focus dial until the image in the viewfinder is in perfect focus and you can see grain in the viewfinder. Then zoom out to the exact framing you want, and every frame will be in focus.

Figure 4.2 Bolex 16mm film camera. (Courtesy of Nick Hilligoss.)

A 100-foot roll of 16mm film contains about two and a half minutes of footage at 24 frames per second. The film must be loaded into the camera in complete darkness, usually done inside a special black bag that blocks out all light. If your film is exposed to light before use, no images can be captured onto it, and if light hits it after shooting, all of your footage will be washed away. There is no way to see what you're doing while loading it, so it's best to practice first with previously exposed scrap film so that you know where the gate, sprockets, and reels are inside. When buying film, you should know that there are two kinds—reversal and negative—available in either black-and-white or color. All Super 8mm and some 16mm is reversal film, which is exposed in the camera, developed, and projected as is. There is only one resulting print that exists, so it is not the best choice for duplication. The only way to make a copy of reversal film is to make a contact print, which works fine for black-and-white, but not for color. Reversal is a less expensive option and good for simple experiments and short film exercises. Negative film is exposed in the camera and developed as a negative image, exactly like still photo negatives that you get from your local photo-developing station. The negative is your original source material and must be handled with care and never projected. A positive image print is made from the original negative, and that is the print you would project.

If your scenes have been shot out of order and editing is needed, the positive print is used as your "work print," which you can splice together into the proper sequence. The film has numbers on the edge between the sprockets, so your edited work print can be sent to a film processing lab along with the original, untouched negative. A technician there will then conform your negative in a special environment that leaves it free from scratches and dust, cutting it to match your work print according to the numbers on the film. The conformed negative is then developed into your "answer print" for projection, and duplicates can be made for distribution. Film processing and conforming is extremely expensive, but, as I said, worth it if you really want to pursue it. Make sure you consult a team of trusted colleagues, your local library, or the Internet to help you, as there is much more to learn than what I have described here.

Video

For more immediate results, and with less stress, slightly less cash, and more creative control, it is best in this digital age to learn the craft of stop-motion with a computer, stop-motion software, and a way to capture images digitally. Before I go any further, I should pause for a moment to emphasize a certain fact: The technology for this kind of digital setup is constantly changing. Even as I write this chapter, software programs are being upgraded and different video formats are phasing out, with new ones rising in popularity. Who knows…in a few years we might be shooting stop-motion with cell phones! This section of the book should help you learn about some different formats and the constant variables you should be aware of, no matter how much things change in the future. As far as what kinds of equipment you use, that is totally up to your personal preferences, budget, and overall purpose for shooting stop-motion. The highest quality possible may be important if you are making a short film for distribution, but only marginally important if you are a beginner just learning how to animate.

Any kind of video camera will work for shooting stop-motion animation, but it's important to know a little bit about the different kinds. Older cameras from the '80s to early '90s are analog only, which means images are recorded onto magnetic videotape, and RCA jacks are used for outputting the image. More recent trends have moved toward digital cameras that record images digitally with better resolution, either in Hi-8 or Mini DV format (see Figures 4.3 and 4.4). Many of them still have analog or S-video outputs, as well as USB and Firewire outputs (see Figures 4.5–4.8). Prices for digital video cameras vary, from the "home movie" purpose handheld camcorder you can buy in your local electronics store to more professional cameras for studio use, which can cost up to several thousand dollars. Another option would be a broadcast video camera that will provide images without a tape-recording mechanism. You will not be recording on tape when shooting stop-motion, so if the camera will not record, it doesn't matter.

Figure 4.3 A professional DV camera.

Figure 4.4 Digital Hi-8 (left) and consumer quality DV (right) cameras.

Figure 4.5 Analog RCA cable.

Figure 4.6 S-video cable.

Figure 4.7 USB cable.

Figure 4.8 Firewire cable.

Make sure your video camera has manual options for focus, zoom, and exposure. When you shoot your animation, always have your camera set to manual focus instead of auto focus. If auto focus is left on while animating, the camera will need a few seconds to adjust after you move away from the puppet each frame. If you then capture the frame too quickly, the camera might not be finished focusing itself. Manual focus alleviates this problem, so you will always know that every frame looks sharp. You can focus the camera the same way you would using film. Having a manual exposure will also allow you to control the brightness of your scene. Light meters can be used to ensure an accurate exposure if you wish, but video is much more predictable than film, and what you see is what you get. Another important setting to adjust on your camera is white balance. Place a white piece of paper or foam board in front of the camera and push the white balance button until the camera sets itself to recognize everything that is white in the frame.

While shooting your animation, make sure there is no videotape cassette inside the camera. Your images will not be stored on tape, but rather in your computer using stop-motion software, which I will go into detail about shortly. When there is a tape inside a video camera that is not recording, most cameras will utilize a function that automatically shuts it off after a few minutes, which you do not want happening while you shoot. Do not use a battery while shooting either, as this will reduce the amount of time allotted to you for shooting. It is far better to plug your camera into the wall with the AC adaptor so that it will always be on. Some cameras have a demo mode that automatically activates when the camera is turned on. Demo mode automatically runs through all of the camera's special features such as titles, borders, no-shake mode, and special video effects. Make sure demo mode is off before you start shooting.

Digital SLR Cameras

The option of shooting stop-motion with a digital still camera is currently a growing trend for professionals and hard-core indies who are intent on getting the best resolution possible. SLR (single lens reflex) cameras are not cheap. Certain brands of cameras like Canon Powershots provide a cheaper alternative but may not have all of the manual settings found in more high-end models. The settings on many digital SLR cameras are all manual, and they are extremely complex to use. An SLR camera connected to your computer can capture each frame as a high-definition image to a directory straight on your hard drive, and the image quality will match that of film. For stop-motion, using a digital still camera alone will not provide you with a live video feed necessary for using the functions of stop-motion software such as frame grabbing or onion skinning, which I will explain further in this chapter. It must be equipped with a video assist method that will give you the live feed for using the software to register your movements. (See Figure 4.9, and read the interview with Nick Hilligoss in Chapter 12 to learn about his setup using a digital SLR camera.) Recent upgrades to certain stop-motion software programs include automatic plug-ins for

Figure 4.9 Digital SLR camera with spycam video assist. (Courtesy of Nick Hilligoss.)

certain brands of SLR cameras and the opportunity to keep the image directory and video assist synced, with a remote function to capture frames using the software. This option is a huge technological breakthrough that has made its way from the industry into the modern home studio for professional use, and the implications for shooting stop-motion in beautiful high-definition are very exciting. If you want to create films in this manner, keep your day job and save up for buckets of hard drive space and the SLR camera itself.

Webcams

If you cannot afford a film or video camera, the cheapest and most straightforward method for capturing your stop-motion images is to use a webcam (see Figure 4.10), which can be fed right into your computer with a USB connection, with no need for a capture card. For simple beginner exercises, webcams work very well and also use up less physical space. Most of them do not provide full resolution, but there are now a few on the market that do, so do your research, as this technology will only continue to improve as time rolls on. If you use a webcam, do not use the little cradle stand they typically come with. The camera will not be held steady this way. You need to get one that has a tripod attachment, and, as with all cameras, lock it down so it will not move at all.

Tripod

There are no "handheld" shots in animation! The most important thing about your camera, especially for the exercises in this book, is that it must not move, because any movement will cause your final image to shift around when played back at speed. Any kind of tripod (see Figure 4.11) will work to accomplish this, but make sure it's a good one without loose parts. A tripod has different dials and knobs that are used to adjust its height and position. Once the tripod has been set up the way you want it, tighten the knobs as far as they will go, taking care not to use so much strength that you break them off. The knobs can be rather delicate on some models. Some tripods will have a level feature with a tiny air bubble to help you ensure it is parallel with the ground. Check your image in the viewfinder or on the monitor to make sure your picture is not crooked. The tripod needs to be secured to the floor so that it will not shift during your shoot, so the floor in your studio

Figure 4.10
A webcam.

Figure 4.11
A tripod.

space must be level and flat. Loose wooden floorboards or uneven foundations in a room will cause your tripod to shift as you or anyone else walks around. Floors made of tile or concrete lend themselves best to securing a tripod. A cheap method is sticky tack (if the tripod legs have smooth rubber tips), hot glue, or the ever-handy duct tape solution. The tripod can always be nailed or screwed into the floor as well. To keep it steady, a good extra piece for your tripod is a spreader that attaches to each leg and can be nailed, taped, or glued down, or weighted with sandbags. If your budget allows, it's worth it to invest in a really nice professional tripod from a photography or film supplier.

For more elaborate shots in stop-motion involving camera movement, a geared tripod head will allow you to animate the camera to create simple pans or tilts, if you want to create shots like this. You can attach a dial with markings that will serve as a guide for moving the camera slightly for each frame. This must be done with extra special care but can add a lot of cinematic life to your animation. Moving shots can also be done with a dolly that moves the camera along for each frame. Professionals on million-dollar films like *Corpse Bride* use a motion control camera rig to create any kind of moving shots. Motion control involves a computer that can be programmed with the exact start and end position of a camera move, including everything in between, even zooms and rack focusing. Exposures are plugged into the motion control so that after each frame is exposed, the camera is automatically moved into the next stage of its programmed movement. For our simple purposes, this is all pretty high-end stuff, but it's worth building into your studio if you want to go more high-tech. It's a good idea, at least, to experiment and know how it is done.

Computer and Capture Card

Whatever kind of computer you currently have, it can likely be used for shooting stop-motion once you have a video capture card installed and a good software program. If you want to shoot your images at full resolution and have them play back at the proper speed, you should ideally have something close to at least 1GB of RAM in your computer. Make sure you have as much hard drive space as possible, as your files can get very large, especially if you are shooting a short film with many scenes. Ideally, you should have a separate hard drive just for your stop-motion media files, either inside the computer or as an external drive that connects by Firewire. You can also save your files to your internal hard drive and use the external as a back-up drive.

Currently, capture cards can be purchased rather inexpensively, especially ones that give you the option of analog inputs. A popular brand that works well for stop-motion capture is the Osprey card. It's now becoming more common for computers to come with a straight Firewire connection so that a capture card is not even entirely necessary. The convenience factor behind Firewire has much to do with its popularity, although the image it creates for live video is actually a compressed image that has an effect on the color seen by the camera. An analog S-video connection will not give you compression, so in many cases this might give you the most accurate capture of what the camera actually sees. If your stop-motion program allows for frame averaging, or if you are shooting with an SLR camera, this may also balance out any drawbacks to using a Firewire connection. Again, this is one of those areas where you just have to do your research and roll with the times as the technology changes. We are currently entering the age of HD (High Definition) video becoming standard, and this will likely surpass the quality of S-video and Firewire.

Software

A new revolution was born the moment that specific software for stop-motion animation was developed and made available for home or professional use. One of the first software programs to come along was Stop Motion Pro, a PC-based program created by a company out of Australia. I first purchased it many years ago for use on a student film and have used it for my own work and my part-time course at VanArts ever since. For Mac users, one of the earliest programs developed was FrameThief, which places such as Cuppa Coffee Studio in Toronto still use for their productions. Since the development of these pioneering tools, many other programs have become available. Many of them are similar, but they vary in price and special features. Almost all stop-motion programs can be downloaded and purchased over the Internet. Some are for PCs only, and some are for Macs only. Some of them work only with a USB or Firewire connection, and others will work with an analog connection. There are now stop-motion programs that are compatible with certain brands of digital still cameras. Each software program will have its own Web site with information on its features, technical requirements, and usually a free trial download. The free trial will allow you to use it on your computer, but not always necessarily save your files. There will usually be a watermark or a line through the viewfinder to prevent you from creating any finished animation files without paying for them. Once you have tried a software package for a limited number of times as a free trial, you can pay for your own license by filling out an order form on the Web site. Once the license is paid for, a code may be e-mailed to you enabling you to fully activate your software and use it for saving your own animation files.

To make full use of this book and to have the most convenient means to create your animation, the software you use should have, at the very least, the following features:

Frame toggling. This is a term that means the same thing as frame grabbing or frame storing. As you start capturing frames, you should be able to "toggle" between the last frame you captured and the live frame you are animating. This is the stop-motion equivalent to flipping two sequential drawings, as in 2D animation. Toggling your frames allows you to check each movement before capturing it. This is the most common feature that any good stop-motion software must have, and it is something that Lunchbox frame-grabbing systems could do before any of these software applications became available. Even programs that are not the most ideal for stop-motion will have ways to accomplish frame toggling. As with this feature and many others, it helps if your software of choice has keyboard shortcuts to help speed along production.

Onion skinning. This feature allows you to see your current live frame as a transparent "ghost" image superimposed over your last stored frame (see Figure 4.12). It's especially useful for making very minute registered movements, and it also comes in handy when mishaps happen such as bumping the camera or set. You can also completely remove your puppet or object from the set to manipulate it, and use the onion skin reference to place it back in line

Figure 4.12 Onion skinning.

with your previous frame. It is very much like using a light table for 2D animation, which allows you to see two or more drawings superimposed over each other. Some programs have an option for changing how many frames you can display as onion skin at once. For most intents and purposes, all you really need to see is the one previous frame. Seeing too many frames blended together can sometimes be confusing to look at.

Instant real-time playback. In addition to being able to compare your last stored frame with your current live frame, you should be able to view all of your previously stored frames in sequence at the proper speed. This will further aid you in making sure that your scene is turning out exactly the way you want it. The most standard frame rate for animation and playback is 24 frames per second, so make sure your software is capable of shooting at this frame rate.

Frame editing and looping. It's very common to make mistakes while shooting your animation. You might get punchy with the capture button and shoot a frame before taking your hand or head away completely. You might also accidentally leave a sculpting tool sitting on your set when capturing. When mishaps like this happen, you need an instant way of cutting out frames with mistakes in them so that you can reshoot them. You can also take advantage of frame editing if you wish to go back and reanimate a certain series of frames to get a better result. A frame-editing function should also allow you to copy and paste frames, so if you animate an action that you want repeated in a cycle, you can copy/paste to repeat frames so they do not have to be animated again. When you play back your scene, it's extremely helpful to have a loop function so that the scene will repeat itself after reaching the last frame. This allows you to sit back and analyze the movement, or simply enjoy it, without manually repeating the Play button.

Markers. Before these programs were available, animators with a video monitor could draw marks on the screen to help plan their animation. This can still be done on a computer monitor, in addition to a built-in feature in the software itself that is now possible. Markers are simply computerized dots that can be placed on the screen to help register and plan out your intended movements (see Figure 4.13). Most programs allow you to create markers by simply clicking on the screen. It's useful to be able to change colors and sizes of your markers if you are trying to keep track of several different parts of your puppet's movement. You should be able to delete or move individual markers on the screen. The markers will not show up in your captured animation when it plays back.

Figure 4.13 Markers.

Exporting into movie files. The raw data of captured frames is created with the software and can only be edited or added to within that software. To view your animation outside the software used to create it, and ultimately create a version that can be used for post-production and editing, you must be able to export your animation as an independent movie file. The more options you have for different file formats, the better, because they give you flexibility depending on how you plan to distribute your animation. Here is a summary of the most common formats for movie files:

◆ **Avi.** This is a standard video media file that will typically export as an uncompressed movie. The quality is very high, but the file size is also very large, so playing the exported avi by itself for viewing purposes will not usually play back without chugging, even on a fast computer. An uncompressed avi file can be imported into any editing software (like Adobe Premiere) for editing and adding sound or music. From this uncompressed, edited footage, the editing program can export it as an Mpeg or QuickTime file for delivery.

◆ **Mpeg.** Some stop-motion programs will export movies as Mpegs, which are smaller than avi files and more suited for playing back your animation in real time. They only export at half the resolution of an avi, so although they work fine for playing back your animation, an Mpeg file is not the best to use for editing. Mpeg1 format is the standard for VCD, and an Mpeg2 file created by editing software at full resolution from an uncompressed avi is the final delivery format for DVD.

◆ **QuickTime.** This is a file type that carries over from Macs but can run on a PC as well, usually with the extension .mov. The QuickTime player software will also play avi files if they are created with the right codec. For playback on the Internet, QuickTime files are the best files to use.

It's also useful if your software is able to export each frame as an individual file, such as a Targa, Jpeg, or Bitmap file. If you export your entire animation scene as a sequence of frames, you can import them into an editing program like Adobe Premiere and maintain a high level of quality. Targas provide the best quality, with each frame being sharp and clear if being exported from the actual stored frames in the stop-motion software. Exporting individual frames is useful if you want to manipulate certain frames in Photoshop for adding effects like motion blur, fixing mistakes, and removing support rigs or wires.

Frame averaging. I mention frame averaging as a useful feature for professional work, where you certainly want the best picture quality possible. Frame averaging improves the quality of each frame as it is captured while animating, and can be set to varying degrees for different levels of picture quality and video noise reduction. If your subjects are lit very well, frame averaging may not always be necessary, unless you are extremely particular about sharp images. The only frustration with frame averaging at a high level is that it can take anywhere from 10 to 30 seconds to average each time you click the Capture button, and this waiting can slow down the animation process. The speed of your computer will also have an effect on how long frame averaging takes. The wait is worth it for a low-cost alternative to fancy cameras to achieve high resolution.

Audio sync. This function is needed only if you are animating to music, sound effects, or dialogue with a prerecorded track, which I will discuss in more detail in Chapter 9, "Puppet Animation." It gives you the ability to see your animation and sound together and make sure they are truly in sync, without the added step of compositing sound and picture together in another software program.

Rotoscoping. This is a very useful feature, but I mention it as the last "requirement" feature because I don't think it should be used too literally. Rotoscoping is a technique that has its origins in 2D animation, first patented and utilized in the 1920s by the Fleischer studio, which was famous for Popeye, Betty Boop, and Koko the Clown. It consisted of shooting live action on film and tracing over each frame on paper to create animation with an exact resemblance to real live movement. Some very innovative and surreal effects have been created throughout history with the rotoscope technique. The problem with it, however, is that it too often creates dull, lifeless animation due to the lack of exaggeration. Animation is not fulfilling its full potential when it strives to literally duplicate reality to an exact degree. There needs to be an element of exaggeration injected into it if it is to be believable. It is also a somewhat wasted use of animation, if the point is to mimic live footage that has already been captured. Many stop-motion software applications now have a synchronized rotoscope function that allows you to import video clips and superimpose them frame by frame as a transparent image over your animation. The clip may be reference footage of yourself or another actor shot with a video camera or webcam. By lining up your puppet with the actor in the video clip, you can literally copy the movement for a life-like effect where the puppet will move exactly the same way. In some cases for very complicated actions, this could possibly prove a great benefit, but I would not suggest relying on it too much. The reason I do not recommend using the rotoscope feature too literally for animation, especially for beginners, is because it can become too much of a crutch and can stifle the learning process. Live-action timing is not the same as animation timing, and if copying live action is done too accurately per frame, you will never learn to develop your own sense of timing for animation. So I would suggest using the rotoscope window as a way to have live-action reference there in front of you as a guide, but not as something that always needs to be superimposed over the frame for exact replication. Have your reference footage in the rotoscope window alongside your animation so that you can analyze it frame by frame and figure out how to create the same motion with your puppet, but with a degree of exaggeration, too.

I think a much better use of any superimposed rotoscoping for stop-motion is if a 2D animation sequence is used for matching the puppet, because this is still an animated reference. In 1994, an animated short called *The Big Story* was created by Tim Watts and David Stoten, featuring clay characters modeled after a Kirk Douglas caricature. The film was animated in rough 2D animation and then replicated frame for frame in clay animation, and the results were superb. Since I also work in both mediums, I have found 2D reference extremely useful for my own animation (see Figure 4.14), and I enjoy experimenting with making stop-motion do whatever 2D can do, while still taking advantage of the medium.

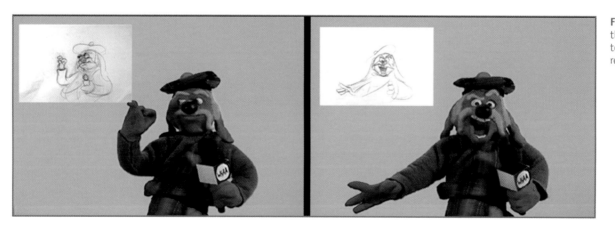

Figure 4.14 Using the rotoscope window to view 2D animation reference.

Chroma-key. Many stop-motion software programs now have a built-in feature for chroma-key, which means compositing video footage into any area of the frame that is a specific flat color. It is the same technology used for weather reports on TV and blue-screen or green-screen compositing in movies. For learning animation, it is not a necessary feature, but more of an extra bonus for cool effects or filmmaking, so I will discuss it more later on.

So these are the major software features I would say are the most important for having a convenient set of tools at your disposal for a good animation experience. Another feature that many stop-motion programs have is a time-lapse feature, which is not really relevant to the exercises in this book but fun to experiment with all the same. Time-lapse photography is a film method in which frames are taken at intervals of seconds, minutes, hours, or days apart, to simulate a long period of time passing in a matter of seconds. It is commonly used in music videos and commercials to create effects like fast-moving clouds, blooming flowers, and building construction. There was once an independent filmmaker who made a time-lapse film by pointing a film camera out his window looking out at a garden. At the same times every day for a few years, he took a frame of film, and the result was a fast moving look at the seasons changing. If your stop-motion software has a time-lapse feature, you can set it to automatically capture frames at any interval you wish. It's a fun technique to play with, and it's useful for science class demonstrations, too, to show the process of anything that normally develops over a long period. Time-lapse photography has opened our imaginations to the wonders of our natural world in a very unique way.

Whichever software or camera you use along with this book or for your own future projects is up to you, according to your personal preferences and, ultimately, your budget. Some programs are free, but they will not likely have as many bells and whistles as the ones that cost money. Overall, most available programs for stop-motion are not very expensive. I will not go into much detail on the different packages available, as stop-motion expert Lionel Ivan Orozco has already done a great job on this page of his Web site: www.stopmotionworks.com/stopmosoftwr.htm. As the site mentions, you can download free trials of different software to your computer, try it out, and uninstall the program after using it, before purchasing an actual license to save your own work. Remember, software changes, and upgrades are released all the time, so it's good to move with the times and try to take advantage of new technology as it grows.

Set

For simple animation exercises, a set does not need to be elaborate. It can be as simple as a tabletop. The important thing is that whatever you use as your stage, ideally it should be set up so that you can have everything you need within reach, especially the objects you are animating. Most ready-made desks and tables are designed to have a waist-level surface since that best suits the purpose they were made for. To have your puppet at this level can be hard on your back, so it's preferable to have it closer to eye level. This height also gives you a better sense in real space of what your puppet should look like on camera. You can build a table from scratch at a height that works best for you, or you can build a separate tabletop set to place onto a standard desk. The examples shown in Figures 4.15 and 4.16 show how a slot has been built into the set for fitting a sheet of Plexiglas, which can be placed either behind or in front of a puppet on stage to achieve certain effects. The advantages of a separate tabletop are many, in that you can keep supplies underneath it where they are accessible and out of the camera's view. You can also easily drill holes for tie-downs, which are screws that go through your puppet's feet to anchor it to the ground. A wooden platform can be used as a simple surface, and any kind of additional surface can be attached to it. Having a sheet of

Figure 4.15 An example of a wooden tabletop set, seen here from the back. (Built by John Worth.)

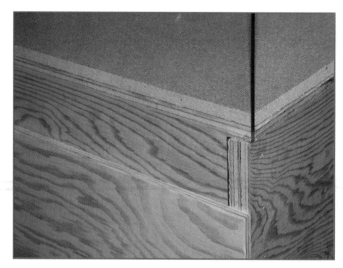

Figure 4.16 Here is a close-up of how the Plexiglas has been cut to fit neatly into the back of the stage.

cork bulletin board material is useful because any holes drilled into it can be hidden rather easily by filling them with loose cork pieces. Clay does not stick to it well, but thumbtacks can be stuck in with the clay surrounding it, giving it extra stability. The cork board can be screwed into the wood so that it can be removed if a different surface is desired. Sticky tack is also a very handy material for adhering anything that should not move, including the tabletop to the desk. Your computer and monitor should be close by so that you can have easy access to the keyboard for capturing.

Overall, how much space you use for your set determines how much space is available to you. Whether you are setting up in a small apartment or a large basement, you must work with what you have. The most important thing to remember is to make sure you choose a room without windows. If you do not have such a room, you will only be able to animate at night when your outdoor lighting conditions will not change. There must be no sunlight cast onto your puppet stage, because the light will change over the span of your shooting and will affect the lighting in your animation. Above your stage, it is useful to have a shelf installed, which can serve many purposes—for example, setting up a plate of glass or strings rig for flying objects, and attaching lights.

Lights

To get a high-quality image on camera, whatever lights preexisting in the room in which you shoot will not be enough. You will need extra lighting on your subject. If your set is too dark, your images will be grainy on video and hardly visible at all on film. For simple exercises, lighting does not need to be extremely elaborate. All you really need is enough light to illuminate your puppets and make them look good on camera. You can easily use any kind of cheap lights that you would find at your local hardware or furniture store. I have found simple halogen floods useful, as well as adjustable desk lamps from Ikea that have a snake neck for extra filler light. A very popular option among stop-motion animators is pinspot disco lights (see Figure 4.17), which can be found at DJ or party supply shops, because they are a comfortable size and can be adjusted to a variety of settings for the amount of light projected. For studio productions, some popular lighting kits include Dedo kits and Pepper kits, with Quartz lights that maintain a comparatively cool temperature, which is a plus for stop-motion.

If possible in your space, it is convenient if some lights can be suspended above your stage, rather than on the floor surrounding you. This setup avoids the possibility of bumping into light stands and having extra clutter. Getting the right lighting for your studio space requires a lot of experimentation and patience. You also need to be very careful when handling the lights, as the really bright ones get hot and can burn you badly. Take care to make sure your studio room has enough power to withstand the total voltage you use to light your set. Wattages for simple stop-motion lighting can be low to anywhere between 100 and 650 watts.

There are three kinds of lights for a standard lighting setup:

Figure 4.17 A 6-volt, 30-watt pinspot disco light. (Courtesy of Nick Hilligoss.)

- The **key light** (Figure 4.18) is your main light source and is typically the hardest light used. The direction of the key light is usually from above, at an angle to the subject. A key light from above is especially common in a simulated exterior scene, since it is supposed to represent the sun or moon as the key light source.

- The **fill light** (Figure 4.19) is a softer light used to fill the shadows created by the key light. As an alternative to an actual light, sometimes a white reflective surface, such as a piece of foam board, will serve the same purpose. Or, the light may be pointed away from your subject and bounced off a white surface to wash the set with more ambient illumination.

- The **kicker light** (Figure 4.20) gives a rim of light to the edge of the subject to help separate it from the background.

Figure 4.18 Key light. (Sculpture by Lucas Wareing.)

Figure 4.19 Fill light.

Figure 4.20 Kicker light.

Lighting is used to great effect in creating mood and drama when making your own films, which I will talk more about in Chapter 13, "Making a Film." For the purpose of learning basic stop-motion, just focus on a basic lighting setup until you are ready to take things further.

In the next chapter, there are several exercises that involve animating clay on glass, so you will at least want a good lighting setup to make this effective, as shown in Figure 4.21. You will want to avoid seeing too much reflection from the glass, so you want to light things in a way that the glass will be invisible and the illusion of clay objects defying gravity can be achieved. After much experimentation, a simple lighting setup I have found that works is to have at least one key light pointing directly at the set, with two fill lights at a 45-degree angle (more or less) to the glass, and some kind of backlight behind the set. Use a white or light-colored background (made simply with a piece of poster board or foam board), and it will be nearly impossible to see any reflections or smudges on the glass. You may also find it necessary to angle the glass back slightly (by attaching it to a shelf, perhaps) so that the tabletop surface does not reflect onto it.

Figure 4.21 My stop-motion set at VanArts.

Supplies

Once the stage is set, you need something to animate. In later chapters on animating and puppet building, I will be making many references to the kinds of supplies you will need for different aspects of stop-motion animation. Rather than listing all of them here and explaining what they are for without context, I have spread them out throughout the book so that you can just make note of what you need as you continue to read through it. Since most of the exercises in the next chapter on basic animation will be done with clay, for now I will just focus on clay-related supplies you will need to get started.

The kind of clay to use for animation is oil-based modeling clay that will stay soft and not dry up and become hard when left sitting out. Water-based clay that dries in the air or in a firing kiln is commonly used for pottery and sculpture but is not suited for animation. Read the label and make sure it indicates that the clay will not harden. Clays will come in a variety of different colors. You can also mix your own colors by melting colors together in a pot, or simply kneading them together in your hands. The heat from your skin will also soften the clay as you work with it.

Animation clay is available under several different names and brands (see Figure 4.22). One of the standard brands that originates from the UK is called Plasticine. (In Bristol, the vernacular term is "PlasTERcine.") A very popular North American brand of clay is Van Aken's Plastalina. These two types are very similar and both work very well, although Plasticine tends to be slightly softer than the Van Aken brand. When clay gets too soft, it can sometimes be difficult to work with, especially under hot lights. An even softer brand from Van Aken is ClayToons, which works well, but the

Figure 4.22 Three different kinds of clay commonly used for animation.

color comes off on your hands and is extremely messy. Other countries and manufacturers make different kinds of clay under all kinds of names, so use whatever is most easily found wherever you are, but avoid cheap dollar-store brands that are marketed toward kids, as these will typically be too messy to work with.

Sculpey and Fimo are soft polymer clay materials that can be baked in an oven for hardening and are commonly used for sculpting props or puppet appendages that are not supposed to change shape. Sculpey is slightly harder and less greasy than modeling clay, so it is easier to work with for sculpting, and some of my students have experimented with using it for animation. It can often work for facial features like eyebrows, mustaches, or anything that you want only subtle movement with. The hardness of the Sculpey compared with Plasticine prevents colors from blending together too much, but you must watch out for its tendency to crack and crumble.

You will also need some sculpting tools with a variety of different shapes and surfaces. Experiment with different tools and see what kinds of patterns or shapes can be created with them on a lump of clay. Some tools are best suited for creating intricate patterns or textures for clay sculpture that is not intended to move. Detailed textures such as fish or dragon scales are a difficulty in clay animation, in that your sculpture needs to be handled to give it the illusion of life, and these details will be quickly smudged away after a few frames. If your puppet is to have a detailed texture while still maintaining a clay appearance, then sculpt those parts of your puppet with Sculpey and bake it, leaving the more expressive parts that will move as modeling clay. A classic example of this method is Nick Park's Wallace character (of *Wallace & Gromit*). The green sweater he wore in his first three short films was made of a hard baked clay material so that it would not be smudged during the animation.

Clay is hard to keep clean during animation. You may find yourself needing to clean off your puppets or clay objects often, as dirt and oil from your fingers will find its way onto the surface as you work with it. Scraping off thin layers of dirt with a flat sculpting tool will keep things clean, but take care not to disturb your volumes too much. Keep some baby wipes nearby so that you can keep your fingers as clean as possible. When using different colors together at once, watch out for unwanted blending or running together of the colors. Under the lights, your clay will soften and can cause this to happen.

Once you have a simple set, lights, camera/computer, and something to animate, you are ready to start your journey as a stop-motion animator. As you set up all of these items for your studio space, work with the space you have as best you can to ensure that you have enough room to maneuver and to reach your puppets and capture method without too much trouble. Remember, everything in your studio space must be as sturdy as possible so that nothing will move except your puppet and you. As you weave through your set, taking care not to bump into lights, camera, or stage, suddenly your awareness of the physical space around you becomes different. It is an awkward dance, like walking on a tightrope or eggshells, treating everything as delicate and precious. One false move, and hours of hard work can be lost. So it should go without saying, as a final word of advice: KEEP DOGS, CATS, AND SMALL CHILDREN OUT!

Chapter 5
Basic Animation

Animation is literally defined as "to give life to" or "to breathe life into," coming from the root word *anima*, meaning soul, breath, or life. The responsibility of giving *anima* to something is a serious business. That anima life is completely determined by how much you put into it. It's more than just "moving stuff around." Animators express through their craft just how much they really care about how and why things move as they do. The believability of their animation will fail or succeed based on how seriously they take the process of getting it right, and squeezing every last bit of quality out of the final product. Because animators are not perfect, their imperfections will also be inevitably revealed through their work from time to time, yet those imperfections are what will ultimately make the audience relate to their work, because they're not perfect either! With their trick films and magic acts, early animators were trying to get people to believe in the illusions they were creating. They had the advantage of an audience that was much more naïve to the process of their craft that they could be swayed to believe anything the animator created, even though logic told them it was all an illusion, and there had to be a catch to it. Their logical brains concluded that things must have been done with wires, lighting, or some other very complicated technology, without even fathoming the truth behind the technique. Perhaps some superstitious audience members thought it was all some bizarre form of witchcraft! Remember, this was all something that nobody had even imagined was possible before. If you are new to animation, you are becoming initiated into an ancient craft that is a lot like going to wizardry school, where you get to wield magic before an unsuspecting audience of "non-magic folk."

Are today's audiences more sophisticated? Yes…and no. Animation has been around long enough that most people have a pretty good idea of how it works. They just don't know how much work it really is! They think, "Oh, you just create a few drawings or move a puppet around a few times and it moves," or my favorite saying, "It's all done with computers now, isn't it?" Common folk uninitiated to the animation world practically wet themselves when you tell them for the first time just how many moves or drawings need to be created for each second. Once they learn that, they have a much greater appreciation for the hard work that is animation. This appreciation is multiplied tenfold when they actually try it! Our purpose in the stop-motion medium is to present to our uninitiated audience the illusion of real objects doing things they wouldn't normally do, to give the illusion of believable movement. Where the challenge and creativity comes in is to realize that your audience probably understands that these are simply objects being manipulated between frames, so you need to do it in a way that they will still be able to say "Wow! How did they do that?" The best stop-motion films do this, in the same way that the trick films in the 1920s amazed audiences of their day.

So this is the ultimate goal, but to achieve this believability, there are principles of creating movement that *must* be learned. The basic principles of animation are the same for all mediums, whether stop-motion, 2D, or CG. The exercises in this chapter will help you learn these principles, using the stop-motion technique to do so. I would encourage you to use the animation diagrams as a guide at first and then take what you've learned and apply it to your own experiments. It is important not to skip over these basic principles if you are a beginner. Many animation students want to rush into creating feature-quality animation right away and ultimately fail because they are not patient enough to spend time learning the basics. After *lots* of practice, you can reach a more professional level of expertise if you stay focused and learn how to crawl before you run. Now it's time to learn how to think and talk like an animator.

Timing and Spacing

If a lump of clay or a puppet is your instrument as a stop-motion animator, then your music is found in the elements of time and space. The basic building block of how your animation will be created in time and space is the *frame*, which is our term for each image that is captured and projected. The standard frame rate for animation is the same as film speed at 24 frames per second. Naturally, one would assume then, that objects in stop-motion must be moved 24 times for each second of screen time. In some cases, this is true. However, it is possible to cut the workload in half by shooting each movement for two frames, thereby needing only to move the object 12 times for each second. The final result is almost the same, since the playback speed has not changed. This method of 12 movements per second is called "shooting on twos," whereas 24 movements per second is "shooting on ones." Whether you shoot on ones or twos depends on several factors. Because stop-motion is similar to live action, in that real materials and lights are used, shooting on ones typically enhances the realism of the movement. Ones results in smoother, fluid motion that has a quality all its own if done properly. However, if the animation is not registered well, the jerky quality of the movements will be more noticeable and hard to watch. Shooting on ones is particularly effective for animating fast actions or movements that require a staggering or shivering effect. Any dialogue that is spoken very quickly may need to be done on ones just to get every syllable represented, because it could be that each syllable is only one frame long. Oftentimes, shooting on ones might also be an artistic choice preferred by the director based on the look of the animation. *The Nightmare Before Christmas* and *Corpse Bride* were shot entirely on ones, whereas *Wallace & Gromit* and many TV specials are mostly on twos. Ultimately, it depends on the stylistic choice of the director, and sometimes time and budget are a factor as well.

Shooting on twos is very common for most animation, especially in the 2D medium. Stop-motion looks very good on twos (again, if done properly), so it is a fine method for making the animation effective for a production schedule. Many animators and directors prefer shooting on twos because of the way it looks, still giving the right level of smoothness and taking half as much time as ones. For beginners in animation, I always recommend shooting everything on twos until you really master your own sense of timing. As you become more comfortable with the animation, you can start experimenting with shooting on ones. Most complex character animation is generally a combination of ones and twos, using twos mostly and throwing in some single "ones" where they are needed, depending on the timing and spacing.

When an object on screen remains static for more than one or two frames, we refer to this as a *hold*. A hold should never be any less than six frames. A four-frame hold will most often look more like a camera mistake when played back at speed. The general rule in animation is that it takes 6 frames to feel something, 8 frames to see it, and 12 frames for it to really register in the mind. Remember, 12 frames is only half of one second. The time it takes you to say "one-one-thousand" is roughly one second of time. (Some animators prefer saying "one-thousand-one," or "one-elephant," as Nick Hilligoss explains in Chapter 12.) You can plan the timing of your animation by saying these words to yourself as you visualize the movement or act it out.

So, if 12 to 24 separate movements are shot for each second of film, and the playback rate is constant, it makes sense that the speed at which objects move will depend on the distance between movements. The basic rule of thumb is that when the movements are *spaced close together*, the speed of the object *slows down*. When the movements are *spaced farther apart*, the speed of the object is *faster*. When movements are *spaced in equal distance* from each other, the speed of the object will simply *move at a consistent speed*. This is the most basic principle of time and space in animation (see Figure 5.1).

When an object is stationary and then starts to move, the first few movements should be slower, with the spacing close together. As the movement gradually accelerates, the movements get incrementally farther apart. This is called "slowing out" or "cushioning" out of a hold. Adding a slow-out to your animation gets the eye used to the fact that your object is changing from a static state to a moving state, and it prevents any unexpected jarring movement without preparing the brain for it. On the other end of the scale, if your object is moving and then comes to a halt, the distance between movements should get incrementally closer together, until it stops completely and holds.

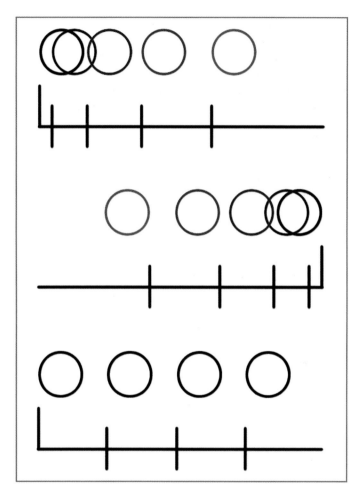

Figure 5.1 Basic spacing: slowing out (top), slowing in (middle), and even spacing (bottom).

This is called "slowing in" or "cushioning" *into* a hold. Slowing in is also vital for communicating to the brain that the object has stopped moving. Without a few frames to cushion into the hold, the object will simply seem to "freeze" and be very jarring to the eye and the brain. It's a very similar concept to crescendos and decrescendos in music, where there is a soft, gradual fade in or fade out in volume. I have always felt that musicians who become animators have an advantage, in that many of these concepts of timing are easier to pick up. Having come from a strong musical background myself before learning to animate, I believe it helped me embed many of the animation principles into my subconscious mind and made the process feel very natural. Just as music is about a relationship between different audible intonations and how they work together in sequence to create a melody, animation is basically a relationship between sequential images to create the illusion of movement. Each pose, or note, leads to the next one to contribute to a whole.

As your first animation exercise to learn how to slow in and slow out of holds, take an object and place it on a table in front of your camera. (Use the camera setup tips described in Chapter 4, "What You Need," to ensure that everything pertaining to manual settings and a secure camera is set.) You will simply be moving the object from one side of the screen to the other, left to right and then right to left. The best kind of object to use is anything that is flat on the bottom with a good sense of weight to it. A chess piece would work well, as would a glass or a tiny sculpture. Round objects will tend to roll away on you, and objects that are too light will risk falling over. Place your object on the left side of the viewfinder's image, not too close to the edge, but about an inch inward. (Traditionally, the field of vision for film is larger than that of television. Since the early television screens were dome-shaped or rounded on the edges, anything on the far edges of the screen would be cut off when displayed on television. Today, most television monitors have moved toward flat screens, so the cropping around the edges is not as severe as it used to be. Nevertheless, there is still a "TV cut-off" area where the action should take place, as anything outside of that area may be cropped and not seen by the audience. Some stop-motion programs should have an option for displaying a TV cut-off grid, as in Figure 5.2.)

From the starting point of your object, determine where its end point will be and create a spacing guide for a slow-out and slow-in (see Figure 5.3). If you are not zoomed in too close to your object, you should have a considerable distance between the two points, which will make it easier to animate. You can create this spacing guide by either drawing directly on the monitor with a dry-erase marker or using marker points in the software if they are available. If you do not want to damage your monitor by drawing on it, firmly attach a

Figure 5.2 A TV cut-off grid shows where the edges of the screen would be on a TV screen.

blank sheet of acetate over it and draw on that. Plan out your spacing guide as best you can, based on the speed you want your object to move.

Before you start animating, here are a few other tips to think about first. The two major software program features used most regularly while animating are frame grabbing/toggling and onion skinning. We are lucky to have these tools today, so we should not take them for granted, since many of us started out shooting blind on film. Remember that in Chapter 4 I compared toggling to flipping 2D drawings and onion skinning to having a light table. When I teach 2D animation to students, I encourage them to flip the drawings as much as possible and try to avoid using the light table too much at first. The light table can become a stumbling block for the fledgling animator, because it takes focus away from the most important factor of the animation, which is *movement*. A 2D animator needs to get into the habit of flipping constantly as he draws, so that he can see the movement start to happen gradually in front of him. If an animator relies on the light table too much without flipping, he will often miss discrepancies in the animation that are not as easily noticeable when seeing the drawings merely super-imposed over each other. The same principle applies to this modern way of shooting stop-motion. The onion skin will become too much of a crutch if relied on too exclusively without toggling to see the actual animation happen. The onion skin is still important and is extremely helpful for ensuring that movements are properly registered in comparison with the last stored frame. You can also use it for completely removing an object from the stage to manipulate it and then put it back exactly where it needs to be. But relying on the onion skin alone is a nasty habit to get into. It simply keeps you too far from studying the flow of your animation as it progresses forward. I have found that the best way to take full advantage of the onion skin is to use it as a guide for registering your movement if necessary, and then turn it off and *toggle your frames before committing to capturing* that frame. This way, you can ensure that your animation is lined up very accurately with your markers and also ensure that the animation itself looks dynamic and free of errors. Little mishaps such as changes in lighting, little lumps of clay left behind on the stage, or improper flow of the path of action will be seen by toggling but will most often be missed by the onion skin. Remember, animation is about the relationship between all of these various frames and how they relate to each other to create a whole piece of movement. There will be many times when you will not need the onion skin at all, especially if you get used to toggling as much as possible from the very beginning.

Figure 5.3 Markers create a spacing guide for a slow-in and slow-out.

5. Basic Animation

Once you have onion skinned and toggled as much as possible, and you know that your frame is perfect, also make sure that you *and your shadow* are completely clear of the frame. If you click the Capture button too quickly while animating, your head, hand, or shadow may end up in random frames and flash into your shot. It's a good habit to count anywhere from 5 to 10 seconds after moving out of frame before you capture. When you move into the frame to manipulate your object, you will block most of the light, so when you move away, the camera will need a few seconds to adjust itself back to the proper exposure and lighting conditions.

Stay focused on those two frames you are working on, with a good idea of where you are headed in context of the whole animation. You can play back your stored frames as often as you like to ensure that everything is moving along correctly. This is also something to watch out for, however, in terms of becoming a crutch when you are a beginner. Partly out of habit, I do not usually like to watch my animation play back until I have worked through it frame by frame to the end. Everyone has different preferences for working, and for me it depends on the complexity of the shot. I often go backward and forward frame-by-frame to check my path of action, but mostly I just take one step back and another step forward, like digging a tunnel to the end of the shot. Once I reach that point, I run it through the preview player or export the animation as an Mpeg so that I can watch it in real time and see if it worked or not. This could be because I started out by using film and didn't have the luxury of instant feedback like I do now. But I also think it's a valuable learning process, getting into the habit of just immersing yourself in the straight-ahead animation and then hoping that you got it right at the end. You may play it back and see things you wish you had been able to change, but you simply move on and apply your lesson to the next shot. Part of the thrill of stop-motion is that sense of suspense where you put a great deal of faith and effort into the process and just pray that it works. When it does work, Oh, the joy! It feels like Christmas. Just remember to pace yourself, and don't rush! I know you are itching to get it over with so that you can sit back and watch your masterpiece, but rushing through and getting punchy with the buttons will only hurt your animation. If you find yourself getting tired, impatient, or bleary-eyed, take a short break. Drink some water, take a walk, stretch your legs, gather your thoughts, and come back to it. Review the frames you have already shot, and get back in there. Athletes need to pace themselves during a game, fight, or run so they don't burn out, and so do animators…sometimes! So now, with these important points in mind, let's get back to the exercise.

Start your scene with an eight-frame hold before you start animating. This will give the eye a fraction of a second to recognize that there is an object on-screen before it starts moving. Then start carefully moving your object by lining up its edge with each successive marker on your spacing guide (see Figure 5.4).

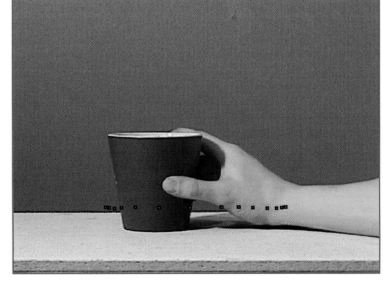

Figure 5.4 Use the markers to line up with the edge of your object.

Your first and last new movements as you cushion in and out should be so minute that you are barely moving your object at all, just lightly nudging it. Keep animating through to the other side, hold for another eight frames, and then work backward using the same markers to move the object back to where you started. End your scene with another eight-frame hold at the end. Then you can watch your first animation play back! When you watch it, you may notice a difference in the way it moves left to right versus right to left, even though you have used the same spacing guide. This is due to the direction in which we read. In Western culture, we read left to right, so any movement on-screen in this direction will have a psychological effect of appearing to move faster or smoother. When objects move across the screen in the opposite direction to how we read, the effect is one of resistance and slowing down. There may be no actual difference in the animation, but your brain's conditioned tendencies will still have an effect on how you see it. Weird, eh?

The Problem of Gravity

The next exercise, the bouncing ball, will involve not only further exploration of timing and spacing, but also the illusion of seeing the ball float through the air. The neat thing about doing this exercise in stop-motion is that it's one of those moments when you can really play with audiences' heads the way I was describing at the beginning of this chapter. The ball will be bouncing across the screen and seeming to defy gravity, and if someone watches your animation knowing a basic idea of how it's done, he will logically conclude that the ball cannot float in midair on its own, so he will become puzzled and wonder, "How did you do that?" The question of how to make things fly through the air in stop-motion is asked of *a lot* of people who work in it. Through the years, there have been several different methods for achieving this illusion. One way is to use very thin monofilament wires or fishing line to hang objects from above.

Any glare given from the lights reflecting can be reduced by going over the wire with a Sharpie marker or painting the wire the same color as the background. This method can be extremely time-consuming, in that it's difficult to have much control over the position of the object, and you must wait for it to stop swinging before you shoot it. (Although, for some frames, a motion blur effect could be achieved by capturing the frame before it has stopped moving.) The wires can also break easily, which is frustrating. Despite these complications, it works very well if done effectively. Other animators through the years have come up with other solutions. National Film Board animator Co Hoedeman sometimes made his characters jump by placing them on a glass cube, which would be invisible on camera if positioned exactly perpendicular to the camera's field of vision.

Another method becoming standard in this digital age is to actually place a rig or wire holding up your object into the shot and then remove it with the computer as a post-production procedure. This can be done by exporting individual frames from the stop-motion software and importing them into a program like Photoshop to do the actual removal in each frame. The removal of the rig is most easily done if the animation is shot against an evenly lit background with one universal color, such as black, white, or a chroma-key green. (More on chroma-key in Chapter 11, "Sets and Props.") A plain white background can be achieved by using a large white sheet of paper or poster board curved inward so that there is no distinction between the ground plane and the horizon (see Figure 5.5).

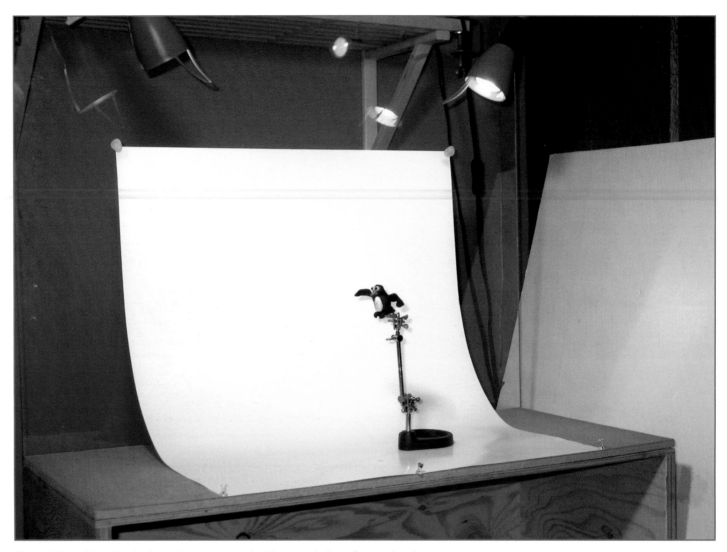

Figure 5.5 A plain white background can be created with a curved piece of poster board.

You then must light the background as evenly as possible so that everything is stark white with no gradient or variation. The rig holding up your object can be placed into the shot and captured as such, and then in each frame you can select the white value and paint out the rig (see Figure 5.6). Your rig will obviously create a shadow, but that can also be painted out so that only the object and its shadow remain. The same procedure can be applied with another universal color other than white.

You can also remove rigs digitally if you actually want to have a real background, like an environmental backdrop or a physical set. The way to do this is to shoot a "clean plate" of your background without your object or puppet in the frame, and then go on with your animation. The empty background plate can be exported separately or edited out of your animation. Export the animation as an image sequence, and open up the individual frames in Photoshop. Paste the clean plate into the individual frames as a separate layer so that it lies beneath the layer with your object and the rig. With the top layer selected, you can erase the rig and its shadow, and the clean plate background will show through. After performing this procedure for each frame, you can flatten and import the frames back into your stop-motion program, or just straight into an editing program to play back the animation without the rig.

Figure 5.6 A rig holding up an object can be removed digitally with Photoshop.

Yet another method is to use a plate of glass to adhere the object to. The glass will be transparent, and the object will appear to be suspended in the air. This method works particularly well for simple clay animation, as the clay is typically tacky enough to stick to the glass. Suction cups can also be hidden behind to stick puppets to the glass. The challenges involved with using glass are keeping it clean from the oily residue left behind by clay and avoiding reflections, which can mostly be solved by the way the glass is lit (see "Lighting" in Chapter 4). I tend to use Plexiglas because it's more durable and less dangerous (in the event it falls over), and it's also important to keep it clean using white vinegar instead of Windex, which will scratch it. While animating, you can wipe off the clay residue with a soft cotton cloth as you move it into different positions, and toggle your frames to make sure it's all clean. If the lighting is done right, you won't see any smudging, but it's important to watch for it, as it will give away the fact that your clay is on a plate of glass.

5. Basic Animation

91

In the context of teaching my stop-motion course, I have typically adopted the glass method as the standard way to achieve the flying illusion because it is the simplest and quickest way to do it. Oftentimes, the most effective stop-motion effects shots are the ones you can do on set without too much digital tampering. For beginners, I also find that the best methods for doing this are the ones that help you learn the animation principle in the most straightforward way. In this case, where we are learning about timing and spacing, I think using the glass helps you focus on the animation rather than too many technical issues. So I would recommend it as a good way to get started, setting up a plate of glass similar to the pictures in Chapter 4 (or a simpler version thereof), and you can then experiment with other methods as well. The other thing to consider, in terms of which method works best for more advanced projects, is the direction that your object or puppet is flying in relation to the camera. If you want to move a puppet in a diagonal path away from or toward the camera, then using wires or digital rig removal might be the better way to go. Ultimately, it depends on the animation and the most cost-effective way to do it.

The Bouncing Ball

This exercise is one of the most basic building blocks for learning animation, because it emphasizes the principle of timing and spacing in terms of how it depicts believable weight. It also introduces the principle of "squash and stretch," which is not always possible with some forms of puppet animation but completely relevant if your object is a lump of clay. A real rubber ball would not literally squash and stretch that much, but this is animation, where anything is possible, and for it to be believable, you need to inject some exaggeration into the movement. The basic goal is to animate a rubbery ball entering the frame, bouncing twice, and exiting. The ball is an inanimate object in that it has no soul or anima of its own; it is simply reacting to the forces of gravity and physics that cause it to move the way it does, in relation to its weight and mass. Whatever happens outside the camera's view will not be seen, but we can imagine that the ball is being tossed forward by someone off camera, and continues to bounce away.

Once you have set up your camera, set, and glass, the first thing to do is to chart out a path of action for the ball to follow, keeping in mind the TV cut-off. The most important part of this action is the arc of the first bounce, so start by determining where the ball will hit the ground and draw the connecting arc on the monitor. From there, you can draw the arcs where the ball will enter and exit the screen. The arc as it enters will obviously be higher, and the exiting arc lower, because the ball is losing energy with each successive bounce. The path of action, most often moving in arcs, is the most vital key to achieving smooth animation. The jerky quality that is often seen in early stop-motion attempts comes from objects not staying registered to an arched path of action. I will elaborate more on this with each exercise, as it is very important. In each frame, the ball should be positioned in such a way that the path of action goes straight through its center. If your stop-motion program allows, once the path of action has been drawn onto the monitor, you can actually trace it with a poly line within the software (see Figure 5.7). It requires a steady hand and is more easily accomplished by drawing with a Wacom tablet (and staying away from coffee, which is a hard task for some of us).

When the path of action that the ball will follow has been established, the next step is to figure out the spacing. Here, by studying Figures 5.8 through 5.15, you need to understand what is going to happen to the ball as it moves. (Most of the pictures shown to illustrate these exercises have an onion-skin image of the previous frame or frames so that you can see the spacing.)

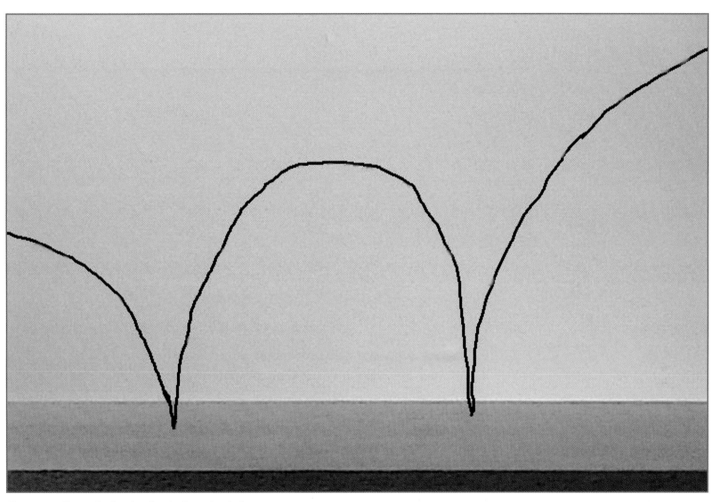

Figure 5.7 The path of action for the bouncing ball.

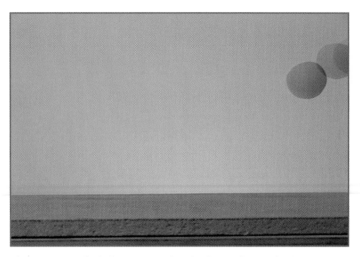

Figure 5.8 As the ball starts entering the frame, the spacing is relatively close together but gets farther apart as it falls.

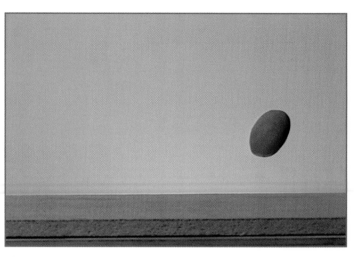

Figure 5.9 Right before it hits the ground, the ball stretches because gravity is pulling on it.

Figure 5.10 When the ball hits the ground, it squashes, and then stretches again in the next frame as it bounces upward.

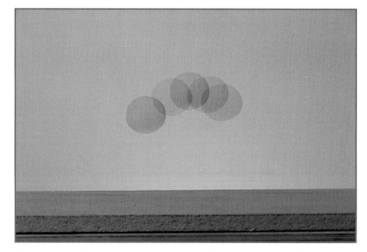

Figure 5.11 The ball returns to its original shape and slows down at the top of the arc, which means the spacing gets closer together.

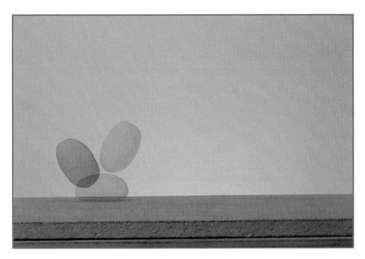

Figure 5.12 On the second bounce, repeat the stretch-squash-stretch again...

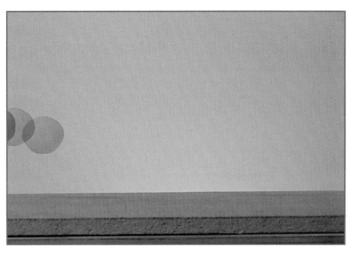

Figure 5.13 ...and then have the ball slow down as it exits the frame.

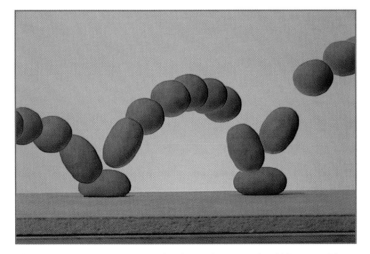

Figure 5.14 The spacing guide for the entire scene should be something like this.

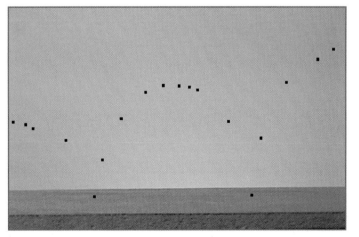

Figure 5.15 On your monitor, or in the software program, you can make marks for where the edge of the ball will be in each frame.

5. Basic Animation

With your spacing guide, it's important to make sure your spacing does not get too even. You should have some variation in your spacing at the top of each arc, and as the ball moves down, the spacing gradually becomes farther apart. If your spacing is too even, the ball will appear as if it has a life of its own, moving by its own anima, which it doesn't have. The movement should be as though the ball is just reacting to the laws of physics. With your spacing guide in place, you are ready to animate, shooting on twos. Start your scene with an eight-frame hold of an empty stage, and then roll a lump of clay into a ball and stick it to the glass, lining it up with your first marker. The ball should be coming into the frame, so part of it will be cut off. Capture your frame and move it into the next position. If you have trouble getting the clay to stick to the glass, give it a little twist and press firmly, being careful not to squish it. This is one exercise where the onion skin comes in handy, especially when you get to the part where the ball stretches. You will have to remove the ball from the glass, change its shape, and then stick it into the next position. Having the onion skin on while you do this gives you a reference point for where the ball was in the last frame. Remember to turn the onion skin off and toggle your frames once the ball is back on the glass, and then capture. You can then turn the onion skin back on, remove the ball, and change its shape for the squash. When placing the squashed ball onto the stage, place it an inch or so away from the glass so that it doesn't look like the ball is just hitting the edge of the horizon. Perspective-wise, the ball is indeed more forward than it was on the glass, but for some reason the camera does not notice this. The depth of field is such that when the animation plays back, you will not notice a difference in size. When the ball stretches upward, place it back on the glass and carry on from there. Check out the CD for a more visual demonstration of how the animation should look when it's finished. If your ball appears to hang too much at the top of its arc, or if it appears to float too much, you can experiment with the timing by hiding or cutting out certain frames, and see if it makes a difference. Enjoy watching your animation play back, and perhaps even import your movie into editing software and add bouncy sound effects to it! The neat thing about this animation is that you are taking the clay material and making it appear like rubber. It's one of those illusions of matter that makes stop-motion so unique!

Once you have mastered the art of the rubber ball, try some different variations on it. Place a box or wall into your shot and have the ball enter in and bounce off of it. Or, you can create a different ball out of several colors of clay to make it look like a beach ball, and as it bounces it could rotate as well. You can also try animating a heavier ball, like a bowling ball. This will have some significant differences. For one thing, the path of action is completely different for a bowling ball. It would not sail across the screen in long arcs, because it is too heavy to do so. Instead, it would make one large steep bounce, and a little hop, and then roll to a stop (see Figure 5.16). A bowling ball would not stretch or squash at all, because it has a different mass and texture from a rubber ball. With these differences in mind, use the same procedures for charting a path of action and a spacing guide and try animating a bouncing bowling ball. See the CD for an example to study. Have fun!

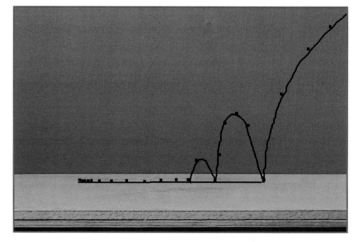

Figure 5.16 The path of action for a bouncing bowling ball.

Overlapping Action and Follow-Through

Now it's time to learn another two animation principles that often go hand-in-hand: overlapping action and follow-through. *Overlapping action* means that when an object moves, not every part of that object will move at the same time. There will be overlapping and staggering of actions, with each part of that object one step behind another part. This principle is very common in character animation, so I will emphasize it again in Chapter 9, "Puppet Animation." One such example would be if a character turns from left to right: His head would start to move, then his shoulders, then his hips. Rather than turn the whole character around at the same time, there is overlap between parts of that action. In a quick action, it is not always something that is noticed by the audience, but it's much more subtle and gives a natural feeling to the animation. Without the overlapping action, the movement would feel very stiff and robotic. Computer animators who have not learned this principle will always have stiff, lifeless animation, because the computer only understands "move point A to point B" and will not overlap parts of a model unless the animator makes it do so.

Follow-through is when an object causes another part of that object to trail along behind it, with an overlap to the timing. A character animation example would be if a character with long hair moves from left to right: The hair would stay in the same position when the head starts to move, and follow through with its movement behind it, and then stop moving a few frames after the head stops. The rhythmic action of the hair would have an overlapping movement like a wave, often referred to as the "wave principle."

Thumbnailing is a common practice for animators in all mediums, named as such because the sketches are no bigger than your thumbnail. Thumbnail sketches take only seconds to draw and are designed to help you analyze the steps of an animated movement (see Figure 5.17). You can study them or create your own to understand the concept.

Figure 5.17 These thumbnail sketches illustrate the wave principle.

5. Basic Animation

The Animated Vine

The next exercise is for getting used to the idea of overlapping action and follow-through with the wave principle. This movement is seen often in animation for the action of a character's tail following through as it walks, or for the tail of a dinosaur, or any other Harryhausen-type tentacled creature. To learn this principle and animate it, use a piece of wire that will bend easily for fluid movement. For other materials (see Figure 5.18), there are many options, such as gluing the wire into a piece of wood perhaps, but the important thing is that the wire needs to have a solid base that will not come loose or slide around. The wire must be rooted down tight and be the only moving object in the shot.

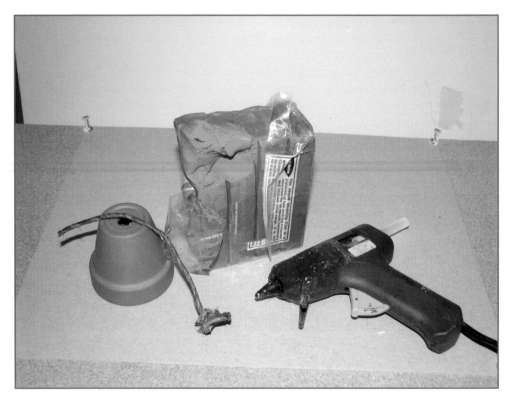

Figure 5.18 Some possible materials for creating the animated vine.

To accomplish this, my solution (with some help from my ever-so-creative wife) was to use a miniature terra cotta flower pot (easy to find in craft or plant stores) and stick the wire through the hole in the base. I used craft wire (typically used for making wreaths) because it has great flexibility and is wrapped in twine to give it the appearance of a vine coming out of the bottom of the flower pot. Then I tied a knot in the piece of wire, put some hot glue on it, stuck it through the hole, and filled the pot with clay to hold it in (see Figure 5.19).

Then I hot glued the flower pot to a piece of cardboard tacked down to my cork board stage surface (see Figure 5.20). The cardboard solution is a handy way to make a quick and dirty floor when you don't want to damage another surface. Making simple sets like this is part of the problem-solving aspect of stop-motion, and it's where a lot of the creativity comes in.

Figure 5.19 Clay fills the flower pot to hold the wire in place.

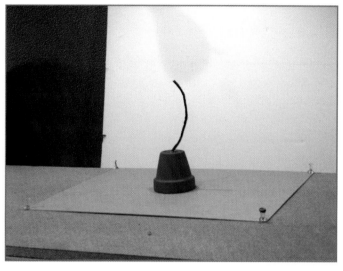

Figure 5.20 Securing the set holds the vine in place for animation.

This animation exercise, which consists of the wire or "vine" swaying back and forth with overlapping action and follow-through, is also a *cycle*, which means that the last frame of the animation must hook up smoothly with the first frame. It's not the same kind of scene as the bouncing ball, which has a beginning, middle, and end. An animation cycle can be put on a loop so that the drawings will repeat themselves infinitely. Cycles are not something very common to stop-motion animation, since for most of its predigital history, it would have been impossible to achieve without a reference point for the first frame or without being able to play it on a loop. To help you make sure your animation will be able to cycle back into the beginning, trace over the position of the vine in the first frame on your monitor to give yourself a reference point as you reach the end (see Figures 5.21–5.36). The best way to animate the vine is to grip it with both hands and push against the base with your thumb, while moving the tip in the opposite direction with your fingers (as illustrated more specifically in Figure 5.29).

The path of action on the tip of the weed is like a figure-eight pattern, so keep this in mind while animating to ensure that your arcs are smooth. If you follow this many positions as a guide, then shooting on twos should give you 28 frames of animation. In your stop-motion program, copy and paste your frames so that they will cycle through twice. This way, if you want to look at your animation frame-by-frame in playback, the "hook-up" between the last and first frame will be in the middle of your scene. Once you learn this basic wave principle at this speed, experiment by shooting it on ones or animating it with more frames to slow it down. The results are fun to watch when played back in a loop, and they're rather hypnotic, too. (Watch your animation if you have trouble sleeping.)

The Art of Stop-Motion Animation

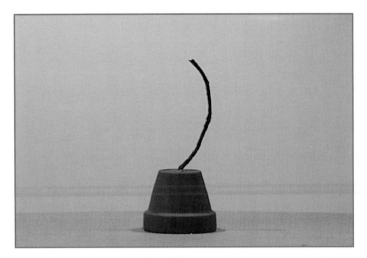

Figure 5.21 Start with your "vine" in a smooth curved position, and trace this position on your monitor.

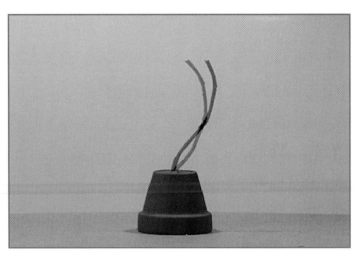

Figure 5.22 The base of the vine starts curving in the opposite direction, which causes the tip to move over.

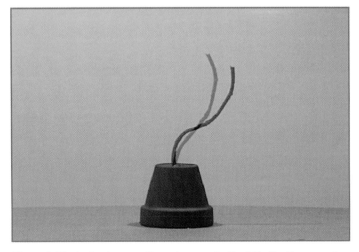

Figure 5.23 As the base continues to curve to the left, the tip moves to the right, following a curved path of action.

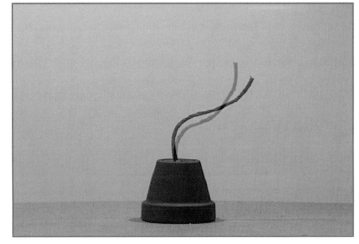

Figure 5.24 The movement continues, with the base moving left and the tip curving to the right.

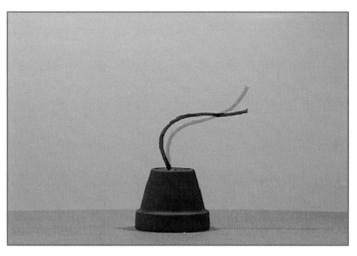

Figure 5.25 The curve that started in the base is starting to take over the whole vine, as the tip starts moving down and to the left as well.

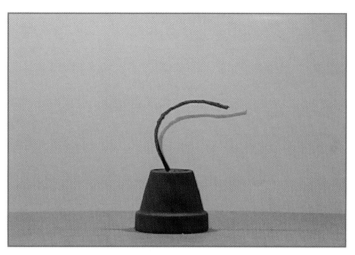

Figure 5.26 Now the entire vine is moving the same way, as the tip of the weed catches up with the base.

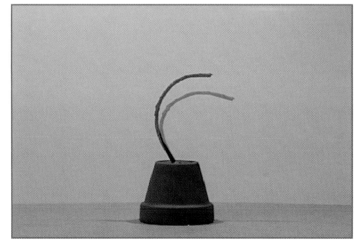

Figure 5.27 The vine continues moving in this position to the left.

Figure 5.28 The weed is now in the exact opposite position it started in, as if it is a mirror image.

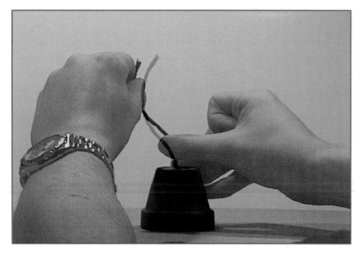

Figure 5.29 The same process is now going to repeat itself going in the opposite direction.

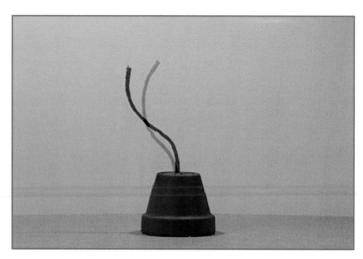

Figure 5.30 The base curves to the right, and the tip to the left.

Figure 5.31 The base continues right as the tip comes down.

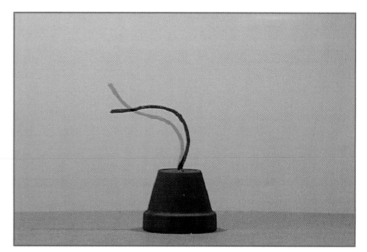

Figure 5.32 The tip catches up with the base.

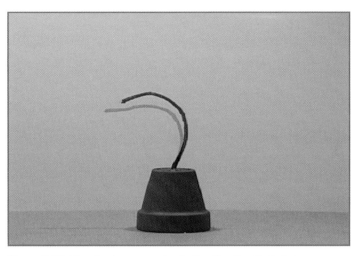

Figure 5.33 The vine is now curving in the direction it started.

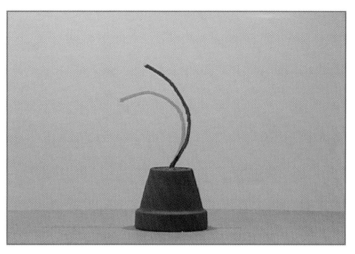

Figure 5.34 It continues moving closer to the mark made on the monitor to reference the first frame.

Figure 5.35 Here is the previous frame onion-skinned on the left, the current live frame in the middle, and the frame 1 position drawn in marker on the computer screen.

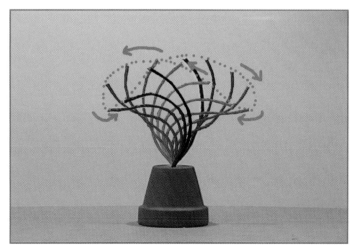

Figure 5.36 This diagram shows an overview of the whole animation.

5. Basic Animation

Bouncing Ball with Pigtails

Here is another cycle exercise that illustrates how follow-through can be applied to a moving object. You will have to break out your clay and glass again for this one. The animation will be a rubbery clay ball, bouncing straight up and down, with some "pigtails" attached to it. The pigtails will move a step behind the movement of the ball for some smooth follow-through using the wave principle, overlapping the action of the ball. The ball will squash and stretch as it jumps, slowing in and out at the top of its path. You can create markers to give yourself a spacing guide as the ball slows down at the top of its jump. Make sure you are moving the ball in a straight line as it bounces up and down to avoid unwanted jittering. To build the pigtails, sculpt them around a small piece of twisted aluminum wire to stick into the ball. It works best to take the pigtails off to reshape them, and the ball when it changes shape, for each frame, as there will be holes left behind on the ball to keep them rooted in the same place. See Figures 5.37–5.47 for an illustration, and use the CD to watch the finished animation. (Note that the animation was shot on twos, but the frame in Figure 5.39 was only captured for one frame, for a snappier action.)

Figure 5.37 Start with the ball in its "squashed" position as it makes contact with the ground. The pigtails are pointing upward because the ball has fallen downward and dragged them along behind them.

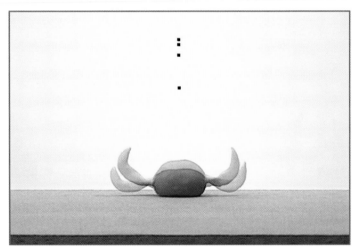

Figure 5.38 The ball starts to transition into its stretched shape before it bounces back up, and the pigtails fall to catch up with the landing.

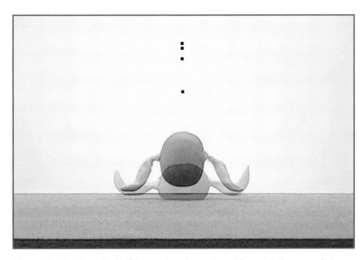

Figure 5.39 Now the ball is on the glass, stretching as it bounces into the air. Notice how the pigtails are lined up with the path of action in the previous frame.

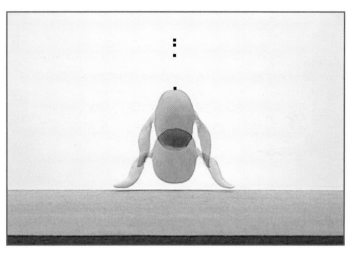

Figure 5.40 The ball stretches more, lining up with its marker, and the pigtails drag behind.

Figure 5.41 The ball changes to its original roundness, and the pigtails slowly start to catch up to it.

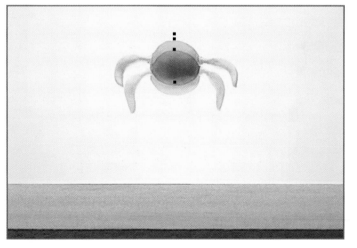

Figure 5.42 The ball begins to slow down at the top of its jump.

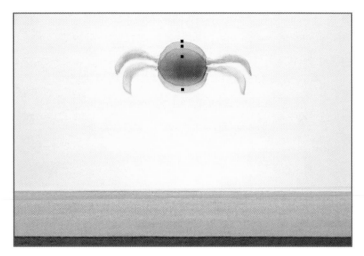

Figure 5.43 The ball has now reached its highest point.

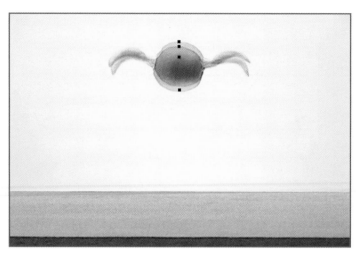

Figure 5.44 Now the ball is moving down, so it is slowing out from the top of its jump, and the pigtails have caught up with it.

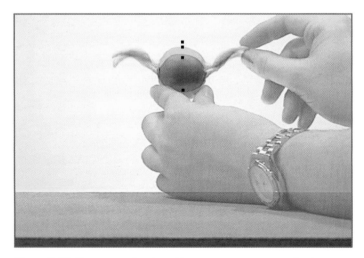

Figure 5.45 Here are my hands making a cameo appearance, to show sliding the ball down the glass into the next position.

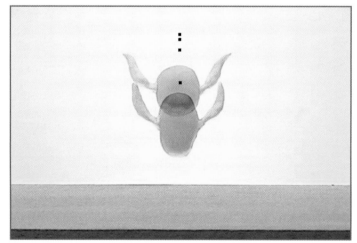

Figure 5.46 The last frame should show the ball stretching as gravity pulls on it, with the pigtails trailing behind it.

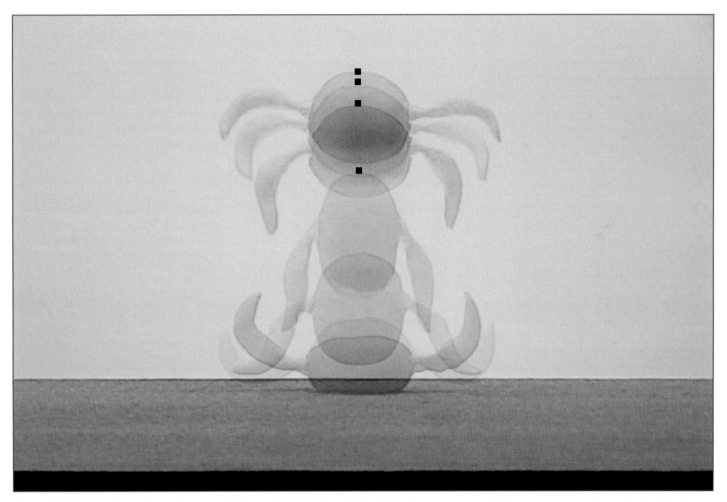

Figure 5.47 Copy and paste these frames so that the cycle repeats itself at least twice in your scene, and then export your movie to play back in a loop. Enjoy!

Anticipation, Action, Reaction

Many of the principles I am introducing in this chapter were primarily discovered and used to great effect by the Disney Studio in the golden age of the 1930s. It is through these discoveries, as they were displayed through their groundbreaking cartoon films, that the same principles began to be demonstrated with stop-motion animation. Another such animation principle was that of *anticipation* and *reaction*. Anticipation grew from the idea in theater that all actions needed to be extremely clear to the audience, since they couldn't very well ask the actors on stage to repeat an action if they were not prepared for it. In the same way, a film moves ahead through time with no intention of going back, so every action must communicate clearly the first time. To prepare the audience for an action, a character would *anticipate* the action before going into it. For example, a character throwing a ball would move it back in the opposite direction before throwing it forward. After throwing the ball, there would then need to be a *reaction* to the throw, which might be the body gaining its balance by recovering and settling into a final neutral pose.

To demonstrate the principle of anticipation–action–reaction, one of the most useful exercises is *the jumping sack*. The idea here is that the sack has an anima of its own, not that there is something inside it. The sack will start on one side of the screen, anticipate its jump by squashing down, jump across the screen and land on the other side, reacting with a recovery and a settle. The recovery and settle is kind of like a little inhale/exhale at the end, moving upward slightly as a bounce reaction to the landing, and settling down into its final pose. Stretch and squash should be put into the poses so that the sack feels flexible and not stiff.

In any animation pose, no matter which medium you are using, there must be a clear *line of action*. The line of action acts as the spine of your pose, capturing the essence of the position your character or object is in. The thumbnail sketches in Figure 5.48 demonstrate the basic key positions of the anticipation, action, and reaction of the sack.

Figure 5.48 Notice how the line of action changes in each pose, starting with a simple curved line, going into an S-curved anticipation, and changing as it stretches and squashes.

Obviously, since the sack is jumping through the air, you will need to set up your glass plate to stick it to. Start by sculpting a sack out of solid clay, giving it a little knot on the top. Any color will work fine, but a dark gray or green will make it look like a garbage bag. A white color would look like a flour or sugar sack. The imagined contents are not important, but it should look like whatever is inside is heavy. Because the sack is heavy, it will need to exert itself with a lot of force to propel into the air. Try jumping yourself, and pay attention to the forces of gravity on your body. You must anticipate your jump by crouching down to give yourself leverage, and then when you land, your body must recover upward before settling back into position.

Place the sack on the left side of the screen and hold its first pose for at least eight frames at the beginning of your scene (see Figures 5.49 and 5.50). The number of poses it will take to move into its anticipation I leave up to your own experimentation, depending on how fast or slow you want it to move. Remember to slow out of the zero pose and slow in to the anticipation, and have the sack move downward in an arc (see Figures 5.51 and 5.52). If you have lots of frames cushioning into it, you can hold this pose for six or eight frames if you wish. Another common term used in animation lingo for having many in-betweens cushioning into a pose is *favoring* the pose. Any pose you really want the audience to notice and have linger in the brain needs some cushion positions favoring it so that it creates a kind of *moving hold*. When the sack takes off into the air, it should stretch and feel like it is pushing itself into the air with all its strength. If you had too many frames, the action would slow down too much, and it would feel like the sack is floating rather than jumping (see Figures 5.53 and 5.54). At the top of the arc, the sack will slow down. The more positions you create at this point, the slower the sack will move. It is often better to create more frames than you think you need, especially in stop-motion, since it's much harder to add them in later. If you want to change the timing, you simply remove frames. The sack squashes at the top of its arc, because its bottom has caught up with its top, causing the action to overlap. Like the bouncing ball, the sack stretches as it comes down, and the spacing increases to make it land hard (see Figures 5.55–5.59). After landing, the sack recovers from the impact of its landing by pulling itself up against the force of gravity and settles into a more relaxed pose. For the recovery and settle, Figures 5.60–5.62 show only the main key positions, so you can experiment with how many in-betweens you think you need based on the timing. You can also study the animation frame by frame on the CD, if it helps you. To make sure the sack returns to a pose close to its original volume and shape, you can go back to frame 1 and line it up with the onion skin to compare.

This exercise will likely require a fair bit of experimentation and trial and error to perfect, but treat it all as part of the learning process, and once you learn it you will find it useful for more advanced stuff down the road. You can try variations on it, such as animating on ones or trying a different shaped sack. You can even try applying the same principles to making a small clay figure jump. Thumbnail the basic movements and think of the overlapping action in the arms and legs. You will undoubtedly need to resculpt your character often, and you will probably have to reinforce the clay with little wires in some areas. One trick for getting a clay figure to stick to a plate of glass is to tear off its arm on the far side, stick its torso to the glass, and line up the arm with the body on the opposite side of the glass. The separation should not be noticeable if lit and positioned properly. A certain toy that is very popular with stop-motion animators is Stikfas, which are little posable action figures that have a wide variety of joints. You could use one of these for a character jump as well, using any method you want for holding it in the air. One way that combines a few different methods is to attach the Stikfa to a tiny suction cup sticking to a plate of glass, and any part of the cup that shows up behind it can be removed digitally. Just keep experimenting!

Figure 5.49 Plan out your animation by drawing a layout on your monitor and referencing the line of action for each main key position.

Figure 5.50 Here is the sack in its first position, what is also referred to as the *zero pose*.

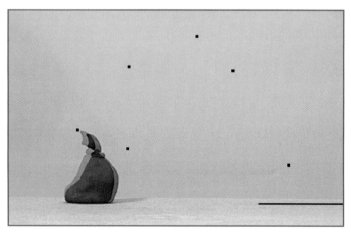

Figure 5.51 This is one of many in-between poses that will carry the sack from its zero pose into the anticipation.

Figure 5.52 The anticipation pose, with an S-curved line of action.

Figure 5.53 This pose can be shot for one frame only, to give a quick fluid snap to the action.

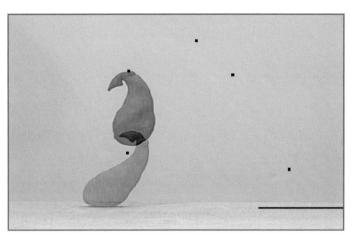

Figure 5.54 Now the sack is in the air and stuck to the glass, continuing in an arc and overlapping on the knot.

Figure 5.55 The sack slows down at the top of the arc, just like the bouncing ball.

Figure 5.56 As the sack moves down toward the ground, the movements get gradually farther apart.

5. Basic Animation

Figure 5.57 Gravity pulls on the sack, causing it to stretch!

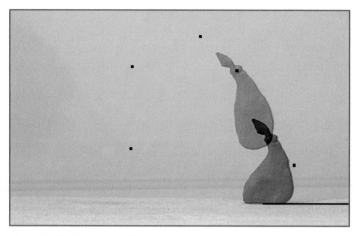

Figure 5.58 The sack is off the glass now and is resting on the surface (captured for one frame only).

Figure 5.59 Squash! The sack lands. Notice the S-curved line of action again.

Figure 5.60 The recovery and settle is the trickiest part of this exercise. Think back to the movement of the weed, and use that as the basis for your line of action.

The Art of Stop-Motion Animation

Figure 5.61 This is the recovery pose, which is like a mini-stretch or an inhale performed by the sack.

Figure 5.62 After the recovery, the sack settles into a final pose, with a little bounce at the end.

The 80-Frame Morph

This is a fun exercise designed to take full advantage of the fluid quality of clay, but also to teach you how to plan ahead your animation within a specific limit of frames. Often in an animated film, there may be only a tight space to fit the actions for the animation in a specific shot. Pretend you have been given an assignment by a director to make an object change or *morph* into another object, and you have only 80 frames (or 3 1/3 seconds) in which to accomplish it. To make the transition smooth, you should plan out your timing on an exposure sheet.

An *exposure sheet* is like a road map for the animator to plan out the frames and actions in a scene. It is also referred to as an *X-sheet* or a *dope sheet*, which is what I like to call it. The "dope" sheet name has nothing to do with stupidity or substances, but rather comes from an old slang term common in the golden age of animation, when people would often ask "What's the dope on that scene you're working on?," meaning "How is it going, and when will it be finished?" On the CD, there is a sample dope sheet for the morph exercise (in .pdf format). Note the numbers from 1 to 0 down the side column. These are your frame numbers, so you can pencil in numbers by 10s. Each sheet has 80 frames, so if you are working on a scene with more than one sheet, you can continue on page 2 with 81 and continue on to 90, 100, and so on. Each little square in the columns alongside these numbers represents a frame, and they are divided into sections of eight, so three of these sections equals one second (24 frames).

The additional columns represent different layers or levels, which are mostly relevant to 2D animation but can be used for some stop-motion, too. A 2D animator might have two or three different characters or part of one character on separate levels as a way to economize the animation. In stop-motion, these different levels can come in handy when animating a group scene or two characters at once, and keeping track of their various movements. There is also a dialogue column that I will show you how to use in Chapter 9. In addition, there is also a blank dope sheet (courtesy of VanArts) on the CD for you to print out for use in your own future projects. (It will print out at standard 8 1/2" × 11" size or can be sized to print larger.)

On the sample dope sheet for the morph, notice that I have placed a frame number in every other frame, since this animation will be shot on twos. In this case, I am animating a man morphing into a bunny. (I was originally going to morph him into a fish, but while I worked on it, the clay shapes started looking more like a bunny, so I changed my mind rather spontaneously. Weird things like that happen often in stop-motion. I can't explain it.) I would suggest using your own idea for your morph, using this dope sheet as your conceptual timing chart. Perhaps a cat into a dog, or an animal into a piece of furniture…whatever you want. Remember, the rule is that you cannot go beyond 80 frames!

Start out, as we do with every scene, with an eight-frame hold. On the dope sheet, this is indicated by drawing an arrow straight through eight frames. Now, the frames from 9 to 25 are your "slow-out" frames. Use this region of frames at your discretion to plan a slow-out of the hold, making your first few movements very small and gradually becoming more extreme. By the time you reach frame 25, your original object should have changed position but still be in the form of whatever it is. Some of the details may be squished or may have deliberately lost their definition, but it hasn't really changed its overall shape yet. The purpose of the slow-out, as always, is to give the eye a chance to notice that the object has started moving before going directly into the drastic changes about to occur.

The frames from 27 to 55 are where the morph takes place. Anything goes in this region, so long as the movements flow nicely from each frame to the next, with a smooth path of action. Starting with frame 27, you can make your movements more extreme than in your slow-out phase. This part is fun because you literally get to destroy the beautiful sculpture you spent much tender loving care in creating. Twist, squash, and mash your clay and give it texture. By themselves, these frames will not be noticed by the naked eye, but rather will flow into each other. By the time you reach frame 55, your morph needs to have reached the point where it has taken on the shape of the object it will become. It should not be clean, polished, or final by any standard, but you should be able to recognize its shape. This is where the planning part takes effect, and you must refer to your dope sheet often as you work through it to make sure you plan your movements to see how many frames you have left until frame 55, and make sure your morph does not complete itself too early.

Frames 57 to 73 are your "slow-in" frames, so use these frames to gradually smooth out the clay, add details, and polish it into a final sculpture. Throughout the cushion frames, end certain parts of your puppet's body earlier than others in terms of when all the detail is finalized, so that the animation overlaps and doesn't all come to a stop at once. The final results should be a fluid and beautiful transformation between two completely different objects or characters. Then hold the object or character for eight frames, watch the animation play back a few times, and go to bed.

Figures 5.63–5.73 show how I used the timing I just described to create stages of my 80-frame morph of man into a bunny. The final animation with all of its frames can be watched and studied on the CD.

Figure 5.63 Frame 1 (holding for eight frames). Here is the human subject at the start of his morph.

Figure 5.64 Frame 9. There is only a very slight difference on this frame, as the subject is just starting to cushion out of his hold.

Figure 5.65 Frame 25 . Up to this frame, the man has moved slowly backward, as if anticipating the transformation he is about to undergo.

Figure 5.66 Frame 29. Now he is coming more extremely out of his cushion, still in "man-form" but decidedly starting to be deformed.

Figure 5.67 Frame 33. The subject's face is squashed into his body, and his arms come up further.

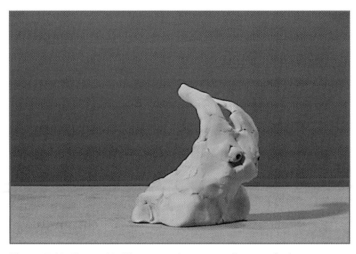

Figure 5.68 Frame 41. We are starting to get glimpses of a bunny shape, but it's still undefined and messy.

Figure 5.69 Frame 47. Almost there! It's starting to look more like a bunny now, but there's still some room for further refinement in the next few frames.

Figure 5.70 Frame 51. This is the tricky part of the animation, where decisions have to be made on the final appearance of the bunny.

Figure 5.71 Frame 55. He is now a bunny, and much of his personality is already there in his face.

Figure 5.72 Frame 63. Now I am smoothing out details, polishing the clay, giving the bunny more of a facial expression, and starting to grow his tail.

Figure 5.73 Frame 73. All done! Hold for eight frames at the end.

117

The man's eyes were made of wooden beads, and the rest of his body solid clay, although I did stick some pieces of wire behind and inside him here and there to keep him from falling over. His feet were sculpted around two thumbtacks sticking into the cork board surface to give him extra stability as well. By the point he reached his bunny stage, I had removed most of the wires that held him up when he was a man, except for inside the ears where I have thin pieces of aluminum wire inside to hold them up. I made up the bunny's design as I animated, and I literally made the bunny decision in the middle of the shot as well. I even removed his head completely a few times so that I would have an easier time resculpting it, and then smoothed it back into place.

Have fun with this exercise, as it truly is one of the most amazing ones to sit back and enjoy. There's no reason why this should end with only one morph, so continue with as many transformations as you want! I would suggest keeping the 80-frame rule consistent with each one, to maintain a rhythm to your animation. (This means each successive thing the object morphs into will hold for 16 frames in total.) Make enough morphs, and you'll almost have yourself a little film. Or, take a blank dope sheet and change the timing to see if you can fit three morphs into 80 frames! What really makes it work is the timing with the cushions and proper planning, with enough room for spontaneous ideas along the way.

Basic Performance

Keep in mind all of the other principles from the other exercises: squash and stretch, line of action, path of action, anticipation and reaction, overlapping action, and follow-through. These lessons will make your animation not just about "moving stuff around" aimlessly, but about real natural movement. You should start looking for these principles while watching animation and live-action films, and study them frame by frame to see how they are used. If you see something that grabs your attention and you think, "Wow! What a great action that was!," go back and figure out how the animator did it. See how long a character will hold for different reactions and expressions. After you study any action frame by frame, always go back and watch it play at real speed. You will notice how everything you just analyzed plays back and see how it all ties together. Another really useful method for studying movement is watching TV with the sound off. When you are not distracted by the sound, you will be amazed at how many subtle movements you notice, particularly if you watch something you have already seen. This can apply to stop-motion animation films, plus any other medium, including live-action. Watching sitcoms with the sound off is a fascinating study in character animation (and in some cases, it's more entertaining that way).

Once you get used to the idea of animating with holds, cushions, and anticipation, you can start experimenting with using these principles to "act" using common household objects. One of the great things about stop-motion animation is that you can animate ANYTHING! Every piece of furniture, kitchen utensil, toiletry, tool, toy, or food item in your house can be made to move on its own, and with a little creativity, not just move but *move the audience*. To accomplish this, you need good animation combined with a good story, which gets you into the realm of making a short film. I will cover the subject of storytelling and filmmaking in more detail in Chapter 13, "Making a Film," where you can learn some tips for using objects or puppets to entertain and enlighten your audience.

As a final exercise for experimenting with basic animation, one household item you can play with is a desk lamp with a posable goose-neck (see Figure 5.74). It may be a stand-up one with a base, or a clip-on lamp attached to a table or shelf.

These lamps work great for stop-motion animation because of their flexibility and capability to hold their position in very intricate measurements. The challenge is to think of the lamp as a character, with a head but no facial expression to tell us how it is feeling. Its attitude must be expressed entirely through the way it moves. By posing the lamp in tiny increments, its movement will be slower, which may indicate that it is sad, dim-witted, or sleepy. Posing it with movements that are farther apart will result in faster, snappier movement, which will make it look alert, happy, or shocked. (A good film to study for reference is Pixar's short *Luxo Jr.*)

If your lamp has a base, use hot glue or poster putty to firmly attach it to your set, so it doesn't slide around and cause unwanted jerks in your animation. Remember the importance of arcs and holds while animating. All objects move in arcs, so chart out an arced path of action on your monitor if you have trouble visualizing it in your head. If your lamp is moving from side to side, it must stay along a curved path of action to avoid jitters. The personality of your lamp will also come through largely by how long it holds. If the lamp is sleepy and slowly turns its head to react to something, it might hold for at least one or two full seconds before going into a shocked "take" or surprised reaction. Oftentimes in animation, less is more, meaning that a good pose without movement can still say a lot to your audience. Try experimenting with just some basic animation of the lamp to see if you can get across the idea that it's thinking. Perhaps animate another object moving into the shot to give it something to react to. Keep it short and simple; the possibilities are endless!

Figure 5.74 Lamps are great tools for stop-motion animation.

Chapter 6
An Interview with Dave Thomas

Figure 6.1
Dave Thomas.
(Photo by
Anna Keenan.)

Dave Thomas (see Figure 6.1) is a senior director at Cuppa Coffee Studios in Toronto, Ontario, Canada. He has worked on several bumpers and promo spots for clients such as Teletoon, Prosieben, and Major League Baseball, and television series such as *Crashbox, Henry's World, JoJo's Circus, The Wrong Coast,* and *Little People*, and has received several film festival awards. Samples of the studio's work can be seen at www.cuppacoffee.com. I first met Dave at the 1998 World Animation Celebration in Los Angeles, and I ran into him again 7 years later at the Ottawa Animation Festival, where one of his films was screening.

KEN: *How did you get started with stop-motion animation?*

DAVE: I attended Sheridan College in the late 1980s and majored in media arts and film production. While I was there, I started doing some clay animation with a college friend, having been a big fan of *Gumby* and stop-motion in general, especially *Davey and Goliath*. I found I had a knack for it. I think the reason I got into it is that it's a merging of the freedom of animation with live action. I like constructing sets and lights and working with cameras. There's a lot of planning you have to do, as with all animation, but at the same time there is a lot of flexibility once you set your camera up, in terms of last-minute ideas or changing camera angles. In my second year of college, I made a combined clay animation/live action film (*Claydreaming*), which I had the extreme fortune to sell to HBO. I was only 20 at the time, so it was like hitting the jackpot, and my parents were pleased that I might have a future in this business. After graduation, I tried to get work in the live action field, but I wasn't having much luck, so I gradually broadened my search into animation studios. My first job was as a production assistant at a 2D commercial studio called Lightbox Studios. There I did a little bit of everything from ink and paint to animation checking to answering the phone. It was a great learning experience. I learned about dope sheets there! When I did my college film, I didn't use any dope sheets. I just guessed all of my timing based on 24 frames per second. So when I came to the studio, it was good to see that they actually took notes. [laughs]

So a couple of years later, I got a grant to make my 17-minute animated film, *Rodent Stew* (see Figures 6.2 and 6.3), which was mostly plasticine with some 2D elements and effects, which I burned into the original negative. I shot it all on 16mm and of course had to wait for weeks to get it back from the

Figure 6.2 Clay boy from *Rodent Stew*. (Courtesy of Dave Thomas.)

Figure 6.3 Clay boy with pig from *Rodent Stew*. (Courtesy of Dave Thomas.)

lab, so I used to unravel it on the train back home because I couldn't wait to see if it had worked! I spent many years in my parents' basement making that film and contacting TV stations on my own, getting to animate some interstitials for Global and other local broadcasters. It was all a great learning curve, figuring out quick and dirty ways to create things on film with low budgeting, which helped me immeasurably later on when getting into bigger-budget shows. Stop-motion involves a lot of problem solving in front of the camera.

KEN: *So how did this lead you to work at Cuppa Coffee Studios?*

DAVE: It was all through connections, really. I was doing some animation for TV Ontario, and one of the producers recommended Cuppa Coffee to me, so I contacted them and had an interview with Adam Shaheen, who is Cuppa's president and executive producer. Shortly afterward, I got a job animating dinosaurs for Hall Train Moving Pictures, which was some of the most difficult animation I've ever done, because the dinosaurs had to look absolutely alive. Hall Train was an excellent teacher and sculptor, so I worked for him for about a year, and some of my animation is still on display at the American Museum of Natural History in New York. Around that same time, I was interviewed for a show on animation for TV Ontario, and people at Cuppa Coffee saw me on TV, remembered who I was, and they called me back there because they were looking for someone who could animate plasticine, and I've been there ever since. It's been great, and I've gotten to work on a lot of different projects: pixilation, stop-motion, Flash, TV series, commercials, everything!

KEN: *Do any of these projects stand out as those that you're most proud of, or that have been the most challenging?*

DAVE: Well, in terms of challenges, each one is its own beast, you know? I often say that no matter how long I've been working in the field, I'm constantly learning new ways to do things. You get through a project and you can say, "Now I understand this," and then the next one comes up and it's like, "I don't know a thing!" So the challenges of each project have been enough to keep me up at night and keep learning. I guess one of my favorite projects was *Crashbox* for HBO Family. It was Cuppa Coffee's first major series and one of the things that was great about it was the clients were very flexible and open to ideas. It had a handcrafted look, with many of our puppets being built with found objects, painted foam core, tissue paper, stuff that you buy at Michael's or Home Depot and throw together. *Crashbox* combined all kinds of media, and it was a total blast running on adrenalin for about nine months on that show. More recently, another favorite project was an episode of *The Newsroom* with Ken Finkleman.

KEN: *What are you working on now?*

DAVE: Right now the studio is working on the third season of *JoJo's Circus* for Disney and prepping for more projects. I just wrapped a preschool series for Mattel called *Little People* and am involved in prepping some of the new projects that Cuppa is developing internally. The company had a busy summer with three series going at once. Our broadcast design department is busy working on a variety of commercials and other projects. The studio has a great structure where people are encouraged to try different things, and there is flexibility for people to move between departments. We've had people who start as sculptors and then slide into animation, so they get to animate puppets they've built themselves. We even had a production assistant who really wanted to learn animation, so she spent her evenings practicing in a spare studio, getting tips from the other animators, and that's what she does now.

KEN: *Tell me a bit more about your exact role in the company, and the responsibilities of an animation and series director.*

DAVE: I am a senior director at Cuppa Coffee, and I have performed different roles within the studio structure. Much of my work is either as a series director or as an animation director, which are different positions, especially on large productions. Series directors oversee the whole production, whereas animation directors are responsible for the animation teams themselves. Both jobs require a lot of work and really keep you hopping. As series director, I work with the storyboard artists to block out the script. We lock the boards down and move on to animatics, with client approval every step of the way. Once all questions and concerns have been worked out, I meet with the animation directors and go through the storyboards and animatics, which don't explain absolutely everything about how you want things to move, so there's a lot of acting things out. We each carry different colored highlighters to make any last minute notes or changes. The animation director takes it from there and supervises the daily shooting in all the studios with the animation team. As the series director, I am involved with every department, working with the designers, puppet crews, sculptors, giving directions on materials and so forth, add a little here, subtract a little there, etc. So my days during production are kind of like a high school class schedule, meeting with each department for an hour or so at a time.

KEN: *That leads into my next question: What would a typical day at the office be like?*

DAVE: Well, as an animation director, if you want to talk about that role, you're on the floor pretty much all day. On the first season of *JoJo's Circus*, for example, I was one of the animation directors, and I was there from 6:45AM until about 4:30PM when the afternoon shift came in. We had eight studios running at that time, so my job was to check the animation from the night shift before, check the day's list of what we hope to achieve, and then meet with the animators as they come in. Rather than having them all arrive at once, we stagger their times coming in, because you can only talk so fast, so if you spent ten minutes with each animator, some of them would be waiting for two hours just to talk to you. So we discuss framing of shots with the director of photography and lighting crew, and block out the scenes, plan everything out, and make sure everybody understands how each shot should look. It really is a team thing. Nobody's perfect, and people, including myself, will miss things, and other people need to be there to point things out and double check everybody's work. So the animation director moves along to each set and does this with every scene. I actually have a scooter at work that I ride from department to department all day long. Someone made a basket for my scooter to carry my clipboard and my Coca-Cola, so I can just keep going. You're constantly getting called in to approve things, discuss things, and before you know it, it's 7PM and your lunch is still sitting in the fridge. It's nonstop. When I am series directing, it is the same kind of thing, only spread out in the different departments, having meetings, figuring things out. At least in editing, you get to sit down for a little while, but you still forget your lunch from time to time.

KEN: *How long does one episode of a TV series take?*

DAVE: That's a hard question. It depends on how many animators you have, and what your daily quota is. On feature films, it's typical to create two seconds a day, four seconds a week, that kind of thing. TV series are a whole different ball game, a constant balancing act between schedule, content, and quality, trying to do the best job we can on time. So if I had to ball-park it, eight animators working on an 11-minute show would take about two-and-a-half weeks. Sometimes, the animators will shoot 20 seconds a day, other times 2 seconds a day, depending on the complexity of the shots. A group shot with 50 characters moving at once will obviously take longer.

6. An Interview with Dave Thomas

KEN: *I understand that group scenes will still usually be done by only one animator. Is that still the case on a TV show?*

DAVE: Yes, generally one animator will animate an entire scene. I prefer to work alone when I'm animating, as most do. But sometimes we will have more animators work on a shot together. On the *Crashbox* show, the opening was a Rube Goldberg environment, with cogwheels, conveyer belts, tiny robots, all on this big set that filled a whole room. We had three animators in there for two weeks, each moving 15 things, and then they would duck and one person would capture each frame on the keyboard. Then they all stand up and move 15 things again.

KEN: *That almost sounds like a dance.*

DAVE: You know, it's interesting you say that! I really find that to do stop-motion well, you need to think of it as a dance, like a ballet. I think stop-motion has more to say about performance and acting. You really have to understand human movement. We've found that people who dance, or do martial arts, Tai Chi, or yoga, make very good stop-motion animators. It's all in their head; they don't really have to think about how the character is going to move; they just have a feel for it.

KEN: *What other kinds of backgrounds do the animators at Cuppa Coffee have?*

DAVE: It's a really big mix. In addition to people who are seasoned stop-motion animators before they come to Cuppa, we also have people with film production backgrounds, 2D animators who cross over into stop-motion, people with acting and theatre backgrounds, dancers. We hold auditions and assess who has potential. We start them with something simple, like maybe moving an arm up and down. After leaving them to work for an hour, we come back, critique them, and build up from there. Cuppa Coffee will train the people we feel are dedicated and who demonstrate the skill base the work requires. So there's no one avenue—it's all about desire and dedication, and you just gotta love toys. It's like playing with toys very, very slowly.

KEN: *Of all the different materials you've used for puppets, which work best for a typical production environment?*

DAVE: That can depend on the aesthetic of the show. *Crashbox* had a crafty kind of look, and we made puppets out of pink insulation foam covered with tissue paper and painted. They were very effective, and I still have a few of my favorites which were a joy to animate with (see Figures 6.4 and 6.5). Right now on *Jojo's Circus*, it's mainly been foam latex bodies and silicone limbs, with heads cast in plastic. Clothes are either sculpted and cast in foam latex, or we use fabric, which I really like because it adds another dimension of texture. Pieces of clothing like veils, for example, can be wired and animated, too. Armatures will be either ball-and-socket or wire, or a mix, and it all hinges (pun intended) on budget and schedule like everything else. There are pros and cons to both. Ball-and-sockets have good durability, but I love the flexibility of wire and the possibilities that offers. We've done a lot of experimenting with ways to make things fixable when wires snap, using Allen keys and

Figure 6.4 Dave Thomas animating a puppet. (Photo by Daniel Robinson.)

Figure 6.5 A frame from an animation test for a short film. The puppet is built from wire, carved pink insulation foam, and painted, collaged paper. (Courtesy of Dave Thomas.)

other devices to replace sections, pop in new wires, and keep going. We're still learning. We've used plumber strapping for hinges, because you can bend it many times without any snapping, and works very well for a low-cost foot joint.

KEN: *So what are your thoughts on the future of stop-motion in these CG-saturated times?*

DAVE: I really think it's just another tool, another medium. There's fantastic CG work out there, and some of it really comes close to approximating the stop-motion look, but it's really apples and oranges. Stop-motion has its own aesthetic and charm to it. Not to say CG is charmless, just that it is a different kind of charm. I think there will always be a market for stop-motion as long as there are the right kinds of projects and the right people behind it. The success of recent features bodes well for producers putting money into it, and children's series are doing well. One great thing I liked about *James and the Giant Peach*, which is almost 10 years old now, is that it was a convergence of different media; they used everything (live action, puppets, cutouts, CG). That's where the secret lies—don't disregard it because it's "old school." You may as well say that CG will replace live action, which it never will. We use CG in our own work at Cuppa Coffee. *JoJo's Circus* is a stop-motion series, but there are CG and 2D elements in it, too, so it's just a matter of seeing what medium works best and going ahead with it. The important thing is to keep showing it as an option. People with training in other mediums can come here to work in stop-motion; it's just another way to do it.

KEN: *What other advice would you have for aspiring stop-motion animators?*

DAVE: It's so much more affordable today to get the technology and just start practicing. The people who come down to Cuppa Coffee for auditions are encouraged to get a program for their home Mac or PC, hook up a camera, and just use anything. I've animated dominos and given them personality. Or just get some plasticine or put a rough puppet together. I would also say, watch movies, not just animation but live action, and watch them not as an audience member, but from a filmmaker's perspective. As an animator, you need to understand not just the scene you're working on, but where your scene comes from and where it's going. Don't think it's beyond you financially; just pick up something and start moving it around. Stop-motion is a real "learn by doing" technique.

Chapter 7
Building Puppets

I think too many people take puppets for granted. Stop and think for a moment about how surreal and amazing the concept of a puppet is. It resembles a person or an animal but has no life of its own. It is simply an inanimate object, a lifeless lump of material. But when a real person manipulates it somehow, it brings forth the illusion of life. Puppets have been with us since ancient times, and, for me, they have always been a fascination in one form or another. Having grown up in the late 1970s through the '80s, Jim Henson's Muppets were a constant source of entertainment. I vividly remember seeing them on display at the Detroit Institute of Arts in 1981, and seeing live puppet performances from different world traditions there as well. In elementary school, we had a puppeteer who brought his marionette plays to the gymnasium every year, starring a dragon named Applesauce. Since I had toy puppets of my own, I knew how they were operated, yet at the same time I believed they were alive. Another obsession of mine from growing up in the '80s were the animatronic animal rock bands at places like Chuck E. Cheese's and Showbiz Pizza Place. These also seemed to be alive, but they were not operated by live puppeteers. Instead, they were programmed by a computer synced with audio tapes behind the stage, delivering a performance that had been premeditated to repeat itself. In all of these various forms, the same illusion was being achieved: The puppets had *anima*, but their *animators* were nowhere to be seen, hidden from view, or absent entirely.

In stop-motion animation, the same illusion of life is achieved in a different dimension of time. The animator is touching the puppet and making it move, but his work is not seen by the audience in real time. It exists only between the frames that flash before our eyes. A stop-motion puppet performance is a combination of premeditated planning and improvisation by the animator, in a thought process that takes several hours of our time, and condenses it to mere seconds of screen time. Because of the amount of control offered to the stop-motion animator over what can be achieved in this time dimension between frames, there is a wider spectrum of possibilities for naturalistic movement compared with most other forms of puppetry. A stop-motion puppet, for instance, can walk with a more realistic sense of weight, which is more difficult to achieve with a marionette. That does not necessarily lessen the challenges involved, nor does anything possible in stop-motion make other puppet art forms inferior. As always, story has priority over technique when it comes to reaching your audience.

Whether a puppet animator is moving a hand puppet, marionette, stop-motion clay figure, or a realistic creature like the kind seen in the Jim Henson/Frank Oz film *The Dark Crystal* (1982), there will always be obstacles to overcome in making the performance believable. Working with puppets in any way always requires much creative problem solving. For this reason, the design of the puppet in appearance and construction is vital to how effective it will look before an audience. There are thousands of materials, methods, and techniques that can be used when it comes to making stop-motion puppets, and it will always take much experimentation and trial and error to get them working. As you attempt this, be humbled by the words of Thomas Edison, who said, "I have not failed. I've just found 10,000 ways that won't work." There is not necessarily any right or wrong when it comes to building puppets; there is only what works and what doesn't work as well. Even professional puppet builders with years of experience come across obstacles and problems, and through their experience, they find which methods work better than others. Through experimenting with different techniques and materials, animators and puppet builders find personal preferences they continue to work with. One of the neatest things about stop-motion is the opportunity to throw things together with whatever you have easy access to in your home or school. This applies to building sets as well as puppets. It is often referred to as the *MacGyver* method of filmmaking. (For younger readers who missed out on 1980s television, MacGyver was a kind of intellectual action hero who made weapons and traps out of whatever materials he happened to find around him.) All aspects of stop-motion filmmaking are a constant challenge in problem solving, and sometimes the best solutions are found by the seat of your pants.

This chapter will help you design your own characters and build them into puppets to be animated in stop-motion, based on what has worked well for me and others in the field. I will cover several different methods for making puppets so that you can choose which method will work best for the kind of characters you want to create.

Character Design

The main difference between stop-motion puppets and other kinds is that they have an *armature* inside. An armature acts as the skeleton of the puppet and must be built so that it can hold its position without slipping for each frame captured. A stop-motion puppet must also be built in a way that will prevent it from falling over or breaking during a shoot. To prevent mishaps such as these, your puppet should be as lightweight and durable as possible. With all of these points to remember, the most important principle is that *your puppets must be designed based on what they will be doing, and what kinds of movements will be required of them*. It is the simple rule of form following function. What do your characters do? Will they be walking or jumping, or will they only be seen from the waist up? Will they speak or express their feelings solely through body language? Will they need to hold a prop in their hand? Your story or overall purpose for animating will be the ultimate factor in how your character is designed and built.

To design a character, you must first be familiar with what *design* actually means. Design really boils down to communication of an idea that is being relayed—in this case, to the audience watching your character move on-screen. Most animated characters are designed based on a set of symbols and clichés based on reality but exaggerated to emphasize certain aspects of their personality. The most basic symbols used to communicate to the audience about a character are the shapes of the mouth: If it is curved upward, the character is happy; if curved downward, the character is sad. Adding to these symbols would be the position of the eyebrows, indicating whether a character is worried, angry, or devious (see Figure 7.1).

These symbols go all the way back to the first scribbles we all made as children, so they will always be recognized by our subconscious mind. However, these symbolic facial expressions can be used by any character depending on his mood, so other symbols must be employed to suggest more about who that character is.

Figure 7.1 Basic face symbols instantly communicate various expressions to an audience.

Proportions and body shapes are commonly used to communicate certain character types to an audience. By taking life drawing classes and studying the human figure, you can learn more about the proportions that make up a human or animal figure and then exaggerate them for an animated character. The human figure is typically measured in height using the height of the head as a measuring stick. The average adult human

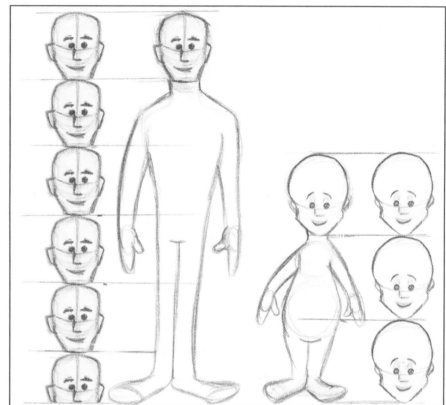

Figure 7.2 Proportions of a human figure are measured according to the height of its head.

is about seven to eight heads tall, with the head being balanced in proportion to the rest of the body. Small children, however, have larger heads in proportion to the rest of their body, and as they get older the proportions balance themselves out (see Figure 7.2).

Since audiences will subconsciously pick up on this fact, it must be exaggerated when creating animated characters, so that the age of the character can instantly be communicated through the design. By designing your character with a huge head in proportion to his body, he will look more childlike, so you would want this kind of design if you want to create a baby or child character, at about two or three heads tall. A good example of this principle in stop-motion design is in Art Clokey's *Davey and Goliath*, where Davey and his friends are designed with much bigger heads compared to the adult characters in the show.

Other character design principles related to proportion and body shape will vary depending on the type of character (see Figure 7.3). Big "tough guy" or heroic characters are designed with emphasis on the shoulders and chest to show they are strong, because in real life a strong person would have wide shoulders in proportion to the rest of his body. Fat characters will have huge stomachs and short, stumpy legs, so that the girth of their body looks even fatter in proportion to the rest of them. Often, effective character design comes from taking that one element of the character that says the most about *who he is* and making it the most central part of the design. Also think in terms of costuming and props, and how these can be used to tell the audience about your character. Whoever your character is on the inside will have a big effect on what he looks like on the outside.

At its simplest level, all animated characters are made up of a hodgepodge of circles, squares, triangles, and variations on these basic shapes. Study characters from all kinds of animated productions and analyze their silhouettes, looking for the shapes and patterns that make up the shape of their body. These principles apply to characters in all mediums, so they are important to experiment with. In stop-motion animation, there is one major difference, in that once a character is designed, it must also be realized in three dimensions and made simple enough to animate. 2D characters have much less to worry

Figure 7.3 Different typical body types for animated characters.

about in terms of gravity, for instance, since they are not necessarily enslaved to it. A character with a big head and chest, but with thin legs and tiny feet, might work as a drawing, but problems could arise if the same character were made into a puppet, because it could become very top-heavy, making it difficult to maintain its balance. In this case, it would definitely need to be extremely light and be built with strong support in its feet to balance it. Your designs might need to be modified to make them suitable for stop-motion. One way to test this would be to draw your character in different poses, or, better yet, make a tiny sculpture of your puppet in solid clay and try posing it into a few different positions to get a feel for how it will work in 3D. Imagine any problems you foresee with working with it as a larger scale puppet, and plan accordingly.

Again, I must emphasize that your design will depend on what your character does in your animation. If your character must reach for an object behind or above him, make sure his arms are long enough to do so. If he is to be walking, make sure his feet are not too big or too small in proportion to his body. Puppets designed mainly for action shots like walking or jumping will need more emphasis placed on the construction of their body. For puppets that will have a stronger focus in character animation, the eyes and hands will most often be the most important element. The eyes are the first thing the viewer will gravitate toward when looking at your character, so make sure they are placed well on the face to bring the viewer into them. Study the eyes of different stop-motion characters and think about how important they are to the overall design. Eyes are especially crucial to mute characters, such as Nick Park's Gromit, who makes all of his expressions using his eyes and brow. Hands are also very important for establishing character when posing and speaking, as many of us typically gesture with our hands when we speak. One of the best animations to study for how the eyes and hands work together with character design and dialogue is in *Creature Comforts*, both the original film and the series.

Dialogue is achieved with puppets in a number of ways, and how to animate dialogue is discussed more in Chapter 9, "Puppet Animation." The most common methods are either through the construction and manipulation of one mouth or a series of replacement mouths (see Figure 7.4). A single mouth on a character might possibly be sculpted in clay and need to be resculpted and shaped for each frame, a technique commonly seen in Will Vinton's Claymation films. Alternatively, the puppet might have one mouth that is formed with wires that simply open, close, and reshape themselves for certain syllable shapes, such as the Oogie Boogie Man in *The Nightmare Before Christmas*. Replacement mouths require different individual mouths for each syllable that are removed and replaced for each frame. They are very popular in stop-motion due to their efficiency for production, and they are used in many shows like *Davey and Goliath* and *The PJs*. Replacement mouths in clay animation are sometimes blended into the face for each frame so that they continually appear to be part of the whole face.

With all of these different design elements, it all boils down to what will be most convenient to your budget and the process of animating your puppet. In some cases, the materials used for building a puppet will also be determined by the personal preferences of the animator. Keeping all of these factors in mind during the design stage will save you from the common problem of investing lots of time, money, and energy into building your puppet, only to realize it's impossible to animate what you want it to do.

Figure 7.4 Replacement mouths and puppet by Darren Lee.

Evolution of a Character: Hamish McFlea

It is very common for characters to evolve as you work with them. You might start with an initial sketch of an idea and have it go off completely in another direction, which is good, because that is typically how the best ideas come about. As an example, I thought I would show some of the process behind a character I developed for my unrealized student film *Bad News*. The original film idea was about a news report concerning a doomsday cult's prediction of an alien Clockwork Monkey coming from outer space to destroy the world. (I have always been simultaneously terrified and fascinated with clockwork monkeys banging cymbals, and I figured if anything came to destroy us, that would be it!) I thought it would be funny to have a Scottish news reporter talking about it on location, since I do have some Scottish heritage, and because I love Scottish accents and thought it would be fun to animate. So, with these rough ideas in mind, I just started sketching ideas for a character that would ultimately be created as a stop-motion puppet.

My initial concept for the news reporter, who I named Hamish, was to make him human, so I started drawing him in different poses I imagined for the animation. His personality was that of a very nervous, dim-witted character who half-believed the rumors of the alien monkey, so I drew him in poses suggesting panic and fear (see Figure 7.5).

Figure 7.5 The first sketches of Hamish explore his personality.

135

As this project continued to evolve, for some reason I don't quite recall, I decided that all of the characters in the film should be animals, so I turned Hamish into a dog. I began experimenting with his facial expressions, still drawing him as a naïve, energetic character, but also trying some expressions of anger and smugness (see Figure 7.6). I find this to be a good method for fully exploring a character's potential. Do not limit yourself only to the moods that you envision your character displaying within your story, but show your character in every disposition imaginable. Through this process, I found myself gravitating toward the drawings of Hamish in a bad mood, and his personality transformed as such (see Figure 7.7).

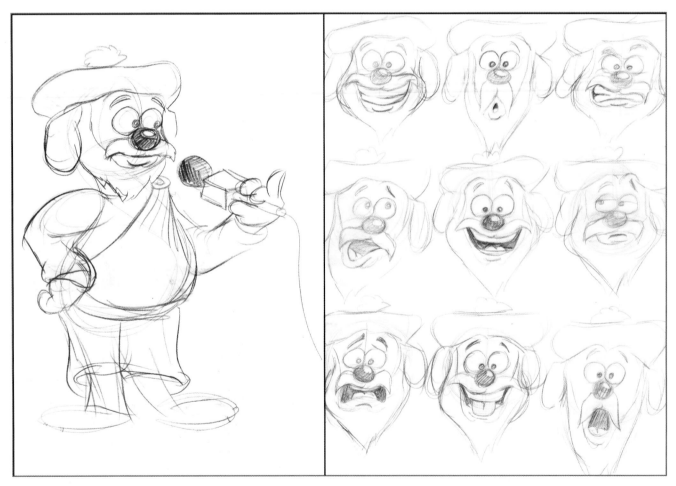

Figure 7.6 Early sketches of Hamish as a dog, exploring his facial expressions.

Hamish didn't believe in the rumors at all and was annoyed at the whole prospect of being outside on location to report on it. Being a dog, I decided he should also have a flea problem; hence his last name, McFlea, which would make him even more irritable. Knowing these things about his character helped me in writing his dialogue with the off-screen news anchor, commenting about how all the police have left for the pub and how the whole situation was a load of…(you get the idea). In the middle of his rant, the monkey appears and attacks him, which adds to the comedy and suspense of his disbelief. I felt that now Hamish was a real character ready to be made into a puppet! (The finished animation of this scene is part of my demo reel on the accompanying CD.)

Since Hamish was only going to be seen from the waist up, I decided I would not waste time building him legs, but rather have him attached to a wooden base. I started by making a solid clay sculpture of him for scale purposes, to make sure he would be the right size compared to the Clockwork Monkey of the Apocalypse (see Figure 7.8), who I had already started building (more on him later).

I used a plastic beaded doll armature found in a local craft shop (David Bowes, who is interviewed in Chapter 3, "An Interview with David Bowes," had found these and told me to go check them out.) These armatures are designed for doll makers for the purpose of posing them for window displays or catalogs, and they also work great for stop-motion animation. They already come in a human body shape and hold their position extremely well, so they are perfect for simple puppets designed for medium shots and dialogue. The materials used for building a puppet will always be determined by the look you want and what the animation calls for. Hamish's head and hands would be made of clay, since they were to be the most expressive parts with the most fluid movement. The rest of Hamish's body would

Figure 7.7 Additional concept sketches developed his character further.

Figure 7.8 Hamish is built as a solid clay sculpture alongside his puppet costar.

be made of fabric, to keep him lightweight and avoid deforming his shape while being animated. Making puppets with real fabric clothing adds a great sense of texture and realism to the final look.

I pulled the legs off the armature and adhered the armature to a balsa wood base (see Figure 7.9) with epoxy putty, also referred to as the popular brand "ProPoxy." This is a two-part compound putty found in hardware stores that is normally used for masonry and concrete repair. I will explain more about using epoxy putty while describing other puppet building methods.

Because Hamish's hands would move around and his mouth need to be changed often while he talked, those parts worked best if they were removable. This way I could resculpt them or manipulate them without causing unwanted movement in the body of the puppet. At the ends of Hamish's arms and his neck, I attached small pieces of K&S tubing with epoxy putty so that the head and hands could be attached to wires that slide inside. K&S tubing can be purchased in hobby shops and cut to whatever size is needed.

To create the bulk of Hamish's body, I covered his arms and torso with mattress foam (see Figure 7.10). The foam was cut into strips, wrapped around the armature, and held in place with glue, thin wire, and a bit of tape. Extra layers were wrapped around his belly area to give his body a pear shape and indicate that he has a large gut. His clothes were then sown together, with his green shirt made of felt and his tartan sash made of a scrap of plaid flannel fabric (see Figure 7.11).

Figure 7.9 A plastic doll armature adhered to a wooden base.

Figure 7.10 The armature is covered with mattress foam.

Figure 7.11 Clothes made of fabric are sewn over the armature.

The base for each hand was a lump of epoxy putty with a twisted wire stuck into it (before it dried; see Figure 7.12). The clay was built up around it and sculpted into a hand shape. Having the putty base not only makes it possible to attach a wire for sliding into the K&S tube, but it also cuts down on the weight. The fingers were left just as solid clay, because they are thick enough to hold their position without wires inside, which would just poke through the clay and make the animation difficult.

Hamish's head was built over a Styrofoam ball with a twisted wire stuck into it. This was also done to make the head lighter, and the wire would allow his head to tilt in any direction, once stuck inside the K&S tube. To give his ears extra stability for animating, they were built out of a wire mesh. Socket holes for his eyes, which were made out of Sculpey and painted, were gouged into the Styrofoam. Eyes can also be made with wood, plastic, or glass beads and should always have a pinhole in them so that they can be animated (see Figure 7.13).

Over the Styrofoam ball, Hamish's head was sculpted with a thin layer of Plasticine clay, with a Sculpey nose. For his dialogue, I would sculpt replacement mouths that would need to be changed for each syllable of his speech patterns, and his mustache provided a frame around the mouth. His hat was made of fabric over a wire frame, which had two pieces of wire sticking out of the bottom, so that they could go through his head and keep it from falling off (see Figure 7.14). Finally, his prop microphone was built out of Sculpey, cardboard, and an actual miniature foam microphone cover.

Figure 7.15 is a shot of my bringing Hamish to life, and Figure 7.16 shows him acting for the camera. See Chapter 11, "Sets and Props," to read about how I composited Hamish and the monkey into a live-action background.

Figure 7.12 Plasticine hand sculpted over epoxy putty base.

Figure 7.13 Styrofoam head with Sculpey eyes and wire mesh ears.

Figure 7.14 Plasticine is layered over the head.

Figure 7.15 A slightly younger me at work.

Figure 7.16 Hamish McFlea on set.

Other Characters with Doll Armatures

The plastic doll armature (see Figure 7.17) is a fantastic tool for creating a very durable puppet that will last you a long time, and these armatures have grown to be a favorite tool of mine. Surprisingly, they are not very popular or widely distributed (at least no longer here in Vancouver). The local craft stores that used to carry them where I live stopped selling them, so I ended up buying them in bulk from the original distributor. They cost only a few dollars a piece, and different versions of them can also be ordered from a few distributors on the Internet. They have always been extremely popular and convenient in teaching my stop-motion course over the years, already made and ready to be dressed and animated, so they are great for kids as well. For new animators, doll armatures are particularly suitable, because they eliminate the extra step of making an armature from scratch, so that the focus can immediately be on just animating. Unlike wire armatures, which run the risk of breaking during animation, the plastic beads can be popped back together again if they come apart. Although doll armatures come premade as a body shape, they can also be cannibalized for extra parts such as tails, tentacles, or other appendages. You can also shorten their arms or legs for more stocky characters (see Figure 7.18, built

Figure 7.17 Plastic beaded doll armatures.

Figure 7.18 Leprechaun puppet by Nicole Tremblay.

on a plastic doll armature with felt clothing and head made of Sculpey on a Styrofoam ball) or use them for four-legged creatures (see Figure 7.19, built on two plastic doll armatures with papier-mâché head, beads for eyes, and wires inside the fingers).

The Clockwork Monkey in *Bad News* was also built on a plastic doll armature, using the full figure. After designing him with a series of concept drawings, I built the bulk of his body with mattress foam just like Hamish: cut into strips, wrapped around the armature, and stuck on with glue. (Hot glue or spray adhesive glue will work fine, reinforced with a little bit of strong tape here and there.) I found a furry brown fabric and glued it onto the foam and made some felt clothes for him (see Figure 7.20). His hands were ready-made plastic doll hands painted the same color as his feet. My friend Meeka's dad is an award-winning metalsmith/jeweler, so she was kind enough to have him fashion some homemade cymbals for me. He also had a tail made from more beaded plastic armature pieces and covered with furry fabric.

Figure 7.19 Centaurette puppet by Stephanie Mahoney.

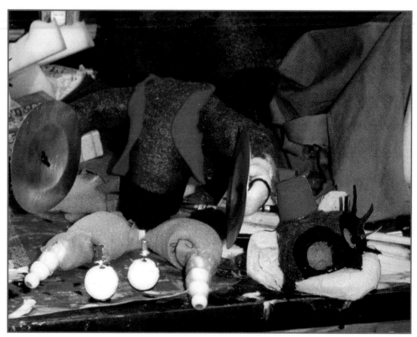

Figure 7.20 The Clockwork Monkey in progress.

The Clockwork Monkey's feet were made of baked polymer clay that I pressed the ends of his legs into before baking, so that there would be an exact indentation to hot glue the armature to afterward (see Figure 7.21). To make his head, I used a Styrofoam ball and attached different pieces of mattress foam (covered with fabric and paint) to make his ears, face, and muzzle. His muzzle was covered with a thin layer of Plasticine so that I could make him curl up his lips in a sneer or move the corners up for a wider smile. The teeth were made of baked polymer clay and glued to his foam muzzle, and his bottom jaw was attached with wire so that he could open and close his mouth.

The eyes were wooden beads painted white with a pinhole poked into them, so that a toothpick or thumbtack could be used to animate them moving around. The foam eyelashes on only one eye were a play-on-words homage to the Alex character from Stanley Kubrick's film *A Clockwork Orange*, since he was, after all, a Clockwork Monkey.

I wanted Hamish's head to be removable, so the wire sliding into the K&S tube was the best option for serving that purpose. In the case of the monkey, there was no need to remove his head, so it needed to be firmly attached to the body. I have found the steps in Figures 7.22–7.25 to be the best method for creating a puppet on a doll armature with a permanently attached head.

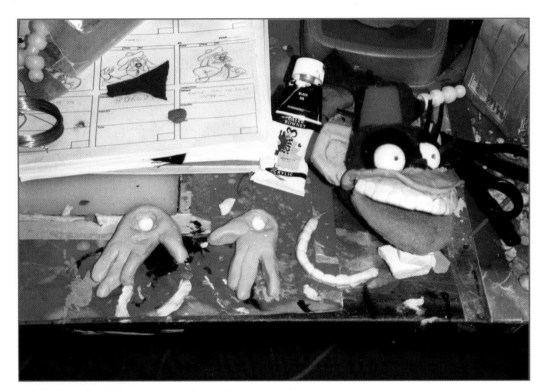

Figure 7.21 The Clockwork Monkey's feet and head, in progress.

Figure 7.22 Break off three beads from another doll armature and attach them to the top with epoxy putty for a neck piece.

Figure 7.23 Gouge a hole into a Styrofoam ball with the plastic neck piece so that it creates a hole exactly the right size.

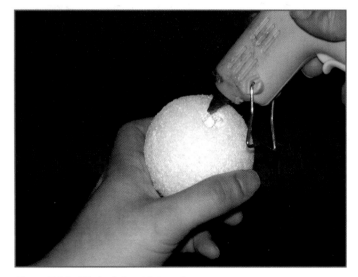

Figure 7.24 Fill the hole with hot glue.

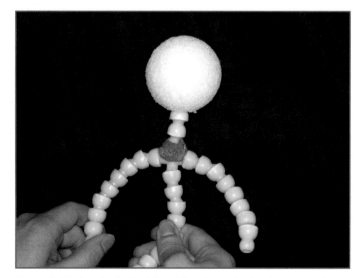

Figure 7.25 Attach the head by sliding the neck piece into the hole, and let it sit for a few minutes to cool off.

You can put some epoxy putty around the neck joint if it needs some extra stability. You can then cover the neck piece with fabric, Plasticine, or whatever flexible material will match the look of your head, and you now have a puppet with a head that will be able to rotate, tilt, and hold its position extremely well.

I used this same method of attaching a head for another puppet I built for my current film-in-progress, *Storytime with Nigel*. Nigel (see Figure 7.26) is a children's storyteller who narrates a story told in 2D animation and is voiced by Academy-Award winning animator Bob Godfrey. He was built on a plastic doll armature with a Styrofoam head and wooden beads for eyes. I covered his head with a material called Rigid Wrap, which is basically a roll of gauze caked in plaster. Rigid Wrap can be found in craft stores, cut into strips, dipped in water, and layered onto the head. When dried, it will be rock solid and ready to be painted. Nigel's dialogue was done with clay replacement mouths, which were placed onto a pinhead sticking out of the middle of his muzzle. The only elements that moved on his face were his mouth, eyes, and eyebrows (stuck on with Sculpey), so his head was simply a solid object that would move in sync with the inflections in his dialogue.

Nigel's hands were built on a poxy putty base adhered directly to the doll armature, which would allow them to move in any direction. Wires for the fingers were stuck directly into the putty before it dried, and they were covered with felt gloves that were sewn together and stuffed with fiber fill to give them some bulk. His clothes were made of felt.

Figure 7.26 My Nigel puppet, also built on a doll armature.

All of these puppets were built with the plastic doll armatures because they proved to be the best kind of armatures for the size needed and suited themselves well to the design. These methods may not necessarily be as convenient for other character designs. The important point here is that the puppets were designed based on what would be required of them to perform in front of the camera, which was mainly dialogue or simple character animation from the waist up. I would highly recommend getting your hands on a few armatures like this for your first puppet experiments. Here are a few resources, and you can always Google search for more or scope out your local craft store:

◆ **www.varietydistributors.com.** This is where I tracked down the armatures that stopped being distributed in Vancouver craft stores, and I began buying in bulk for my students. They may not have many more in stock but still may be worth contacting to find out. The item number is 17130.

◆ **www.modularhose.com.** This new site sells the beaded armature pieces that can be used to custom-build a doll armature. For an example of the armature design on their old site, go to the "Loc-Line Doll Armature" link in the "Workshop" section under the Library at StopMotionWorks.com.

◆ **www.miniworlddolls.com/TS9Armature.htm.** This is a site from which to buy plastic doll armatures, in different sizes and design styles.

◆ **www.crawforddesigns.net/acces.html.** This is another site from which to buy plastic doll armatures.

Ball-and-Socket Armatures

In studio productions, the most popular kind of armature is the ball-and-socket (see Figures 7.27 and 7.28), whose use goes all the way back to the original *King Kong*. Ball-and-socket armatures were also used by Ray Harryhausen and Phil Tippett, and for the puppets in films like *The Nightmare Before Christmas* and *Wallace and*

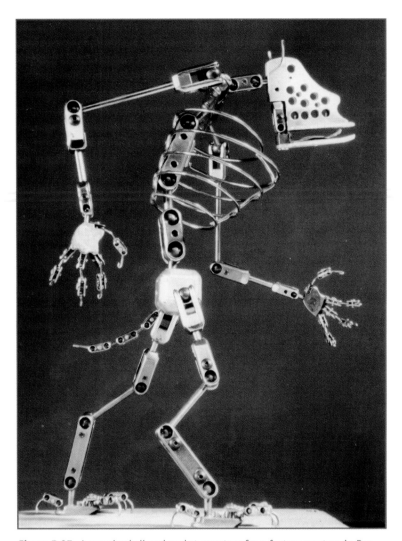

Figure 7.27 A complex ball-and-socket armature for a fantasy creature in Ray Harryhausen-esque tradition. (Copyright Stop Motion Works.)

Figure 7.28 Four-legged ball-and-socket armature for a Stegosaurus. (Copyright Stop Motion Works.)

Gromit. A ball-and-socket armature is typically made of metal—either brass, steel, or aluminum—and can be relatively simple or extremely complex. Its popularity comes from the fact that it is extremely durable, holds its positions well, and can be custom made to accommodate nearly any character design. The level of subtlety in movement that can be achieved is also quite remarkable, in that the tiniest movements can be animated to cushion in and out of holds with ease. Certain joints can be tightened or loosened to provide the best movement for the animator's liking. One of the most prolific ball-and-socket armature building studios in the world is MacKinnon and Saunders, based in the UK, which has built armatured puppets for productions ranging from *Bob the Builder* to *Corpse Bride*. The fabrication costs for many of their puppets go up to several thousands of dollars!

In a ball-and-socket armature, there are different kinds of joints that make up the parts of the body that connect. The logic behind them is based strongly on actual human anatomy. Ball joints (see Figure 7.29) are universal joints that consist of two metal plates with ball bearings fit snugly between them, allowing for any kind of movement: left-to-right or diagonally for easy posing. Hinges, another kind of joint, bend only in one linear direction. A human knee or elbow joint can bend only in one direction, so it's common for a hinge joint to be used for these parts of a human armature. The whole armature, and the different joints associated with it, should be planned carefully against diagrams of the character and its anatomy (see Figure 7.30).

My reference in the Introduction to Ken Southworth's description of an animator being an artist/actor/engineer is especially relevant in stop-motion animation when it comes to building a ball-and-socket armature. Building an armature such as this from scratch requires the skills of a machinist engineer, but it is also a delicate art in itself. A great deal of studio space and equipment may be required, and the tools needed such as mills, lathes, saws, drills, and a blowtorch can get rather expensive. An easier route to take would be to purchase a kit that has all of the pieces you need and just put it together. Kits are not cheap either, but they save you work building all of the pieces yourself. If you want to specialize in puppet building, getting hard-core into ball-and-socket armatures is a good area to consider, since most studio puppets are built this way. It is usually done by a special department of skilled machinists who communicate with the animators to make sure they are adjusted for the best kind of fluid movement. The process is so involved that people who specialize in building these kinds of armatures from scratch *and* animating them are a unique breed. But if you have the cash and the patience of a technician,

Figure 7.29 Hip joint designed by Tom Perzanowski, with a notch in the socket for greater freedom of movement. (Courtesy of Larry Larson at Center for Creative Studies.)

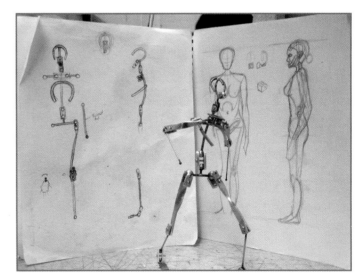

Figure 7.30 Full body armature and plans by Tom Perzanowski. (Courtesy of Larry Larson at Center for Creative Studies.)

the results will give you the best kind of armature for fluid animation. Lionel Ivan Orozco has some helpful tutorials for building your own ball-and-sockets in the Workshop section of www.stopmotionworks.com, and the links page at www.stopmotionanimation.com (see Chapter 8, "An Interview with Anthony Scott") lists many suppliers for armature kits and assembly sets. As always, plan your character design well so that you know that the armature will best suit the animation you want to create.

Wire Armatures

One of the most popular methods for building a custom-made armature for stop-motion, for beginners, hobbyists, and some studio professionals, is to use bendable annealed (or softened) wire. The wire must be strong enough to support the weight of whatever covers it and be able to hold its position without slipping. Wire is made out of many different materials, and in different thicknesses. Generally, wire comes made out of aluminum, lead, or steel. Steel wire, as long as it's not too thick, can be bent into any shape to hold its position but will often have problems with springing. This means that if you move a piece of steel wire into any position, it will often spring back slightly, which is difficult for animation if you are trying to capture precise movements. Lead wire, which is commonly used for soldering, is also very flexible, but it breaks very easily and is also toxic. Lead will come off on your hands when handled and will create a dirty mess when mixed with clay or any other materials. So, these inconveniences related to lead and steel wire leave aluminum as the champion wire material among stop-motion animators everywhere. Wire can be bought at your local hardware store, but make sure it says aluminum on the packaging somewhere. You will need to build a wire armature if your character design is smaller or thinner than what a plastic doll armature will allow you to create, or if a ball-and-socket armature is outside of your price range or preference.

Aluminum alloy wire that is at least 1/8 inch in diameter will work as a single strand for making the limbs of your wire puppet. Any wire that is thinner, say 1/16 inch or less, will need to be doubled up by twisting to give it more durability and longevity. It's likely that your wire, no matter how strong it is, may eventually break after much handling through the animation. The point is to build it so that you can prevent that breakage as long as possible. I have tried different kinds of wire found in craft and hardware stores, and some of them have worked well, although certain kinds of utility wire from hardware stores tend to be too brittle for animation. Another source is sculpture supply houses, which may carry a brand of wire called "Almaloy," used for clay sculptures but with the right properties for animation puppets as well. Marc Spess' online shop at www.animateclay.com sells very effective brands of aluminum wire that can be trusted to work well for stop-motion animation. I find that online resources such as this, which are specifically geared toward stop-motion, will often provide you with very good products. Buying materials from hardware stores is useful (particularly for constructing rigs, sets, and props), and it's inevitable that you will need to buy things from them, even if what they sell for puppets is not necessarily with stop-motion in mind. Again, it's all about experimentation, and looking for the right materials can sometimes be like a scavenger hunt, scouring out different things at craft stores, hardware stores, dollar stores, etc., and the Internet. Unfortunately, you cannot find a one-stop Quick Mart for stop-motion.

Building a Simple Wire Puppet

Let's build a basic human puppet from scratch! There is no ready-made armature in this case, so in a sense, you are creating something out of nothing, which is a creative privilege. Be proud! These steps demonstrate how to build a character out of simple, cheap materials.

Start by making a drawing of your character standing straight up in a generic position. This drawing will be used for scale purposes and to make sure you build your armature with the right proportions. Make your drawing roughly the right height you want your puppet to be. A few millimeters here and there won't matter; it's there as a guide. In this case, the puppet is going to be about 8 to 9 inches tall, which is a good size to work with.

Use your drawing to estimate how long of a wire piece to cut, starting with a loop for the legs, for instance. Take this length and fold it into itself so that you have two sides the same length (see Figure 7.31). Give yourself a few extra inches, as it's always better to make your piece too long and then crop it if you need to. Making your piece too short will be a waste of wire.

For your wire pieces, slide the cut ends into a power drill, so it can be evenly twisted to make it stronger (see Figure 7.32). On the looped side of your wire, you need to anchor it somehow. Leave a good-sized loop at the end, and grip the wire tightly with some pliers, clamp it into a vice, or place the wire under a heavy object. Once the wire is secure, slowly rotate the drill forward so that the wire will twist good and tight. Don't go too fast or too far, or the wire will start twisting over itself and get tangled. For really small wire pieces, you can simply hold the looped end with pliers and twist it with your hands. Now you should be able to bend the twisted wire and lay it over your drawing (see Figure 7.33). Adjust the length of your wire and where it bends so that you can leave at least an inch bent upward for the feet.

If your puppet is being designed so that it can walk, the feet are very important and are one of the most difficult problems to solve in stop-motion puppets. You want the feet to be able to flex their shape slightly, as a real foot does while walking. A simple method and material is foam, which in this case is cut from a foam finger commonly seen at sporting events (see Figure 7.34). Cut the foam so that it has a hole where the ankle joint would be. Bend the wires for the feet downward and gently poke the wires through the foam, so that it can be bent back into a right angle (see Figure 7.35). The wires should be glued firm and snug in the foam to provide a good ankle joint, as there may be times when the ankle supports the weight of the puppet. Try to avoid the wires poking through the top or bottom of the foot. The foam can then be carved into a shoe shape.

Continue measuring cut pieces of wire for the torso and the arms, and use smaller pieces of wire or hot glue to hold the various limbs together (see Figure 7.36). For this puppet, I want the head and hands to be removable so they can be manipulated independently from the body if need be. Wires can be attached to the head and hands and slid into holes in the armature. To achieve this, use K&S tubing from a hobby shop, which is typically sold in one-foot pieces. Cut some pieces about an inch in length for the neck and hands. The best tool for doing this is a tiny saw with a miter box (see Figure 7.37) that will help you cut in a straight line for a clean cut. To keep the wires adhered to each other, you can cover the places where they connect with epoxy putty. Epoxy putty comes in a tube, so tear off a chunk and knead it until the two compounds blend together into a uniform gray color. The putty is very bad for your skin, so always wear latex gloves (cheap disposable ones are fine) when working with it. Work in a ventilated area, and try to avoid breathing the fumes; it's stinky stuff! You will need to work fast at kneading it and applying it to the armature (see Figure 7.38), as it will starting drying right away and will be rock solid within 20 to 30 minutes. You can also use the epoxy putty to create "bones" for the armature in those places where there should not be bending, leaving the exposed wire to serve as your joints. Place the K&S tube pieces into the putty as well, before it dries completely (see Figure 7.39).

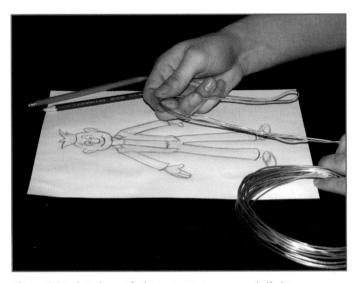

Figure 7.31 Cut pieces of wire to create your puppet's limbs.

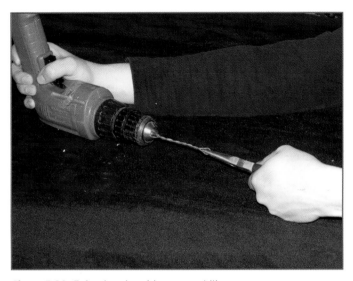

Figure 7.32 Twist the wire with a power drill.

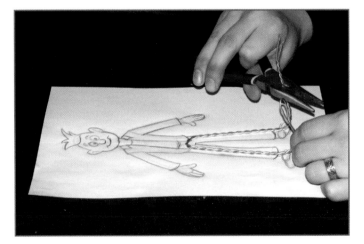

Figure 7.33 Bend and cut the wires into shape using your drawing as a reference.

Figure 7.34 Feet can be made from pieces of foam.

7. Building Puppets

151

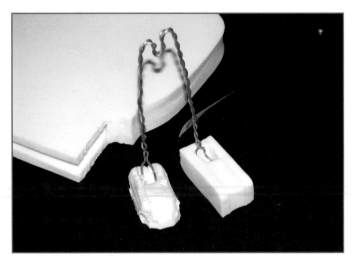

Figure 7.35 The wires are glued into the foam feet, which are carved into shape.

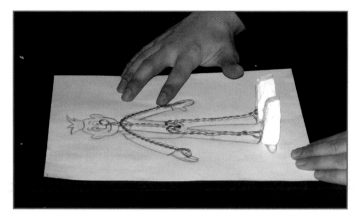

Figure 7.36 Lay the other wire body parts over the drawing.

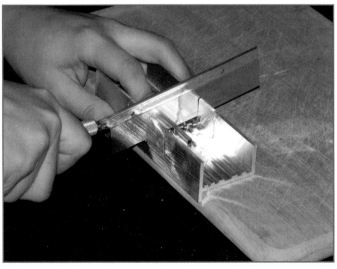

Figure 7.37 Cut pieces of K&S tubing for the head and hands to slide into.

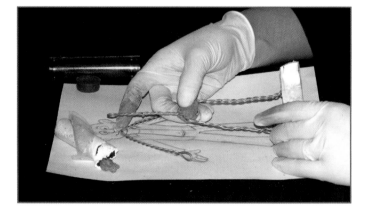

Figure 7.38 Adhere the wire pieces together with epoxy putty.

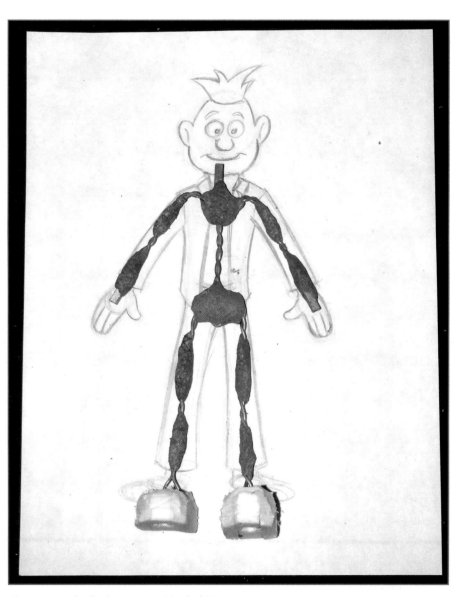

Figure 7.39 The final armature with all of its epoxy bones.

The puppet's feet, especially if it will be standing or walking full-figure on camera, will need tie-downs built into them. Tie-downs allow the feet to be firmly anchored to the ground and prevent the puppet from falling over. Carve holes into the foam feet and super-glue nuts into them, making sure they are flush with the bottom surface of each foot (see Figure 7.40). When animating, bolts can be screwed through holes in the set, up into the nuts in the feet. More on this in Chapter 9. The head and hands can be sculpted out of clay, but to use solid clay would make the puppet too top-heavy, so it should be built around something lightweight. A Styrofoam ball can be sculpted itself by pressing it into a head-like shape (see Figure 7.41). Eyes are gouged into the Styrofoam, and a twisted piece of wire is stuck into the head where the neck joint should be. Use epoxy putty to firmly attach the wire to the head. The base for the hands is a piece of epoxy putty built around a twisted wire (see Figure 7.42). Begin layering thin pieces of clay onto the foam head, lining it up directly with the eyes. Then add additional facial features, keeping in mind that you want to avoid weighing down your puppet with too much clay. Build clay around the hands, leaving the fingers as solid clay (see Figures 7.43–7.44).

To build the bulk, or "muscles," of your puppet, cut strips of mattress/cushion foam (found at craft stores or specialty foam shops) and wrap them around your armature. The foam can be held in place by wrapping and twisting pieces of floral wire around it (see Figures 7.45–7.46). The foam should be wrapped around tightly enough to allow the armature's joints to be able to bend. The feet can be painted black (see Figure 7.47), or any other color you wish.

Figure 7.40 Tie-downs are glued into the bottom of the feet.

Figure 7.41 Sculpt a Styrofoam ball into a head shape.

Figure 7.42 Eyes and a wire neck are added to the head, and hands are made of putty and wire.

Figure 7.43 Build up a thin layer of clay over the head.

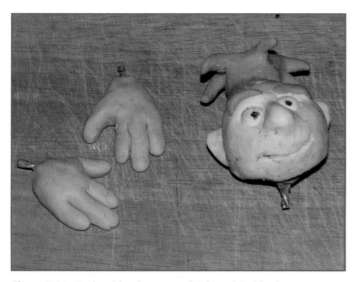

Figure 7.44 Head and hands are completely sculpted in clay.

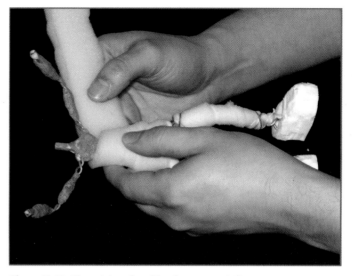

Figure 7.45 Wrap strips of cushion foam around the armature.

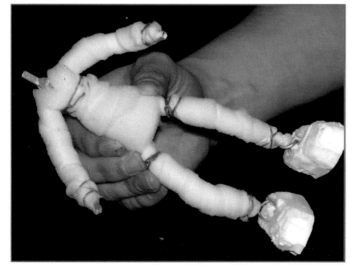

Figure 7.46 Floral wire will keep the foam in place around the armature.

Figure 7.47 Paint the feet black to make them appear like shoes.

7. Building Puppets

155

The foam is hard to get perfectly smooth, but a dark color will hide most of the roughness of the feet and still give them an interesting texture. Cut out pieces of felt or any other kind of fabric, front and back, for the puppet's clothes, and stitch them together over the armature (see Figures 7.48–7.49). Felt has a great texture and hides seams pretty well, so it is a good solution for clothing your puppet. Then the head and hands can be slid into the tubes, with some additional clay added to make wrists and a neck, and your puppet is complete (see Figure 7.50)! If you find the head to be wobbly, or the hands having issues with falling out of the tubes, stick some clay inside the tubes to give them some extra firmness. Refer to Chapter 9 and the accompanying CD to see this guy in action!

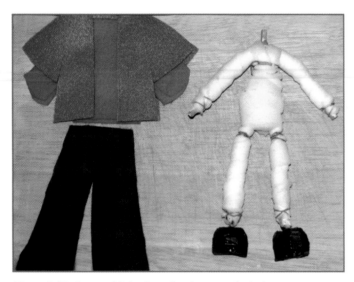

Figure 7.48 Cut out fabric pieces for the puppet's clothes.

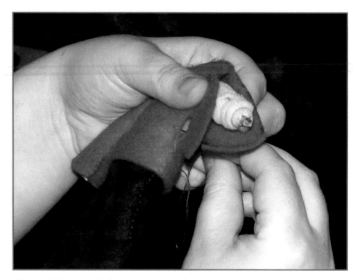

Figure 7.49 Stitch the clothes together over the armature.

Figure 7.50 The fully clothed puppet.

Molds and Foam Latex Methods

For student films, independent projects, or commercials, most puppets are a one-shot deal that are built once, animated once, and then moved on to the Retirement Home for Stop-Motion Puppets. For a stop-motion studio production, *lots* of puppets are needed, often several different copies of the same character (see Figure 7.51). A feature film or television series might have many different scenes with the same characters being animated on separate sets at the same time. This is part of the reason why creating puppets with molds is very popular in the industry. The technique ensures that any puppets created as duplicates or back-up versions (in case an armature breaks) will look the same, so that the character's appearance does not change throughout the show. Another common practice is to create the same puppet in different scales—large-scale for close-ups and tiny versions for extreme long shots. No matter which scale, the only way to guarantee that a puppet will look exactly the same twice is to use molds of one kind or another. Since many stop-motion hopefuls look to the big-budget productions to learn about how these films are made, there is a common misconception that this is the only way to make puppets. As you have seen in this chapter already, it is not the only way, but for studio productions, it usually works best. Independent filmmakers can use these techniques, too, of course, but a word of caution to the beginner: It is an extremely time-consuming and expensive method that must be learned through a lot of trial and error to get right. Many different skills are involved, and to do it conveniently, you should have a dedicated studio space for it. Much of the process is messy and deals with poisonous materials, so I would not recommend attempting it in your kitchen or anyplace else with food around. Adequate ventilation is a must, because the molds are typically filled with foam latex, which is toxic and extremely potent. If you want to specialize in puppet building, I encourage you to do your research and get yourself equipped to try it, and after much experimentation and persistence you will find it rewarding. But if you have a limited budget and want a quicker fix for making a puppet, I would suggest using one of the other simple methods in this chapter.

Figure 7.51 Painting duplicate puppet heads. (Courtesy of Zung Studio.)

The advantage of making a foam latex puppet from a mold is that you can create a puppet with an outside surface that will not flutter or lose its shape when touched during animation. If a puppet's arm, for instance, is covered in clay, then it may squish and lose its shape after many nudges by the animator and will need to be constantly resculpted. If the arm is covered in fabric, there is the possibility that the texture or any loose edges will flutter in the resulting animation. With a foam latex covering, the arm can be squeezed tightly but will then spring back to its original shape. The latex can be painted so that it has an appearance similar to clay, so it is commonly used in clay animation for parts of the puppet that will have less movement. The head and hands/arms may be made of Plasticine clay, but the torso and legs are foam latex, and the two materials work together for a seamless appearance. It is also a popular alternative to clay because it keeps down the weight of the puppet. Aardman Animations, makers of *Wallace and Gromit*, uses this technique for many of their puppets.

The technique of making puppets out of molds in foam latex must be mastered over time with much practice, and there are many different skills to learn throughout the whole procedure. The best way to learn it is to do lots of research and consult some good resources. Taking a sculpture class will help give you some hands-on experience in some of the mold-making steps involved. If you are a visual learner, you may find one of the best resources to be Kathi Zung's excellent DVD tutorial *Do-It-Yourself Puppetmaking 101*, available through her studio Web site, www.angelfire.com/anime4/zungstudio/. For the purpose of this chapter, I will give a basic overview of the process so that you may be inspired to take your research further.

The first step is to make a *sculpt* of your puppet out of oil-based clay (see Figure 7.52). The sculpt should be as smooth as possible with all of the details you want showing up in your final latex version. It can be smoothed out with alcohol or melted clay to ensure there are no unwanted cracks, holes, or lumps. For details on your sculpt, such as the edge of a jacket, sleeve, or collar, anything that is raised up as an extra shape must be sculpted in a way that avoids an undercut. An *undercut* is any texture that will cause problems when it is molded and needs to be separated from the mold. Any raised shape should be sculpted at a 45-degree angle that slopes toward you, not away from you. A shape with an undercut will cause the mold to get stuck underneath it.

Figure 7.52 Kathi Zung refines a puppet sculpt in oil-based clay. (Copyright Zung Studio.)

The sculpt is then laid up inside a bed of potter's clay (the kind that air-dries, not oil-based clay that never hardens) that comes up to its halfway point (see Figure 7.53). Imagine your sculpt is floating on its back in a pool, and make sure the clay bed fills around the entire sculpt without air pockets, as if it were a pool of water. Keys, which are little notches in the clay, are also created on the clay bed (see Figure 7.54) to help the mold stay together with the other half, which will be created later.

Plaster (a common plaster-like substance used is Ultracal-30) or gypsum is mixed and applied onto the sculpt in its clay bed. A common practice for some is to build a wall around the clay bed (out of foam board or milk cartons) so that the mold will have a smooth, uniform shape to it. Many layers are built up over it, inside the wall if there is one, and mixed with sheets of burlap. This is creating the first half of the actual mold. After it dries, the clay bed is ripped apart, and all of the excess clay left on the mold must be washed away with water (see Figure 7.55). Coat the mold, especially the keys, with Vaseline. Then the mold, with the sculpt still inside it, must have another layer of molding material applied to it, to create the second half of the mold (see Figure 7.56). Ultracal contains lime, which can eat away your skin, so wear latex gloves to protect your skin while using it.

When both sides of the mold are dried and finished, they are pulled apart and the sculpt is removed, leaving an exact impression of its front and back. The armature, typically made of wire or ball-and-sockets, is laid inside the mold, ready to be cast in latex (see Figure 7.57). Brass will eat away at latex, so try to avoid any brass pieces in your armature; aluminum or steel is better.

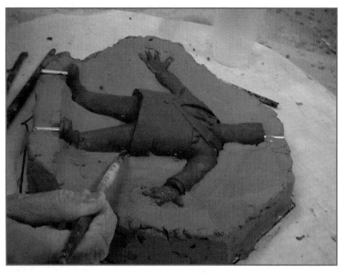

Figure 7.53 Building up a clay bed around the sculpt. (Copyright Zung Studio.)

Figure 7.54 Another example of a sculpt inside its clay bed, with keys sculpted into it. (Copyright Stop Motion Works.)

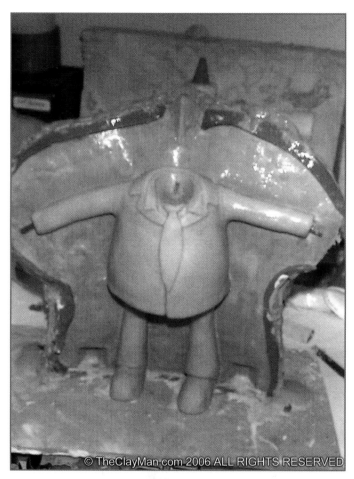

Figure 7.55 The first half of the mold with the sculpt embedded inside. (Courtesy of The Clayman's 3D Cartoon Communications.)

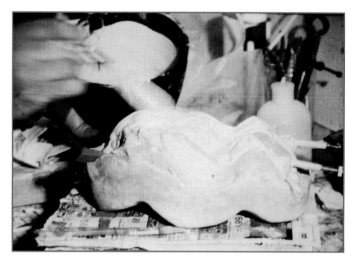

Figure 7.56 Applying a gypsum material to the mold to create the second half. (Copyright Stop Motion Works.)

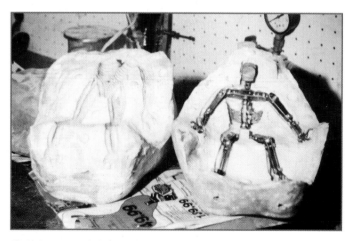

Figure 7.57 Both halves of the open mold, with armature laid inside. (Copyright Stop Motion Works.)

7. Building Puppets

161

Foam latex typically comes in a kit, as it must be mixed together with different agents and solutions to work properly (see Figure 7.58). The kit will have instructions explaining how to mix it, which should be read carefully along with all safety instructions. This whole procedure *must* be done with strong ventilation in the room, as latex contains ammonia and gives off a strong smell that is bad for inhalation and eye contact. The latex base comes in the largest container, because this is the main substance making up most of the solution, with smaller portions of the other agents mixed in. The exact measurements will vary depending on how big of a batch of latex you are making. Mixed with the latex base are the foaming agent and curing agent, which are first measured out and combined in an electric mixer at low speed. For the foaming stage, switch to high speed, then medium speed and lower speed for the refining stage. You might mix at each speed for about 3 to 5 minutes, but the whole process is also dependent on the humidity and temperature of the room. This process may cause you to go through several different batches to get it exactly right. The consistency of the foam should be like thick cream. At the end of your mixing stage, add the gelling agent and let it continue mixing for another minute or so.

Once the latex mix is complete, it is applied into the mold over the armature. The latex can be applied in a number of ways. One way is to clamp the mold tightly together and inject the latex through a hole in the mold with a giant syringe (see Figure 7.59). Another way is to brush a thin layer inside the mold, place the armature inside, and pour the rest over it straight from its mixing bowl.

Figure 7.58 A foam latex kit: base with foaming, curing, and gelling agents. (Courtesy of the Clayman's 3D Cartoon Communications.)

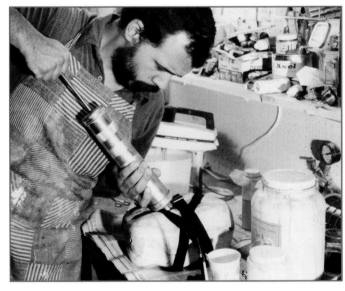

Figure 7.59 Injecting foam latex into the mold. (Copyright Stop Motion Works.)

Once the latex inside the mold has started to gel, it is placed inside an oven for baking and curing. *Do not use the same oven you cook your dinner in!* For making puppets, you need a separate oven that can handle the fumes from the latex, typically referred to as a convection oven. It might be a good idea to check out some local thrift shops or garage sales to possibly find a used one. After a few hours inside the oven, the mold can be removed and pried apart, and you will then have a soft, spongy foam latex version of your original sculpt, with the armature fit snug inside (see Figure 7.60). The latex that has spilled over from being inside the mold will still be attached to it, so it will need to be snipped away with a pair of fine scissors (see Figure 7.61). Then smooth out the seams along the side with a wood-burning tool or soldering gun, but open the window to ventilate the stench it will create. The puppet can then be painted with special brands of acrylic paint suited for latex (see Figure 7.62). When it's all said and done, your puppet is ready for shooting! (See Figures 7.63–7.64.)

Figure 7.60 The mold is pried open to reveal the latex puppet inside. (Courtesy of the Clayman's 3D Cartoon Communications.)

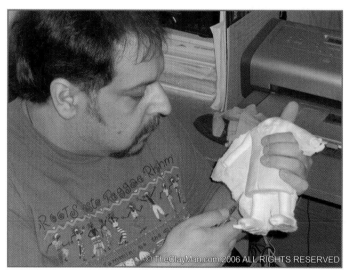

Figure 7.61 Paul Moldovanos snips away excess foam from his puppet. (Courtesy of the Clayman's 3D Cartoon Communications.)

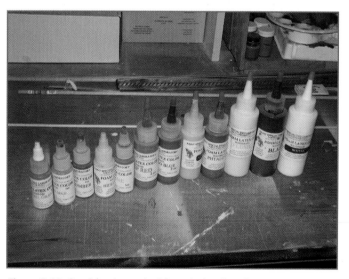

Figure 7.62 Special paints suited for painting foam latex puppets. (Courtesy of the Clayman's 3D Cartoon Communications.)

7. Building Puppets

163

Figure 7.63 Foam latex puppet. (Courtesy of the Clayman's 3D Cartoon Communications.)

Figure 7.64 Foam latex puppet. (Copyright Stop Motion Works.)

A puppet made of foam latex, which is a soft material when cured, requires a hard mold for casting. On the opposite end, any material that is intended to dry hard requires a soft mold for casting (see Figure 7.65). A hard-sculpted object may be a head, or it may be a prop. The process is very similar to the procedure I just described. The original sculpt is done in polymer clay or oil-based clay and laid up in a potter's clay bed. A wall can be built around it and covered with silicone rubber or RTV rubber material, which has a consistency like pancake batter. If the mold has two sides to it, then the first half has more rubber poured onto it to create the second half. The mold will cure itself by air-drying, and can then have a poly resin material poured into it. Within 2 minutes, the resin will harden, creating a hard version of the original sculpt, which can then be sanded down and painted.

Figure 7.65 Soft rubber mold with poly resin sculpture. (Courtesy of the Clayman's 3D Cartoon Communications.)

Latex Build-Up Puppets

If you do not have the time, money, or inclination to make a puppet with a latex skin using the molding method, there is another way to achieve a similar look. The latex build-up technique involves applying the latex skin onto the puppet rather than casting it in a mold. This is the technique that was used to make the original 1933 *King Kong* puppets, of which there were several different ones made for the film. It is not easy to make exact duplicate puppets using this method; in fact, the different original *Kong* puppets varied slightly in their appearance. Latex build-up is a common technique used for humans, creatures, or animal puppets that have a rough, scaly, or wrinkly appearance to their skin (see Figure 7.66). For more detail-specific work and control, the muscles or skin pieces of the puppet may be sculpted or casted in open molds separately and applied onto the puppet in pieces, with liquid latex holding it all together. This process still involves some mold making, but in other cases, the latex may simply be brushed or poured onto the armature.

The following illustrations show the steps I took to make a goblin puppet using the latex build-up technique. Start by building or preparing your armature. Any kind of armature can be used, including ball-and-sockets, but in this case I made another

Figure 7.66 Latex build-up puppet. (Courtesy of Nick Hilligoss.)

wire one (see Figure 7.67), based on the shape of his body. I took a different approach to the goblin's feet (see Figures 7.68–7.69), making them out of polymer clay and sculpting holes for the wires to stick into, and for tie-downs to fit inside. Then I baked them and filled the holes with glue to affix them to the puppet. Heels were sculpted with epoxy putty. The wire between the heel and the rest of the foot, which would allow the foot to bend, was covered in scraps from a pair of doll tights, an elastic material.

The head (see Figure 7.70) is based on a traditional European puppet approach, with very little facial movement. His face is not able to change expression, but rather stays in a permanent grin. (There is something inherently creepy about characters who grin all the time.) The only movement in his face will be subtle changes to his eyebrows and mouth, so I built them out of two pieces of pipe cleaner. (The eyebrows are one continuous piece bent into two brows.) Pipe cleaners are often a nice alternative to aluminum wire for features like this, because they are easy to grip and hold their shape well without ripping through the Styrofoam. The rest of his head was sculpted in polymer clay. I lightly removed the Styrofoam head from the polymer clay "mask" and positioned it as best I could on a tray so that it maintained the same shape, then baked it, along with his chin and horns (see Figure 7.71). Pieces like this can go into a toaster oven for 10 minutes at 285 degrees Fahrenheit. Wooden beads for eyes were painted and filled with hard black Fimo polymer clay, with a hole poked through for easy animating. For detailed work such as heads and eyes, or holding your puppet in place, get yourself a "helping hand" rig from a hobby shop (see Figure 7.72).

Figure 7.67 A wire armature is built against a reference drawing.

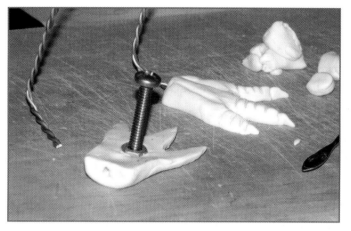

Figure 7.68 Feet are sculpted in clay with tie-downs built into them.

Figure 7.69 Putty and elastic material are added to complete the feet.

Figure 7.70 The head is built of Styrofoam and polymer clay.

Figure 7.71 Clay face pieces are baked in an oven for hardening.

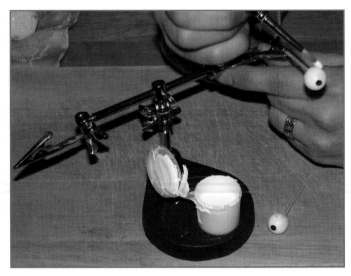

Figure 7.72 Eyes are held in place with a rig for easy painting.

A helping hand is built out of the same joints used for ball-and-socket armatures and is extremely useful. Doll stands will also help for holding up your puppet while working on it.

The rest of the armature was built up with epoxy putty bones, and links of plastic doll armature were used for the neck (see Figure 7.73). Aside from ball-and-socket joints, I think the doll armature pieces provide the absolute best mobility for a universally movable neck joint. Hands were made out of epoxy putty, with single strands of aluminum wire stuck in while still wet. Cut your finger pieces before affixing the putty to the arm, making them longer than you want them, so they can be trimmed later. Use some pliers to make sure the putty is affixed tightly around each wire before it dries (see Figure 7.74). If the wires are too loose, they will slip out. Your armature should be ready for covering at this point (see Figure 7.75).

To begin preparing for the latex build-up process, cover your armature in strips of cotton (see Figure 7.76). An entire roll can be found in your local drug store. Wrap it tightly around your armature in such a way as to suggest muscles or other shapes of your puppet's body. The ends can be tied down with floral wire or tiny bits of hot glue. The cotton will adhere itself to the armature well for a good deal of control over the shape of your body (see Figure 7.77). Pieces of foam could also be used to bulk up your armature more or create more specific shapes than the cotton will allow. It's all going to be covered up anyway.

Figure 7.73 Epoxy putty and a doll armature neck are added to the armature.

Figure 7.74 Hands are built with putty and wires.

Figure 7.75 Here is the finished armature, front and side.

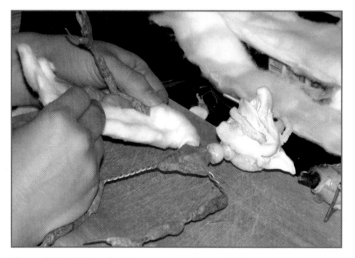

Figure 7.76 Strips of cotton are wrapped around the armature.

7. Building Puppets

169

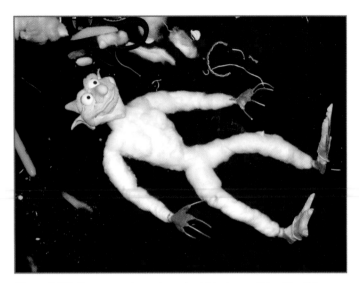

Figure 7.77 Your covered armature should look something like this, depending on your design.

Figure 7.78 Liquid latex rubber is brushed onto the puppet.

Now you are ready to start brushing liquid latex rubber over the cotton (see Figure 7.78). The particular product I used is called Mold Builder from Castin' Craft, which can also be used to create rubber molds, but in this case I used it to mix with the cotton to create skin for my puppet. Add more pieces of cotton and mix with the latex for any parts you want to be bulkier. Do this in a ventilated room, or outside, as the mix contains ammonia and can be hazardous to your skin, eyes, and lungs. Apply tiny pieces of cotton to your hands and over the wires, mixing it together with the latex in layers (see Figure 7.79). To create some abdominal muscles, I found these cotton face cleaning pads that already came with a ribbed shape, much like the muscles I wanted to create (see Figures 7.80–7.81). Continue applying small pieces of cotton to the face and any features that will animate, including eyebrows and mouth pieces. The space between the creature's head and brows will be filled with cotton and latex, so that when the brows are animated, the skin over the top of them will flex slightly (see Figure 7.82). Once your entire puppet is covered in latex (as in Figure 7.83), let it dry overnight.

Once the latex dries, your puppet is ready to be painted (see Figure 7.84). You can use acrylic paint, and either brush or sponge it on, depending on the texture you want. One or two light coats should be enough, so that the texture of your latex skin still maintains its character. Cover any clothed parts of your puppet with fabric, and your puppet is ready to come to life (see Figure 7.85)! As he moves, his skin will flex, bulge, and wrinkle in a realistic fashion.

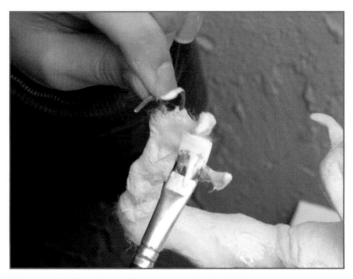

Figure 7.79 Tiny pieces of cotton are mixed with latex.

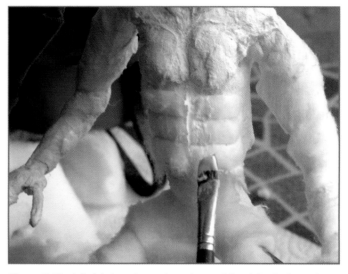

Figure 7.80 A facial cleansing pad can be used for abdominal muscles.

Figure 7.81 Covered with a layer of latex, my goblin is now looking very muscular indeed.

Figure 7.82 More tiny cotton pieces are mixed with latex for facial features.

7. Building Puppets

171

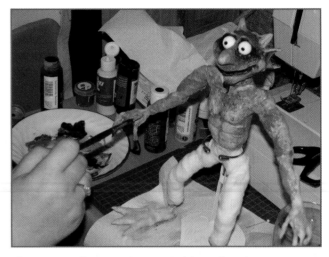

Figure 7.83 Here is the goblin with his feet, body, hands, and head completely painted in latex.

Figure 7.84 The puppet is covered with acrylic paint.

Figure 7.85 The finished goblin puppet.

Clay Puppets

If you want your entire puppet to look like clay (see Figure 7.86), you can use it to create the whole character, much like Will Vinton did with his Claymation work. Depending on your design, it can be all one color or a combination of colors. Clay is a fun medium that can give you lots of freedom in animation, but it also has limitations. Unlike foam and fabric materials, which are lightweight, clay is extremely heavy. If you want to animate walks or jumps, the weight of the clay has potential for problems in fighting with gravity. Clay also gets dirty as you handle it over time, and it will pick up the dirt and oil from your fingers. As your animation progresses over time, the clay might start to lose its cleanliness, resulting in color shifts. To avoid this, it helps to have some baby wipes handy to keep your fingers as clean as possible, and you may also need to lightly scrape off the top layer of clay from your puppet if you notice it starting to get dirty. Keeping your hands clean is also important if your puppet has many different colors, because you don't want the colors running together or causing unnecessary smudges. Clay requires a lot of re-sculpting of your puppet, as it is difficult to retain its original shape and keep it consistent. After being on a set under hot lights for several hours, it also starts to soften and continues to get messier. Because of this, making good-quality clay animation can be a very time-consuming method compared to other materials, but the effort is worth it in the end. If you really want to see what clay is capable of in the hands of a wild imagination, check out the work of Bruce Bickford (Frank Zappa's *Baby Snakes*, *The Amazing Mr. Bickford*, and Brett Ingram's documentary *Monster Road*).

Figure 7.86 "Toyabah" puppet in clay over wire armature. (Copyright Michael Stennick, Space Monster Pictures, laserblast.multiply.com.)

To get around many of the problems involved with clay puppets, you may want to have an armature inside, depending on the design. An armature will give you the freedom to move your puppet into many positions. The stronger and looser the joints are, the less pressure you may need to put on appendages like arms and legs while moving them. You don't want an armature that is too hard to move, because that means you will have to push harder on the limbs, which will cause the shape to squish more. There will always be a certain level of squishing and resculpting of the clay, but any way to keep it to a minimum will be welcomed. You can also combine your armature with other light materials such as Styrofoam to keep the weight down, and place a thin layer of clay over the top so that it still keeps its clay appearance (see Figures 7.87–7.88). Other materials can be combined with clay as well, such as wire or fabric. I would recommend continuing to use beads for eyes, as clay eyes are very hard to move without losing their shape and becoming a big mess.

Most clay animation is done with Plasticine or other brands of oil-based modeling clay, but you can also experiment with animating Sculpey. (The Super Sculpey brand works best.) Sculpey is polymer clay, intended to be baked, but due to the fact that it's less greasy and not as mushy as modeling clay, it can still end up being a convenient material for animation. Or, you can combine them, using the Sculpey for the parts that don't move as much, either baking them or leaving them unbaked. A student of mine recently came up with a neat idea for making a monster puppet completely out of Sculpey (see Figure 7.89). It was created for a dialogue exercise, so the only parts that really needed to move were the eyes, eyebrows, and mouth. Using a ball of tin foil as a base, most of the puppet was built up on top of it and baked so it was hard, then the parts that needed to animate were blended in with unbaked Sculpey and left that way. The mouth was animated through, which means it was resculpted for every frame rather than replaced with different pieces. Since most

Figure 7.87 Armature built with Styrofoam and plastic doll armature pieces, by Katie Nielsen.

Figure 7.88 Finished puppet covered in clay, by Katie Nielsen.

Figure 7.89 Monster puppet created in Sculpey by Matt Hooker. (Photo by Jason Vanderhill.)

of the puppet was baked solid, it prevented the snafu of getting nudged during the animation and causing unwanted jitters. It looked great in the end and was relatively simple to animate.

For some character designs, you can get away with creating a clay puppet in solid clay, without armature. The Booger character in my film *Snot Living* (see Figure 7.90) was simply designed as a blob with arms that slid around the floor and made subtle gestures and facial expressions. For the purpose he served, solid clay worked just fine, so he was a great character to work with and became very real to me. I'm not too sure of his whereabouts now…last time I saw him he was packed away in a box somewhere, which is sad, really. I am not proud, as he deserves more respect than that. Clay puppets are not the most durable or convenient for keeping safe and secure, since they get dirty and stinky over time. But I was glad to have worked with him.

Figure 7.90 The Booger from *Snot Living*. (Copyright Ken Priebe 1998.)

Other Techniques

Stop-motion animation is an art that involves taking elements of the natural world and rearranging them to create the illusion of life. Since the natural world is so rich and varied, so are the possibilities for creating puppets. Anything can potentially be made into a puppet, even a plastic knife and fork (see Figure 7.91)! A valuable pastime is to wander through dollar stores, hardware or craft stores, and just look for materials that might be useful or could be combined with other things to build a puppet. In 1959, Disney animator Bill Justice directed the stop-motion short *Noah's Ark*, which featured puppets made out of regular tiny household objects like pencils, corks, and pipe cleaners.

Through invention and experimentation, my students over the years have come up with many unique methods for making puppets out of different materials. Some of the ideas I've seen include Puppetoon-style replacement heads carved out of votive candles, skins made of a discarded mail bag, and tearing teddy bears open to put armatures inside them. So long as you have a good idea, any object you can find could be made into a puppet, rigged with wires or other materials, and animated. Toys such as action figures, dolls, and Legos have been made into successful stop-motion films, and even series like *Robot Chicken* have been created around the whole premise of poseable action-figure animation. The important thing is to keep the points mentioned in this chapter in mind, regarding weight, appeal, and durability.

Cutout animation is a close cousin of puppet animation, where the puppets are created as flat 2D characters and typically animated on a tabletop with the camera pointing downward. Cutout puppet shapes can be created with joints fastened together with string or paper fasteners, and the drawings can be glued over them so that they do not show. You can also create replacement effects by cutting out different mouths for dialogue or using different cutouts for complete body parts. Television series such as *Life with Loopy* and *Phantom Investigators* by Wholesome Productions have used puppets that are a combination of 3D and 2D. The bodies were made of 3D armatures, but with flat 2D replacement heads and mouths.

Another experiment in combining 2D and 3D elements was created in 1997 by Oscar winner Daniel Greaves (*Manipulation*, Best Animated Short 1991), in a short film called *Flatworld*. In this film, characters were animated entirely in 2D, and every drawing was cut out and mounted on cardboard. 3D sets were built, just like for a stop-motion production, and the 2D cutouts were placed into the set standing straight up and replaced for each frame. *Flatworld* inspired a couple of my students to try the same effect of 2D cutouts on a 3D set (see Figure 7.92). By setting up a glass plate in front of the cutouts, they achieved the illusion of the characters tossing a 3D box back and forth, by sticking the box to the glass.

No matter what you use to build a puppet, the challenge is in making sure that it will not only look good on-screen, but also be easy to animate. Experiment, have fun, find techniques that work for you, and make sure you have something entertaining or important to say with your puppet. A beautifully made puppet will hold the audience's attention for a few seconds, but eventually they will want a good story, a good gag, or beautiful animation to keep them riveted. At the very least, create something original that nobody has ever seen before. If you believe in your idea and see your puppet as a real interesting personality, so will your audience.

Figure 7.91 Puppets by Junko Ogawa.

Figure 7.92 2D cutout puppets by Dharmali Patel and Yatindranath Shinde.

Chapter 8
An Interview with Anthony Scott

Figure 8.1
Anthony Scott.

A nthony Scott's inspiration for wanting to learn about stop-motion came from watching *King Kong* and *Rudolph the Red-Nosed Reindeer* as a child. Anthony (see Figure 8.1) grew up studying art and filmmaking before moving to California to start his animation career. His first job as a stop-motion animator was on the 1987 *New Adventures of Gumby* series, and then on MTV and Pillsbury spots under director Henry Selick. This led to his first feature film animation job on *The Nightmare Before Christmas*, followed by *James and the Giant Peach* and *MonkeyBone*. Anthony has also worked as a computer animator on Pixar's *Toy Story 2* and *A Bug's Life* and *Evolution* at Tippett Studios. He worked as animation director for the WB's TV series *Phantom Investigators* and Clokey Productions' *Davey & Goliath's Snowboard Christmas*. Most recently, Anthony was the animation supervisor on the production of Tim Burton's *Corpse Bride* in London, England. I have admired Anthony's work and visited his Web site for many years, so I contacted him to contribute to this book, and was pleased to learn he was originally a Michigan native like myself!

KEN: *Anthony, after having worked on many of the most famous stop-motion animation productions, what are you working on now?*

ANTHONY: Right now I'm in between projects, taking some time off after working in London on Tim Burton's *Corpse Bride*. I recently visited my family in Michigan and my oldest niece wanted to be the Corpse Bride for Halloween, so I helped her make a costume. [laughs] During this time, I've also been able to work on a personal film project I've been trying to do for years. It's a little early to say much about it, but I've been working on the story, storyboarding, and sculpting maquettes. What it all comes down to is you've got to get the story right before you move forward, and I've gotten it to a place where I'm pretty happy with it. I like to sculpt, paint, and get my hands dirty, so I'd like to do as much of it by myself as possible, but when it comes time to shoot it, I might need some help with building puppets and sets. It's a simple film though, so the next time I have some time off I'll move on to the next step.

KEN: *Will you be shooting the film in your own space or at a studio?*

ANTHONY: Hard to say at this point. It would be nice to have a studio space so I can have different kinds of equipment at my disposal. It will become obvious where I need to shoot it depending on where I'm living and what my resources are. Stop-motion is a funny business, because there aren't too many studios that exist on their own. Most of the projects I've worked on come together and exist for a while, but once the project is over, everyone packs up and leaves. I think Skellington Productions was the only studio that I've been a part of that lasted for more than one project, and that was *Nightmare* and *James*. There was about a year between those two projects when a few animators were shooting their own films inside the studio. Tim Hittle shot *Canhead* during that time; Mike Johnson did *The Devil Went Down to Georgia*; also Justin Kohn and Trey Thomas made films during that time since they had the space and equipment to do so.

KEN: *Which shots did you work on in* Nightmare?

ANTHONY: It's hard to remember every single one, since I worked on so many little shots throughout the film. I worked on some of the "Making Christmas" song sequence, a few shots with Sally, and many shots with Jack. The biggest sequence, and the one I'm most proud of, was the entire "Poor Jack" song bit. That occurred about a year after I was on the show, so I had a lot of time to get accustomed to the puppet and the style of the animation. It definitely took me a couple of months to get into it, because it was my first feature film, and I was used to working on TV shows and commercials. A lot of the commercials were shot in the same style and quality as *Nightmare*, but working on a feature was much more involved, because it's a story, not just a little 30-second spot. So after a year I was really getting into the head of Jack Skellington. I had a good time working on that sequence, because I had time to plan it out, work on it with the director, and it was a part of the film I felt very strongly about. It was a great moment of transformation for Jack, when he realized he had to stop this idea of taking over Christmas and accept who he was. It was definitely my favorite scene to work on, and also the most challenging.

KEN: *Yes, that is actually one of my favorite scenes as well. There's so much emotion and soul that comes through in the animation. There's one particular moment I love right before he jumps off the angel statue, where the animation is so smooth and flowing.*

ANTHONY: Yeah, that was a tough shot to do. Normally we animate on tabletops, but with that shot, to avoid getting the stage ceiling in the frame, we had to put the camera right on the floor, along with the angel statue. I was animating on my knees on a concrete floor. I had knee pads on, but when you're crawling like that for three days, it's still pretty painful. [laughs] Pain is definitely something that comes with stop-motion animation.

KEN: *Yes, I can certainly relate to that, too. How was the transition from those working methods to computer animation while working at Pixar?*

ANTHONY: At first it was tremendous excitement, because I was very curious about computer animation. The first *Toy Story* came about 6 months before *James* did, and it impressed the entire world, including myself. So there was a great curiosity from people who had been doing stop-motion, to figure out how they did it and if we would like the process. I didn't know much about computers, but at that time they needed people who knew how to animate, and they were willing to train us on their software. In many ways it was like relearning animation, because the process is completely different. Pixar was a great place to learn. They know what they're doing; they care about story and characters, so it was quite an education, that's for sure.

KEN: *What are the biggest differences in working on feature films versus working on commercials or TV series? Do you have a preference for one or the other?*

ANTHONY: That's interesting. You would think that I would prefer to work on features, which tend to have more money, but they're also more ambitious, with lengthy production schedules, so I guess the best answer I can think of is, I prefer shows that have a schedule that fits what we're trying to do. I like features because we really try to push stop-motion far. When I first heard of the *Corpse Bride* project years ago, I thought, Wow, they want to animate a flowing dress and veil in stop-motion? Good luck! [laughs] So that was my greatest challenge working on that film, figuring out how to make that work, and it's great when you have the time to try things like that. But sometimes it's also fun to throw yourself at something like the *Davey and Goliath* special (see Figure 8.2), which I had a great time working on. I got to storyboard, I got to animate, and figure out a shooting schedule so we could get it done on time. So it was great wearing several different hats on that one, and getting to use the skills I'd developed over the years. My first animation jobs were in television production, so it's always nice to return to that and learn more. Everything is rewarding in its own way.

Figure 8.2 Anthony Scott with Gumby/*Davey and Goliath* creator Art Clokey in 2002. (Courtesy of Premavision/Clokey Productions.)

KEN: *What are your preferred methods for planning out an animation shot?*

ANTHONY: When you're given a shot, you're given an exposure sheet that breaks it down into frames, and also the dialogue, if there is any, so I use that as a guide to plan it out, as far as where I want to hit certain poses, and things like that. I'll take the sheet and the audio recording and act out the shot a few times with my body if it's a human-type character. Sometimes I'll use a stopwatch to plan the timing and make notes on the exposure sheet. On a feature, I'll typically do a rough animation test, shot on fives or tens, just to give the director an idea of what I'm thinking, to make sure the poses are readable, the lighting's good, and the camera move is working. So between the tests, notes on the X sheets, and meetings in editorial, eventually the director is comfortable to launch me onto the shot. Television is usually a different process, since there's not enough time to test anything, but I still have a sheet to work from.

KEN: *What are the biggest changes you've seen in stop-motion animation over almost 20 years of working in it?*

ANTHONY: Well, we didn't have frame grabbers when I started on *Gumby*. The first time I used one was on a commercial for Colossal Pictures, where you could view two stored frames and your live frame, but not the whole sequence of frames. That was enough to make the animation smoother and also relieve some stress because you didn't have to worry about your shot as much overnight. Years later, when you could review the whole sequence, it was even better.

You didn't have to think about the shot as much over the weekend; just resume on Monday by reviewing it on the frame grabber to get back into the rhythm and continue. Before that, you had to take very careful notes, and it was pretty tedious. The computer, of course, has changed things and continues to do so. We shot *Corpse Bride* digitally, which was great and really sped things up in regards to post-work, removing rigs, and so forth, since it was already in digital format. Computers have really helped stop-motion, allowing people to use things like webcams and shoot their own animation at home. A frame grabber used to be something you had to pay thousands of dollars for, but now anyone with a computer can buy animation software off the Internet, which is great. It's neat to see on my Web site (www.stopmotionanimation.com) that there are kids and other people trying it (see Figure 8.3).

KEN: *Tell me more about your Web site and the inspiration behind starting it.*

ANTHONY: I was just finishing up at Pixar when I started the site, and I wanted there to be a Web site about stop-motion that wasn't just about movies or stuff that I had done, but more of an online community for learning more about it. The whole point of it was to be a resource for people, mainly beginners in stop-motion, to give them the opportunity to learn, share, and ask questions to those who had been working in the field for years. The first thing I included was a stop-motion handbook, and the site has since evolved to the point where the message board is really the center of the whole thing. The site is something I watch mostly from a distance now, since I'm usually so busy, but it's taken off in a big way, and I'm really happy about that.

StopMotionAnimation.com

WARNING: STOP-MOTION IS PROVEN TO BE HABIT-FORMING

Figure 8.3 The home page for Anthony Scott's Web site, www.stopmotionanimation.com.

KEN: *What advice would you have for someone who wanted to be a stop-motion animator?*

ANTHONY: Well, the best advice would be to get on www.stopmotionanimation.com, of course.... [laughs] But really, the best thing is to figure out what it is you want to do, first of all. If you want to specialize in animation, then focus on that. If you want to get into the business, that's usually how you're hired. You're not hired to make a puppet, build a set, and animate it. I know stop-motion tends to be a medium where you do everything, which is kind of cool, but I also know that people get really into building their puppets, which takes a long time, so by the time they animate a puppet, they don't tend to put the time they should into the animation. So if you want to animate, maybe use a simple puppet or get someone else to build the puppet for you, so you can focus on the animation. It's good to know what you want to do, because if you get the opportunity to apply for a job, that's the first thing they will want to know. They only want to hire the best.

KEN: *Do you think there is more room for stop-motion programs in schools?*

ANTHONY: I think if there were more stop-motion jobs, there would be more stop-motion classes in schools. It's just one of those things that's out there on the fringe. It's something I always knew I wanted to do, but I was never sure if there would be enough work. When I left Michigan and came to California (at that time it was 1983 or '84), there was no stop-motion going on, other than Tom St. Amand and Phil Tippett doing some effects at ILM (Industrial Light and Magic). So at the time I was trying to get into something similar to stop-motion, which was special effects make-up, because I like to sculpt, so I had taken the Dick Smith make-up course. I was pursuing that around the time the *Gumby* series came along (see Figure 8.4). I submitted a demo reel of my student films from LCC (Lansing Community College), which is what got me the job. I was just in the right place at the right time.

Figure 8.4 Anthony Scott on set for an ABC spot in 2001, the first time animating Gumby since 1988. (Courtesy of Premavision/Clokey Productions.)

KEN: *What with all the resources and technological breakthroughs offered by the computer, what do you see for the future of the stop-motion medium?*

ANTHONY: I don't see it changing too much. It's always been this strange animation art form and not the most popular, but somehow it keeps breathing and people are still interested in it, so people will continue making stop-motion films. It's just another way to do it, really. Some people like to act on stage, and some like to act in film; people have different preferences, and a little variety is always good. It's like a wave, too. For a while it seems like nothing's happening, and then, next thing you know, two stop-motion features come out in the same month (*Wallace & Gromit* and *Corpse Bride* were released 2 weeks apart)! When I was a kid, Disney would put out a film only every couple of years. Now there's so much more animation in production.

KEN: *Yes, I remember before the days when every Disney film was available on video, it was like a major event when an old feature would be re-issued, or even a new one. It seems stop-motion features are still like that, where every few years another one will come out, so it's more of an "event."*

ANTHONY: Especially *The Nightmare Before Christmas*, which still has a life in theaters. It's amazing! I can't think of too many other movies that still have so much merchandising being created for it after so many years. It's great to have been a part of something with that special appeal to it; it was a great film to work on. Even at that time, we knew we were working on something that hadn't really been made before. There weren't any CG features being made, so it was a cool time.

Chapter 9
Puppet Animation

O nce you have your puppet built, you are ready to put it on camera and bring it to life, which is the most challenging feat of all. Here you are taking the basic principles learned from the exercises in Chapter 5, "Basic Animation," and adding in the element of performance. Your puppet should not just move around aimlessly, but move in a way that it appears believable in its actions, and ultimately appears to be thinking, with a life of its own. In this chapter, I will demonstrate some exercises that are useful for getting warmed up to creating an animated performance in stop-motion, and discuss a few things regarding how to think like an animator.

Posing

Animation is made up of a series of poses made by the character, and how each pose leads to another. Each main action of the character is referred to as a key pose, and the in-betweens connect each pose to the next one. This way of thinking is particularly relevant to 2D and CG animation, where these key poses are created first, with the in-betweens put in later. In stop-motion, each movement must be done in sequence, so there are no keys or in-betweens, in a sense, but it still helps to think about the animation this way. Careful planning of your key poses will keep your animation from becoming a jumbled mess of jittery movement with no forethought to where it's going. Each pose in your animation will probably only be there for a brief moment before it transitions into another one, so it's important for every pose to be clear to the audience. Before animating your puppet, acquaint yourself with it by simply experimenting with posing. This habit will help you explore your character's personality and give you a chance to test out how flexible your armature is. If the actions called for cannot be performed by your puppet, it's better to find out through test poses, rather than during the animation itself.

Proper staging is vital to a pose being readable by the audience. All throughout the history of theater, even going back to the ancient Greek amphitheaters, actors had to make sure their actions were clear to the entire audience, including the people sitting in the back row. The audience members of a play cannot very well stand up and ask the actors, "Can you do that again? I missed what you were doing there!" The same principle applies to film, which cannot be rewound to view actions again while being screened. Watching them now on video or DVD gives us this luxury, of course, but we should not be expected to rely on it to understand the performance we are watching. We should be engrossed in the story the characters are telling through their performance, not confused by it.

One way to ensure proper staging of a pose is to imagine it in silhouette. If a pose can be viewed as a black silhouette without seeing any facial expression or design details, and it is still clear to the audience what the character is doing, it is an effective pose. For example, in Figure 9.1, you see a character holding a skull in front of him, and the resulting silhouette. Judging from the silhouette, it's impossible to tell what he is doing. In Figure 9.2, the same action is posed with the skull held to the side, away from the character's body. In silhouette, this pose reads much better, because it is very clear what the character is doing.

An animation pose should always be built upon a strong and clear line of action, just like the jumping sack in Chapter 5. Thumbnailing in quick sketch drawings is a good way to plan out your animation poses to ensure they are as strong as possible. By experimenting with how much you can exaggerate a pose, even to a ridiculous extreme, and then seeing if it can be replicated by your puppet, you can take a good pose and raise it to the level of a great pose. This is often referred to in animation lingo as *plussing* your pose. Through your line of action, you also want to express the attitude of your character. What mood is your character in? What is going on inside his head? These decisions will influence how your pose looks and make for stronger animation. Often a slight tilt of the head will add a lot of variety to any pose.

Figure 9.1 The staging for this pose is not clear if seen in silhouette.

Figure 9.2 This pose has much better staging, because it can be understood in silhouette.

Act out your animation poses with your body in front of a mirror, or videotape yourself for reference. Pay attention to how your body is positioned for different attitudes. By getting into character yourself and studying how your own body moves, you can learn a lot about how best to move your puppet in a realistic, but exaggerated, fashion.

Look for ways to vary your pose so that it is *asymmetrical*. Nothing in nature is exactly the same on each side. If you cut a tree vertically down the middle, you will not have the same number of identical branches on each half, nor would a person be the same way. When a character stands, it will not usually stand straight up (see Figure 9.3), unless it is a soldier or a robot. There will be a slight weight shift (see Figure 9.4) as the body's weight is transferred primarily to one foot or the other, so the body will lean toward its center of gravity that is supporting its weight. You can angle the feet at approximately 45 degrees to each other and vary the position of the hands and arms. Even the face should not be exactly the same on each side; one eye might be larger than the other, or one eyebrow higher up, or one corner of the mouth might be higher. Thinking about your pose in this way will ensure that your puppet looks natural and lifelike, rather than stiff and wooden. A good way to test out your puppet's posing and personality is to pose it as if it is saying a phrase to an unseen character, and try different variations on the same phrase. For example, show the puppet posing the phrase, "Sit down," both in an inviting way (see Figure 9.5) or in a scolding way (see Figure 9.6).

Figure 9.3 Standing straight up, like a wooden soldier, looks rather unnatural.

Figure 9.4 Shifting the weight and varying the positions of the limbs makes for a much more natural pose.

Figure 9.5 The puppet says "Sit down" in an inviting pose.

Figure 9.6 The puppet says "Sit down" in a scolding pose.

One of the best ways to study animation and posing is to watch as much animation as possible, and look for these elements of staging, asymmetry, and a clear line of action in each pose. Often characters will hold or linger slightly on each pose they move into, revealing their thought process through their posing. The best kinds of films to study for posing are usually ones without dialogue, because the posing tells us everything about what the characters are thinking. Films that have dialogue can be studied with the sound off so that you can just focus on the posing decisions made by the animator. Don't just study animation, however, and certainly don't limit yourself only to other stop-motion films. Learn from 2D and CG animation (Pixar is especially good at effective character posing), but also from live-action. Look for these elements of strong posing in all kinds of films or theater productions, and take mental notes for your animation. When animators rely on other popular animation films too exclusively, there is a danger of things looking too canned or recycled when it comes to posing. The early animators in the Golden Age of the 1930s and '40s looked to the stage and to silent film actors for their inspiration, and so should animators of today. Stop-motion in particular is just like live action in many ways, so studying live-action film and theater is certainly one of the best sources of inspiration for the fantasy worlds that can be created.

Walking

One of the most challenging actions to animate is a walk. You would think it would be simple, since you walk every day, but it's not, especially in stop-motion where you are dealing with the forces of gravity. Therefore, it's crucial for your puppet to be lightweight and to have some way to anchor the feet to keep it from falling over, as there will always be a frame with one foot off the ground. The best way to accomplish this is by using tie-downs. If you have built your puppet with nuts inside the feet, you can drill holes into your set platform and screw a bolt into the nut from underneath, securing it tight with a wing nut (see Figure 9.7). The holes can be planned out and drilled into your set before you start animating. If you are using a wooden platform, the holes can be filled in with a light beige clay so they don't show up on camera. Afterwards they can be filled in more permanently with wood filler. An easier method is using 1/4-inch thick pegboard, usually made of Masonite and available at hardware or lumber stores. These boards already have evenly spaced holes, so you can stick the tie-downs through these holes and drill additional holes only if necessary. No matter which method you use, you can also cover your platform with felt, fake grass, or another material that will hide the holes. Alternatives to tie-downs include magnets or sticky tack, but magnets can often be too strong, and sticky tack not strong enough. Experiment with what works best for you and your puppet.

Before drilling your holes, it helps to know about the mechanics behind the walk (see Figure 9.8). For each step, there are basically four major stages that occur. Each step is measured by its stride, which

Figure 9.7 Tie-downs are the best way to keep your puppet from falling over.

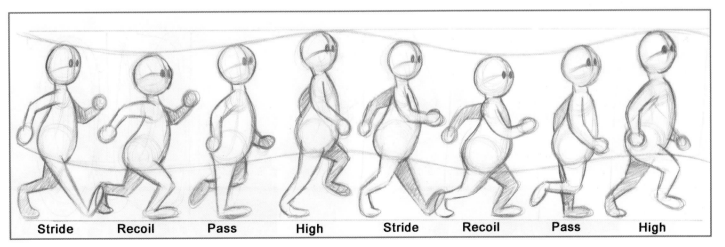

| Stride | Recoil | Pass | High | Stride | Recoil | Pass | High |

Figure 9.8 The basic stages of a walk.

191

means how far apart the feet are from each other when the front heel hits the ground. The *stride* is the first initial pose to a new step, where the front foot's heel makes contact, and the back foot is bent back but still touching the ground. Notice that the front leg is straight in this pose.

The next stage is the *recoil*, where the entire front foot makes contact with the ground, and the back foot is on its toe, just about to touch off. In the recoil position, both legs are bent, which causes the entire body to move down slightly, as the hips, torso, and head are all connected. Walks generally originate in the hip, which is the anchor point for all joints involved. The recoil position causing the body to move downward is important for establishing a sense of weight to the walk. If the body stays at the same level throughout, the walk will feel floaty and weightless.

The next stage is the *pass*, where the front leg straightens out again, pushing the body up, and the back leg starts passing forward to the front. Angling the foot backward creates a nice overlap to the action.

After the pass comes the *high* position, where the passing leg is now completely forward and ready to kick out into the next step. The foot that was forward in the previous stages is now becoming the back foot, which starts to bend up on its toes and propel the body up to reach its highest position. In a realistic walk, the foot may not necessarily push the body up this high, but animation is about exaggeration, so it helps to add some bounce to the movement. The high position is sometimes difficult to achieve in stop-motion if the puppet cannot balance on its toe that way, or if the ankle joint is not strong enough. If you have trouble with your puppet sagging, a quick-and-dirty solution is to prop it up with a rig behind it, or somewhere in full view to be removed digitally. Some stop-motion anima-tors will leave the back foot tied-down flat until the front foot makes full contact with the ground for shorter, more realistic steps, thus alleviating the problem of having the puppet balance on its toe. This depends partly on the design and animation style.

After these four stages for one step, the front leg kicks out again into the next stride, and the same positions repeat themselves, this time with the other leg. While all this is going on, the arms are also moving opposite to the legs: if the right leg is forward, the right arm is back, and vice versa. The body does this with the arms automatically to maintain its balance while walking. So as you can see, a walk is a multilayered action with many different limbs and movements to keep track of.

How fast or slow your walk is depends on how many in-between poses you animate between these major key parts of the action. The stride and recoil positions should always be right after each other, however, unless a slow-motion appearance is wanted or the character is doing a sneaky walk. The number of frames for each step must be the same; otherwise, your character will look like it is limping. The stop-motion walk on the CD has seven posi-tions for each step, shot on twos, so its is a 14-frame walk, which is a pretty brisk pace across the screen, made to look even faster psychologically due to it moving from left to right. If I had wanted a slower walk, I would have animated more frames, so long that the number of frames for each step leading to the stride is the same each time. Planning out the animation on a dope sheet (see Figure 9.9) helped me make sure I was on the right track in terms of which frames the steps landed on.

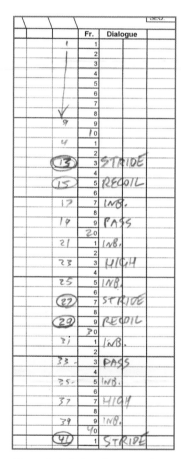

Figure 9.9 A dope/exposure sheet for the walk.

Watch for elements of your character where you can inject some overlapping action and follow-through into the animation. My puppet's hair, for example, drags behind in a subtle manner as his body moves. When his body goes down for the recoil, the hair flips up as if dragging a step behind the head, and it flips down as the body moves upward. The hands also overlap their action by dragging back as the arm moves forward and backward, always a step behind in the opposite direction. Think back to the motion of the vine in Chapter 5, and look for opportunities to reflect it in your puppet. Watch for arcs in the movement of the arms, and make sure the body is always moving forward, not backward or staying in the same position in sequential frames. Losing track of your path of action and arcs will result in a jittery walk. See Figures 9.10–9.19 to study the basic steps of the walk using a stop-motion puppet.

Figure 9.10 The stride position, with a tie-down securing the back foot.

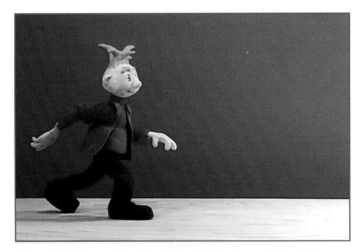

Figure 9.11 The recoil position, where the tie-down switches to the front foot, making full contact with the ground.

Figure 9.12 The front foot is still secured with a tie-down as the back foot starts lifting off the ground.

9. Puppet Animation

Figure 9.13 The pass position with overlapping action on the foot and hand.

Figure 9.14 The leg comes forward more.

Figure 9.15 The high position, which is a difficult pose to hold if your armature's ankle joints are not strong enough.

Figure 9.16 Coming down into the next stride. Be sure to aim directly for the next tie-down hole.

Figure 9.17 Into the stride for the next step.

If your puppet has trouble staying upright coming down into a step, a quick solution is to poke a toothpick through the tie-down hole and hold it there while capturing your frame (see Figure 9.18). A little wiggle while capturing could also result in some motion blur to smooth out the action. The toothpick can be removed later digitally with a different plate as another layer in Photoshop (see Figure 9.19).

Knowing how the puppet will be positioned for the strides and everything in between will help you determine where to drill holes for your tie-downs. As I mentioned earlier, before you animate, it is best to drill all the tie-down holes ahead of time. You want to plan, mark, and then drill where the steps will be. You usually do not want to be drilling your holes while you are animating, as that will disturb or jar the table top stage. Set up your camera so that you know where the frame cuts off, and position your puppet into its sequential

Figure 9.19 The toothpick can be painted out later in post-production.

Figure 9.18 Holding up the foot with a toothpick is a quick solution if it won't stay up.

9. Puppet Animation

strides across the screen. Drill your first hole where his first step coming into the shot would be, and then tie down his foot and move the other leg into the next stride. Make a mark where the nut will land on the next step (see Figure 9.20), and then drill the hole (see Figure 9.21), tie down that foot, and continue with the following step, and so on. Once all of your holes are placed, fill them in with clay to hide them, and get ready to animate.

Figure 9.20 Mark on your platform with a pencil where the foot will land.

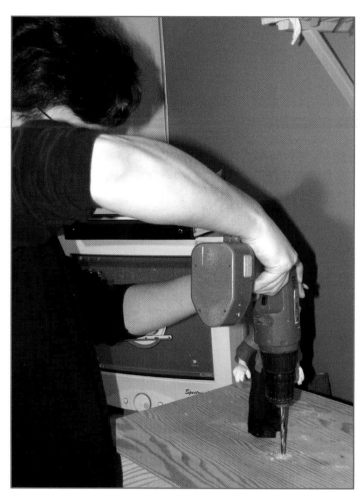

Figure 9.21 Drill holes directly into your platform, with the right size drill bit for your tie-down.

Start with eight frames of an empty stage, and then have your puppet enter the shot and walk across the screen. For the frames where he enters and exits, you can cheat by holding the puppet up with your hand or a rig, as it will be outside of the frame. Once you learn these basic mechanical steps for how a walk is done, you can put personality into any kind of walk, indicating whether your character is sad, happy, proud, afraid, or cautious. Shoot reference footage of different personality walks, and pay attention to how your own body moves. Walks are one of the hardest movements to animate well, so once you have some good practice in it, it will be valuable experience for other stop-motion scenes along the road.

Action Analysis

Once you have tried a walk with your puppet and built some tie-downs into your set, another valuable action to try animating is throwing a ball off-screen. This exercise takes the principle of anticipation–action–reaction (introduced with the jumping sack in Chapter 5), along with other principles, and applies it to a puppet. It can be achieved with any kind of puppet but would probably work best with a puppet built on a wire or ball-and-socket armature and a foam or fabric skin, with a minimal amount of heavy clay, if any. For an action such as this, it's important when setting up your camera to make sure you have enough room on the screen to have the action take place. Once your shot has been set up, place your puppet near the left center of the screen, keeping in mind the TV cutoff. Then try moving it into its anticipation pose and throwing pose, so that you can ensure that he will not go offscreen at any point, and adjust the zoom on your camera if necessary.

Figures 9.22–9.27 show the main key poses of an action such as this.

Figure 9.22 The first initial zero pose.

Figure 9.23 The anticipation.

Figure 9.24 Leading into the throw.

Figure 9.25 Action: Throwing the ball, on a rig to be removed digitally.

Figure 9.26 Reaction: Recovering from the throw.

Figure 9.27 Settle into a final pose.

The Art of Stop-Motion Animation

If you have done the other exercises in this book, you should be familiar now with slow-ins, slow-outs, and other aspects of timing. Use your knowledge of these principles to determine how many in-betweens you think you might need between these keys. Act out the action yourself and time it with a stopwatch, or use video reference footage as a rough guide. The throw should be quick, so you might not need many in-betweens there, but if you want a slower movement leading into the anticipation, then more poses would be needed, with a cushion favoring the anticipation pose. Overlap the action so that the hand stops moving a few frames before the foot does, or vice versa. Perhaps you could hold the anticipation pose or the throw pose for a few frames to break up the rhythm of your action. Look for any opportunity to put overlapping action, follow-through, and a sense of weight to your animation.

Plan your animation by recording the timing of your key poses on a dope sheet. Decide which frames the keys should land on, and you will then know how many in-between poses you will need. You could even shoot a pose test, or pop-through of your animation, just shooting the key poses to match the frames you have determined. Playing it back will show a rough, choppy version of your animation and the timing you want. If you want to change your timing, perhaps holding the anticipation longer, you can delete frames until it is the way you want it, and then change your dope sheet to reflect those changes. Once you are satisfied with your timing, get started on animating it with all of the frames. *The more you plan your animation beforehand, the better your results will be*, but also be open to last-minute ideas that come to you while in the midst of the animation process, much like a one-time live performance.

Facial Expressions

In a close-up or medium shot of your puppet, it is easier to see the facial expression and have that be the focus of your animation. The face, especially the eyes, says a lot about your character. The eyes are typically the first thing the audience will be drawn to. Experiment with your puppet changing expressions and appearing to think, emote, and react to situations that might be seen on-screen or off-screen. A good exercise to try is a *take*, which refers to a character reacting to, or changing his mind about something. Have your character facing one direction, and imagine he hears a sound behind him, causing him to turn his head around. Whatever he sees off-screen causes him to react in surprise, shock, or possibly joy.

Hamish has volunteered his services for a demonstration in this short piece (see Figures 9.28–9.39) available to view in full on the CD.

The key to getting the turn of Hamish's head to look natural is the overlapping action, where different elements of his face start and stop at different times. His eyes start moving, then the head (on a slight arc, not perfectly straight), and then the eyebrows. This very important principle, subtle as it may be, will keep your animation from looking stiff, robotic, and boring. Instead, your audience will really believe your character is alive. There is a scientific explanation for overlapping action as well. The inclination to turn the body in another direction starts in the brain, and that impulse carries itself down the spinal cord within a short flash of time. Since the eyes are closest to the brain, the message to turn goes there first, and afterward travels to the neck, then the shoulders, and hips. It all happens so subtly and quickly that we don't consciously recognize it, but slow down a live-action clip of someone turning his body around, and you will see the overlap. Therefore, since your animation is being created from scratch, frame by frame, you must work it in to make it appear natural.

Figure 9.28 **Frame 1** (held for a few frames). Hamish starts with his zero pose, daydreaming and minding his own business.

Figure 9.29 **Frame 13**. He blinks.

Figure 9.30 **Frame 15**. After Hamish opens his eyes, they start changing direction.

Figure 9.31 **Frame 23**. To create some overlapping action, Hamish's eyes lead the action by changing direction before the head.

Figure 9.32 Frame 39. Hamish's head has started moving on an arc in the other direction.

Figure 9.33 Frame 51. His head is now facing the other direction.

Figure 9.34 Frame 59. After the head stops moving, the eyebrows move up slightly for some more overlapping action, and cushion into a short hold.

Figure 9.35 Frame 69. The eyes widen slightly, as Hamish is starting to react to something.

Figure 9.36 Frame 73. Hamish goes into an anticipation pose, his head squashing down.

Figure 9.37 Frame 77. The actual take pose, stretched and exaggerated.

Figure 9.38 Frame 81. The take pose settles down into Hamish's new expression of shock.

Figure 9.39 Frame 93. After a few cushion frames, Hamish holds on his final pose.

The exaggerated take was accomplished by removing Hamish's original head and replacing it with a couple of replacement heads (see Figure 9.40). The anticipation head is squashed, and the take head is stretched, therefore introducing the principle of squash and stretch into the animation. The original head's facial expression was then changed and replaced to line up with the previous head. The effect of the different heads is not one that the viewer really sees, since it is so fast, but you feel it as you watch it. There is an element of snap and fluidity created by the head anticipating to prepare the audience, and then stretching past the point of his new expression. It is through this series of poses that we feel Hamish's expression change. The replacement head technique may not be necessary for a more subtle take, but for broad exaggerated movement, I like the way it looks.

Try some variations on this with your own character, and pay attention to how the timing is affected by your character's personality. A character like Hamish, who is relatively sharp and alert, may only hold for about six to eight frames after turning his head before he goes into his take. A sleepy, slow, or dim-witted character may hold much longer before reacting—say for 16 frames or a full second—because it takes him longer for his brain to process what he sees. You could also try expanding this exercise to create a double take, which is very popular in comedic timing. In a *double take*, your character would turn to look at something, and then go back to his original position. Then he would realize what he just saw and turn back, going into his anticipation and reaction.

Figure 9.40 Replacement heads to allow for squash and stretch in stop-motion.

Blinks

How often should your character blink? This is something you can experiment with or plan out on your dope sheet before animating. It is easy to fall into the trap of having your character blink too much while animating him. As you are progressing along, you may think to yourself, "He hasn't blinked in awhile, so I'd better do it again." True, it may have been several hours since you last animated a blink, but in screen time, that is only mere seconds. Blinks really only need to be animated for certain occasions, or every 4 to 5 seconds to keep things interesting. If your character is holding for several seconds, throw a blink in to break it up and keep him looking alive. People also often blink when their eyes are changing direction, whether they are turning their entire head or just their eyes are moving. The brain has a hard time handling the sensory overload of an entire room moving before it, so it sends a little message to the eyelids to blink. How often a character blinks will also depend on his personality. If he is nervous or happy, he might blink more than would a threatening or stoic character. The personality will also determine how the character blinks, as there are many different variations that can be played with. Your blink can be open/shut/open for a really fast one, or open/half/shut/open for a slower one (see Figure 9.41). If the character is sleepy or dopey, it might take several frames for his eyelids to come down, and they could possibly be shut for at least six frames before opening. Shutting the eyes for only one frame will not register in playback, but two frames will, especially if combined with some frames of the eyelids down halfway. Eyelids can be created with a tiny slab of clay resting gently over the eyeball, or a presculpted piece of plastic or other hard material.

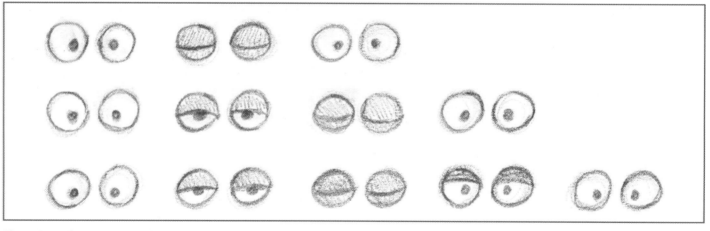

Figure 9.41 There are many variations on animating blinks for character animation.

Dialogue

The final ingredient to making your character seem alive to your audience is to have him speak, or even sing. The earliest known example of animated mouth movement to sound in stop-motion was in a short film by experimental filmmaker Len Lye in the mid 1930s (see Figure 9.42). Its only title was *Experimental Animation 1933*, but I refer to it as "The Peanut Vendor" because that is the title of the popular jazz tune featured in the film. A large monkey sings the song through the use of replacement mouths synced to the soundtrack. Meanwhile, he enters and exits the frame making grotesque faces in full close-up, and then proceeds to dance, remove his tail, and flip it around. It's a cute little stop-motion experiment, but there is also something very disturbing and creepy about it. I often show it to my students, and it gives them nightmares.

Dialogue is animated by breaking down a soundtrack into frames, so that the animator knows how many frames it will take to recite each syllable and sound of every word. Each frame will then have a different mouth shape to sync exactly with the dialogue track. As I mentioned briefly in Chapter 7, "Building Puppets," there are a few different ways to animate dialogue in stop-motion. One way is to treat the mouth like a hand puppet that simply opens and closes without a change in shape. You can also have wires built into the mouth so that it will have a similar effect, but with the ability to change shape for more accurate syllables. Another method, achieved primarily through clay animation, is *animating through*, which consists of building one mouth out of clay and resculpting it for each frame. The main drawback to this method is its time-consuming nature, due to the constant fixing and resculpting necessary as the mouth gets dirty and lumpy throughout the animation process. The final results, when done properly, have a very naturalistic look that is worth the effort.

A way to speed up the process of animating through in clay animation is to create a series of replacement mouths that can be removed and replaced for extremely different mouth shapes and blended into the rest of the face each time (see Figure 9.43). A single mouth can be manipulated for subtle changes until replaced by a completely different shape altogether. This method gives the illusion that the face is still one single entity, when in fact the mouths are separate pieces. Replacement mouths can also be created as a floating pair of lips or round shapes I like to call *donut mouths*, which can be stuck on to a head made of clay, papier-mâché, or any other material. A little bit of sticky wax or putty will hold the mouth in place until it is replaced by another. Figure 9.44 demonstrates the different basic mouth shapes used for dialogue animation, covering major vowel sounds and consonants. The closed mouth for B, M, and P sounds can also serve as a neutral mouth for when the character is holding, or not speaking. Variations on these mouth shapes can also be created without teeth; it all depends on the design you're going for.

Matching the right mouth shapes to each frame to achieve perfect lip sync is obviously important, but it is only a small part of the performance. When characters speak, they use their entire bodies to act out what they are saying. There is also movement in the eyes, the eyebrows, the head, and perhaps even the arms and hands. A common practice in 2D and CG animation is to create a performance for the character using his entire body acting to the dialogue, and then put the mouths in later. If the character can be animated to appear as if he is saying his line without relying on the lip sync, then the mouths are simply icing on the cake. By watching animation with the sound off, you will see this to be true. The characters speak with their hands and their entire bodies, as well as their mouths. In stop-motion, you obviously do not have the luxury of animating dialogue in this multilayered fashion. The mouth shapes, and all other nuances of movement, must be planned out and then animated at the same time. Keeping track of many things at once is the challenge behind animating to dialogue, but in another sense, it is a rather easy task in that all of the timing is done for you. The length of the scene is predetermined, so all you need to do is create the picture to match the sound.

Figure 9.42 "The Peanut Vendor" by Len Lye (1933), easily the creepiest puppet film ever made.

Figure 9.43 Using replacement mouths for clay animation.

Before the process of deciding which mouths to use, the dialogue must be recorded. This can be done by recording directly into your computer or by using a tape recorder and using your computer to capture the sound into digital format. You can also rent a recording studio if you want more professional quality. Your dialogue clip should be in .wav format so that you can break it down frame by frame and then record the sounds on a dope sheet. There are several different software packages used for breaking down dialogue tracks. One popular program is Magpie (or Magpie Pro), which is designed specifically for animation dialogue. Another program that can be used is Sound Forge, along with several others. Each program may have special features. Magpie, for instance, has its own dope sheet that can have the different syllable sounds entered into it, with a

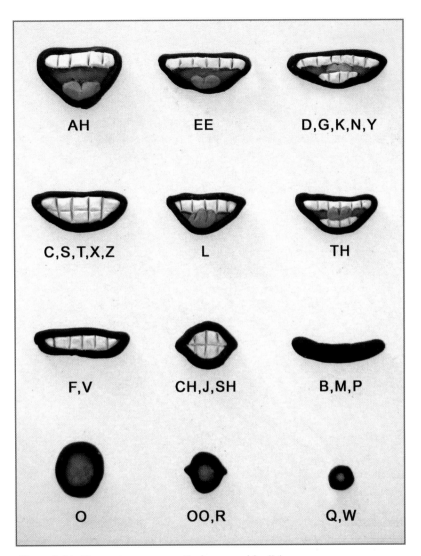

Figure 9.44 The most common mouth shapes used in dialogue. (Sculpted by Janet Priebe.)

series of mouth shapes so that you can test your dialogue and find the right shapes to use. You can also print out your dope sheet directly from the program. The one thing all programs have in common is allowing you to see your soundtrack as a wave form alongside a row of frame numbers so that you can literally see your dialogue and which frames the sounds and accents land on. When breaking down dialogue, remember to make sure that your frame rate is set at 24 frames per second if you plan on animating that way. *If you break down your dialogue at the wrong frame rate, your animation will not be in sync.*

Accents in the dialogue are the moments where certain syllables or words are emphasized more than others. Dialogue has a rhythm to it, just like music. In any melody, certain notes are accented, and each note has a different length: whole notes, half notes, etc. In animating to dialogue or music, the accents should have a strong action to accompany them. My animation reel on the CD has a lengthy dialogue scene with Hamish, so I will use the line where he says, "I don't know, the fuzz ain't even here…they all went down to the pub" to explain the dialogue process. (In this context, the word *fuzz* is a slang term for policemen.)

Figure 9.45 shows the sound wave for Hamish's line in Magpie Pro, with the words "I don't know" highlighted in red. The frame numbers are at the top, and each vertical column represents a frame going through the wave form. By selecting a few frames at a time throughout each phrase, you can listen to the

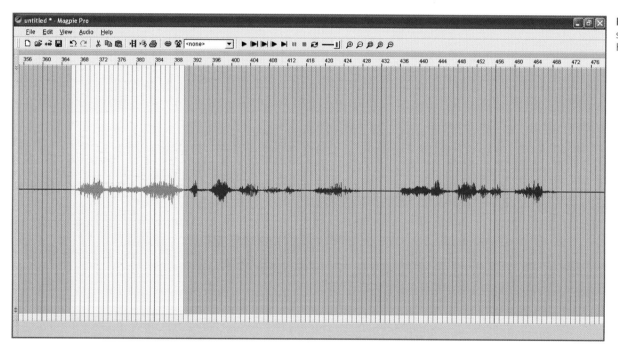

Figure 9.45 The sound wave for Hamish's dialogue.

words by playing each selection only, to determine where the sounds are. It will sound like a bunch of little chirps and fragments of words. By focusing on this one section and breaking it up, I can see that the word "I" goes from frame 367 to frame 373, the word "don't" from frame 374 to 377, and the word "know" from frame 378 to frame 389. This information can be recorded on my dope sheet, which I prefer to write out by hand (see Figure 9.46).

You will notice that the words are not spelled out exactly the way they should be, because they are not enunciated as such. I have to listen to the way Hamish *says* his line. Because of his Scottish accent, he says it more like "AH-e don' NOOOOAAAAH." The individual words blend together into one massive speech pattern and must be broken down phonetically, based on how the words *sound*, not how they are *spelled*. Do not think of the dialogue as words; think of it as sounds and patterns of speech. Listen closely to the way your character says his line, and listen for the accents and intonations, recording your observations on your dope sheet. It helps a great deal, both while breaking down the track and animating it, to listen to the line over and over again. Many animators get annoyed by listening to their voice track repeat all day, but I grew up with an autistic brother who liked to repeat phrases from movies constantly, so thanks to him, I'm rather used to it!

As I continue this process through the entire line of dialogue, I pick up on where the accents are and how Hamish says his line in terms of sound patterns: "AH-e don' NOOOOAAAH, the FAHZZ ain EEven HEEErr. DeyALL wen DAnda thah PAHHB!" There is also a brief 10-frame pause between the two sentences. All of this information is recorded on my dope sheet (see Figure 9.47).

After listening to the dialogue and breaking it down, the next step is to decide on the poses your character will use to act out his line. To do this, you must get inside your character's head and think about why he is saying this particular sentence, and how he feels about it. What is the context behind the scene? Here Hamish is having a conversation with a news anchor in the studio, who is asking him questions. The off-screen voice of the news anchor asks, "Have the police spotted anything unusual?" and Hamish gives his answer. He is annoyed by the fact that he can't answer the question since the "fuzz" have all gone to the pub and left him alone. (It's possible he would rather be at the pub himself.) To get the right posing, try acting out the line

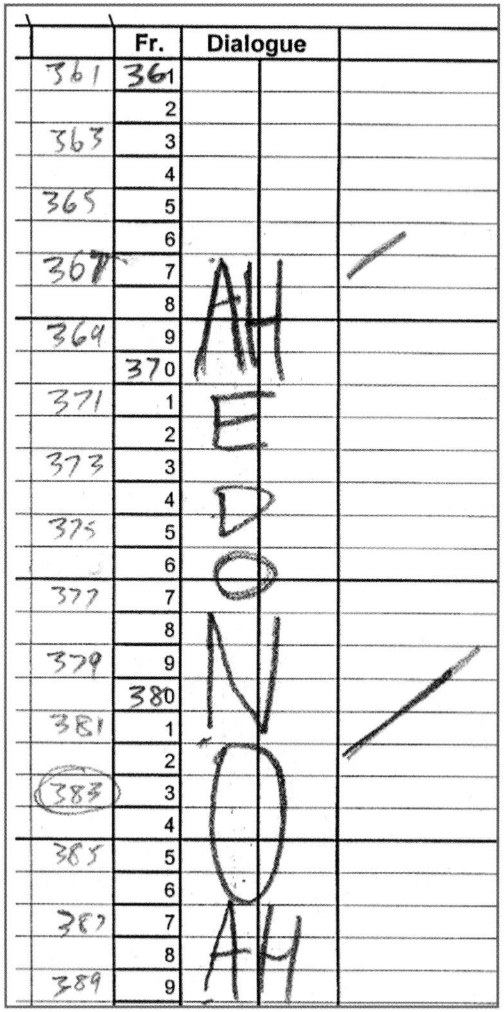

Figure 9.46 The words "I don't know" broken down on the dope sheet.

along with the dialogue to see which poses come naturally to you. What kinds of poses do people usually use to express themselves in this way? By using methods such as acting in front of a mirror, shooting video reference, or making thumbnail sketches, or a combination thereof, explore different options until you find the best one. For Hamish's line about the fuzz at the pub, I decided to assign different key poses to the three main accents in the phrase, on the words ALL, DOWN, and PUB. When characters refer to other people who are off somewhere else, they often gesture behind them with their head or hand. So, I decided to have Hamish cock his head to the side on the word ALL, point with his thumb on the word DOWN, and give him a huge emphatic hand gesture on the word PUB, which is the largest accent in the dialogue (see Figures 9.48–9.52). All of these decisions related to the posing should be thought out before focusing on getting the mouth positions correct. You can watch the final animation on the CD frame by frame to see how it all ties together.

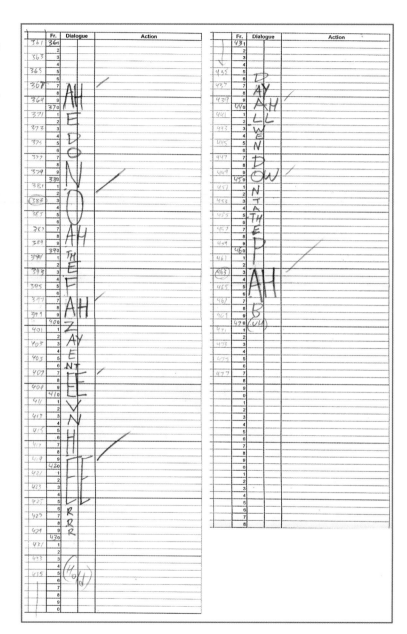

Figure 9.47 The entire dialogue phrase broken down for animation.

Figure 9.48 ALL

Figure 9.49 went

Figure 9.50 DOWN

Figure 9.51 to the

Figure 9.52 PUB!

Here are some general points to remember when animating dialogue:

◆ Dialogue animation can be done primarily on twos, but there will often be cases where it will need to be on ones, for words that are said very quickly or run together. For example, the words "down to the pub" are said very quickly, like "dandathapub," on ones. Consonants like B, M, and P should always be on screen for at least two frames to register.

◆ Animate the lip sync lined up exactly with the frames on the dope sheet, but have body movements hit two to six frames before or after the dialogue.

◆ If the mouth opens wide for a strong accent, don't just make it wide—make it *really wide!* It will add some punch to the dialogue and make the accents stronger. Some frames might look funny by themselves, but remember that the audience doesn't see individual frames—they only see how they work together.

◆ On long sounds expanding over many frames, particularly vowel sounds, hold the same mouth position but keep it moving by pushing the bottom lip up every frame or two so that it transitions smoothly into the following position.

◆ Overlap the movements of the mouth, eyes, and eyebrows so that they start and stop at different times around the accents of the dialogue. For example, if the mouth opens wide on an accent, have the eyes and eyebrows go up a few frames later, rather than on the same frame.

◆ Put holds in your dialogue (minimum six frames) during moments where the voice actor pauses, and find ways to keep the character alive by blinking, looking around, or perhaps fiddling with his hands. The dialogue for Hamish was planned out very carefully, but during one of the breaks while the off-screen voice talks, I improvised on set with a little nose twitch and sniff. This was actually based on the way my wife (who I was only dating at the time) would twitch her nose when it itched, so it was a little personality quirk I threw in there.

◆ Listen for lip smacks, breathing, swallows, and other sounds picked up in the recording, and treat them as extra sounds to animate to. Keep your character alive!

◆ Coming up with lines to practice dialogue is a challenge, but there are many options. You can think of a phrase and record it yourself, or use sound clips from movies if it's only for practice purposes. (Never use copyrighted material for commercial work unless you have permission!) In my course, I give my students a dialogue exercise based loosely on the *Creature Comforts* premise, where I ask them questions and whatever spontaneous answer they give is what they animate. This is a great way to learn dialogue because the speech patterns are very real and natural, and good for experimenting with bits of characterization.

◆ As with everything, study, study, study! Analyze other animated films, live-action films, and stage performances. Watch how actors not only enunciate words but act with their eyes and their hands. Look at your own mouth in a mirror and study how it transitions from one syllable to another. Animation is all about *observation!*

◆ Have fun!

Motion Blur

A common method used in stop-motion to make the animation look smoother is the addition of motion blur into certain frames, particularly for fast actions like a throw, jump, or run. There are several different ways to create motion blur that can be experimented with to see what works best for your projects. The most technical way is to have the puppet move slightly while the frame is being exposed. To move the puppet, you can attach thin wires to it like a marionette, and give them a slight tug while capturing. Depending on the camera you are using, the shutter speed or length of the exposure can also be adjusted to assist in the blurring effect.

Another method I have used is to attach a small plate of glass to the lens of a camera (I did this with sticky tack on the long lens of a Bolex for *Snot Living*) and smear some KY Jelly on the glass where the puppet is in the viewfinder. That creates a smudge that appears like a blurry image on film.

In this digital age, another method is to export the frames you want the blur in from your stop-motion program, and import them into Photoshop. There you can use the Smudge tool to create your blur, and then import the frames back into the animation. Some stop-motion programs now have some motion blur tools built into them, so experiment and see how well they work. Just don't go overboard; motion blur is something the audience should *feel* more than see. Have fun playing!

Chapter 10
An Interview with
Larry Larson

Figure 10.1
Larry Larson.

L arry Larson (see Figure 10.1) has been involved in stop-motion for nearly 35 years, and he currently teaches character animation and puppet building at the College for Creative Studies (CCS) in Detroit, Michigan. Larry was referred to me by my friend and animation mentor Steve Stanchfield, who also teaches at CCS.

KEN: *Please give me a brief bio of your career in stop-motion and how you got started.*

LARRY: The first stop-motion film I saw that changed my life was Lou Bunin's version of *Alice in Wonderland*, which was on television one Christmas. Before that, I saw the odd George Pal *Puppetoon* in grade school, which they would show on 16mm film, and that was always fun to see, but I always was fascinated with how these things were done, because I could see they were real objects. Then when I saw *The Seventh Voyage of Sinbad*, I was at a very impressionable age, about 12 or 13, so then I knew that this was what I wanted to do. Then there were years of working at it and doing things wrong, without much guidance, because there wasn't much information out there. Occasionally you'd see the odd image in a magazine and you'd say, "Ah, so that's how they built it." I made some films, but they weren't story films, because I was so busy figuring out how to do this stuff. My first film with a story was *Pipes of Pan* (see Figure 10.2), which I made at Wayne State University here in 1972. I entered it into a Dallas Fantasy Film festival, and it won first place. I got some money for it, and it aired on public television. In 1973, I moved to Hollywood to find work and ended up getting hired to come back to Detroit! So I came back and worked on *Barrington Bunny* (see Figure 10.3), a short Christmas film where I built puppets and had my name all over it. One of my proudest moments was to have it screen along with a Peter Sellers film, *The Optimists of Nine Elms*.

I then got to work with Bob and Dennis Skotak before they became successful in the visual effects industry, on an unrealized film called *Timespace*, for which I built puppets and helped with process photography and composites. I continued working on short films and features, continuing to use the process projector I had built for projects like *Epic of Gilgamesh*. I did an animation of a local iconic statue called the Spirit of Detroit, which ran for about 15 years on television. I got paid for it, too, which was good. It's important for a filmmaker to start that interchange early on, even if it's not that much. If you start doing that, people will continue to pay you, and I was lucky enough to be paid for my own projects and have them run. So I did a few

Figure 10.2 An image from *Pipes of Pan*. (Courtesy of Larry Larson.)

Figure 10.3 An image from *Barrington Bunny*. (Courtesy of Larry Larson.)

more commercials for Tubby's Submarines, Ameritech, car dealerships, and other businesses. In 1987, I went down to North Carolina and worked on *Evil Dead 2*, which was a terrific experience, working with folks like Tom Sullivan and Rick Catizone. I was hired to help make the stop-motion production work well. Years later, I worked on *The Carrier*, another low-budget film, and *Flesh Gordon 2*, for which I built and animated rubber monsters. In 1992, I got to work as director of cinematography on a film called *That Special Gift*, which was a great experience working with lighting real people after only lighting puppets for so long. In 1999, I picked up a Silicon Graphics workstation and learned the software package Maya, only to learn I really liked working with puppets better than computers. I got to create a CG car for the auto show, and in the meantime having oil painting shows and classes, and doing animation for local poets. Then in 2001, I became a character animation instructor at CCS, which gave me a place to put to use the knowledge I had picked up over the years and help some young people in a way that I didn't get helped at that age. Since then, I've made things like gophers and singing vacuum cleaners for various productions, and continue with teaching and oil painting. I like organic media, and I'm basically in the business of making things for people that work.

KEN: *Out of this entire body of work, which project are you most proud of?*

LARRY: Oddly enough, I like my early work the best. I know most artists would say they like their later work, but I really enjoy *Pipes of Pan, Barrington Bunny*, even the *Timespace* project, for their youthful energy and where they fell in the industry at the time. They had a lot of heart and contained more of what I think puppet animation is about. I found a print of *Barrington Bunny* in an old theater here, and the projectionist ran it every Christmas for the kids, just because he liked it. [laughs] And that means more to me than just doing jobs to order. They're fun, they pay the bills, I learn things, and meet great people, but it's not as engaging as things that come from your heart. Artists should be able to make projects that say something, too.

KEN: *How else are commercials different from films?*

LARRY: Well, they both have extreme time constraints, but there's a little more freedom on feature films, because they will usually let you do something again if you don't get it right. With commercials, they are willing to trade lots of money to save a little time, so that doesn't leave a lot of time for re-dos, so you don't learn as much. It's more like, "Here's the product. Give me the money." Films have a much more creative atmosphere, because the director has a vision, and it's your job to find that vision and add your bit to it. The best directors allow you to be a good artist. I'd rather work on films, although it's hard because you often have to leave town, which was tough because I had a family at home. They had to come down to North Carolina to see me during *Evil Dead 2*. Lots of people have to travel all over the world to be in the places where the film is being done, but I'm more of a home guy. Commercials are usually done in your home town, because there's no time to go anywhere!

KEN: *Especially with stop-motion, you would have to be on set, since it's not like Flash or CGI work that you can just send by e-mail, right?*

LARRY: Right. Plus, if they're spending that much money on you, they want you to be there so they can look over your shoulder and buy you lunch! But now, with the advent of little production companies making big films far from Hollywood, you can make a film with your talent pool spread out over a larger geographic area. For economic reasons, that might make sense, and could become a big trend.

KEN: *Tell me a bit more about your current teaching position.*

LARRY: Well, I'm teaching short courses for character animation in Maya and also in stop-motion, never the same way twice, because nothing's ever perfect. One time in class we focused on building wire armatures and cast rubber figures. Ray Harryhausen, who I know quite well, visited us once (see Figure 10.4).

He favors the ball-and-socket armatures over wires, and when he got here I was teaching ball-and-socket construction and the machining skills needed to make armatures. Many students got to go through the whole process and create finished puppets, which I was very proud of. Just recently I taught about 12 to 15 students— very talented young people—how to animate using surface gauges and learning the importance of tie-downs. We're using a Lunchbox frame-grabbing system, and hopefully will start using a computer software to give us more options. I have my students make a film that is totally from them, so they have that chance to make that personal statement right away, because I think that's important. If I were able to develop an even more complete course in stop-motion, it would be at least a two-year course. Students would build their own puppets and make their films but would also learn the lan-

Figure 10.4 Larry Larson and Ray Harryhausen at the College for Creative Studies.

guage of cinema, lighting, construction techniques, animation, and compositing, which the computer does well. But the considerations would still be the same as they would for an oil painter, like saturation and composition—all the creative decisions that can't be built into a software program. In both mediums, CG and stop-motion, the animation principles are the same, too; it's all about physics and acting. There are people who devote their whole lives to just being actors; it's a noble art. So you add that to the other skills needed to make a stop-motion film, and it's a daunting list of what's necessary: lighting, lenses, exposure, color correction, puppet animation, storyboarding, clay modeling, mold making, casting, plastic, foam rubber, brazing, welding, glazing, matte painting, stage construction, urethane molding (dense and light, soft and rigid), silicone, polyester, vacuum forming, plaster…and this is just a short list of things I've learned how to do.

KEN: *What's the usual format for your classes and the way they are taught?*

LARRY: The only way I teach is by giving short lectures and inspirational pep talks to the whole class, and then I work individually with each student. [The students have] their own needs and their own way of learning, and I have to figure out who they are and how to get it to them. We have four stations in the stop-motion lab, and I have to run around really fast to each of them…I work really hard! [laughs] What's great now is that students can shoot animation with a digital camera themselves and own their own work, so they could do the animation at home and bring it in for critiques. This trend will continue, because people can now express themselves in this wonderful medium without buying $7,000 cameras. One of my students wants to go to Ireland to teach people how to make puppet films! So I say, yes! I want to support that, because he's a good student, and people need to know that stop-motion is accessible. It's a real art, and that's important.

KEN: *What are the main differences you see between the CG and stop-motion mediums?*

LARRY: The computer is a magnificent engineering accomplishment, and I respect it, but the computer only gives you back what you put in. You've got to know a thousand times as much as your audience to get all that other information in there. Whereas when you work with organic media, the media itself helps you. It helps you by fighting back, like when rubber or clay doesn't work the way you want it to, and half the time, that's good. To me, that introduces a little bit of humility into the artistic process. When the computer only gives back what you give, it gets to be a big limitation, because very few people know what to give the computer to get back what they want! I once saw a real scientific study where they tested a guy whose plumbing between his right eye and conscious brain was damaged in an accident; the eye and brain were both fine, but there was no connection. And they discovered through magnetic resonance imaging that there are six more pathways into the human brain that are not conscious. So that means that left-brain thinking, the conscious intellectual information, is only the tip of a very large iceberg. The other part of the brain is where the art is, so how can you put all of that information into a computer without assistance from the wonderful infinite universe and all its variations? [laughs] The limitations with computers are really with the operators, the human beings. You have to import this whole world into the computer, so if you can't draw or sculpt, what are you going to do with it? We've had many years of computer animation films now, and audiences don't really know what they are seeing. Stop-motion has a very important quality about it, because it partakes of this world. It's got a beauty and humility to it because it uses real materials, so I think it will continue and increase.

KEN: *What's the biggest change you have seen after nearly 35 years in this industry?*

LARRY: Nothing significant; it's the same game: artists with a vision working with businessmen making money. It's the same thing it always was! [laughs] The problem has always been, how do you have a vision, maintain it, express it, and then make a living? A wise man once said, "Life is about learning how to live and how to make a living." So we all face the same problem. If you're gifted and burdened with a vision, and a passion to do this, how do you live in this world? That's the task. In the industry, there will always be people who don't understand what you're doing, so you have to deal with them as best you can, collect your paycheck, and run the gauntlet. But you have to keep your original vision alive! I tell my students (see Figures 10.5 and 10.6), your big trick when you were little was to turn over, and then you learned how to walk, and so on. At some point in this little drama of life, you decided to make something good, so hold on to that moment in your life, when you decided to make something that *you* liked, and that maybe other people would like. If you can carry that same vision through your whole life and never lose it, you'll have a pretty good life.

Figure 10.5 Larry Larson with student Megan Harris and her puppet.

Figure 10.6 Larry Larson with student Tom Perzanowski and his foam puppet.

10. An Interview with Larry Larson

221

Chapter 11
Sets and Props

Depending on the type of film or animation exercise you are making, your puppet may need to be complemented by some kind of background or environment. A stop-motion set, which provides this environment, can be very simple or very elaborate, but most importantly it should enhance the surroundings of your characters and not distract the viewer away from them. Your scene or story may also call for some props for the characters to grab or interact with. Building sets and props is another multifaceted process that requires many different skills that could each make up a book of its own to do it justice: woodworking, sculpting, metalworking, drafting, and the list goes on. Building stop-motion sets professionally is like being a carpenter or interior designer, with all of the same skill sets required. The only difference is that everything is in miniature scale! On a more independent or beginner level, the process of creating sets can sometimes turn out to be a fun experiment in MacGyver-style filmmaking. In this chapter, I will briefly cover some basic things to think about when making sets and props for stop-motion.

Setting the Stage

On a practical level, the most important element to consider when designing your set is how much physical space you have available. Whether you live in a tiny apartment or have a house with a spacious basement or spare room will ultimately determine the scale in which everything is built (see Figure 11.1).

As always, work in a room without windows to avoid incoming sunlight that will change throughout the day. The size of your puppets will also be a determining factor. You certainly do not want your puppets to look too small or too large in comparison to your background. These considerations should be the first step before any production on your project begins. You also want to think about where the camera and lights will need to be placed. It's rather pointless to build a huge set and then realize there is no more space left in your room to fit other equipment. If you are making a film that will feature several different camera angles, refer to your storyboard when designing your set so that you can ensure that all of your angles can be achieved without getting unwanted material in the shot, such as lights, the ceiling, or bits of your surrounding studio space. It's also a good idea to design your set with removable walls or backdrops, so that the set can be modified to accommodate changing camera angles. If you plan on having any close-up shots of your puppet, then parts of your set might require more detail if they too are shown in close-up. Remember, your work may be shown on a huge screen, where everything is more readily noticeable than on a computer or TV monitor. You also must make sure that you will have convenient access to your puppets, and can reach them without disturbing the set. Keep everything at a height and depth that will give the best range for lighting and camera, and avoid extra strain on your back while animating.

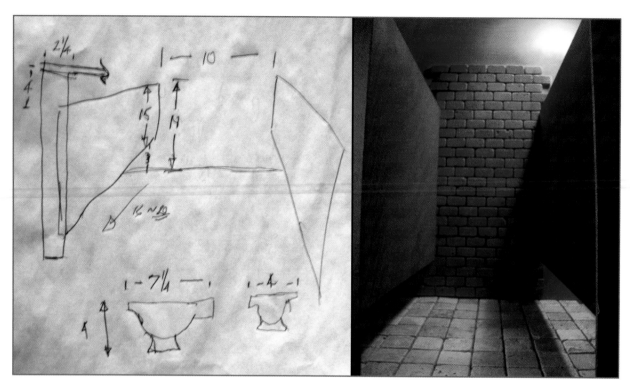

Figure 11.1
Diagram and actual set-in-progress. (Courtesy of Darren Lee.)

As you plan your set in terms of the materials you will use, think about the shots required for your project. Will your characters only be shown from the waist up, or will they be full figure in the frame? Will they be shown walking or jumping? These factors will determine how the ground or floor surface is built and whether you will need any overhead rigging for hanging objects from wires for jumping shots. If the characters' feet will never be seen, it doesn't matter how the surface appears. If they are walking full-frame in any shots, you will need tie-downs for your puppet's feet, and the holes in the floor must be hidden somehow.

As a good way to test out any issues that might come up during your shoot, a common practice is to build a smaller-scale mock-up of your set first (see Figure 11.2). Use light materials such as balsa wood, cardboard, or Styrofoam to build walls or floor surfaces. Perfection and attention to detail are not important here; you could even just use pieces of junk or household objects to suggest elements of the set. For puppets, you can make smaller clay models or flat cutouts for scale purposes. You can use a still camera or viewfinder to view or take pictures of the various angles you will be shooting to get a sense of how they will look in the final version. In this digital age, another way to plan out your set is to create a virtual version of it using any 3D modeling software such as Maya or 3ds Max.

Figure 11.2 Mock-up of a city set on a 4' x 8' table. (Courtesy of Michael Stennick, Space Monster Pictures.)

Securing the Set

In addition to making sure that your camera, lights, and yourself can fit in with your space, the most important quality of your actual set is keeping everything secured. The base must be sturdy and heavy enough to avoid sliding around if pushed or leaned against. Most sets are built on a steel or wooden base, which can be glued or screwed down to the floor, or weighted down to prevent movement. The actual surface on top of the base will be partially determined, as I mentioned previously, by whether or not you will need tie-downs for your characters' feet. A wooden base is still a good option, regardless of this factor of your animation. Make sure that the materials are durable enough that they will not warp over a long period of time. If your shoot takes several weeks or months, any gradual warping of your set will show up on camera as a time-lapse feature. Try to keep the temperature in your studio consistent to avoid this. Any props in your shot such as furniture (in an interior set) or foliage (in an exterior set) must also be secured tightly. Basically, anything that does not move in your scene should be secured with strong glue, putty, or some kind of tie-down from underneath. If they are not secured, it is very common for some props to lose their footing so slowly that you might not notice it while animating. It is only noticed when you play back your animation and see a top-heavy prop gradually slipping or drooping throughout, which can be distracting, not to mention stressful, if your character animation turns out well. Another type of prop to avoid in any kind of set is real plants. If your set has trees, bushes, or house plants in it, use ready-made fake ones or build your own from scratch. Over the span of animating, real plants will gradually either wilt or bloom, especially under hot lights. When I saw Ray Harryhausen speak in 2001, he recounted some incidents on some films he had worked on where the set designers used real plants that blossomed in time-lapse during the shoot. Watch for any elements like this that may show up over a long span of time, including dust and lighting changes.

Interior Sets

An interior set is for any scene that takes place indoors, whether it be a shop, bedroom, or office building. Typically, an interior set will be created with at least two or three walls, so that corners can be shown in different camera angles to give some depth and variety to the composition. "Flyaway" walls can be designed to be removed if the camera switches position. Good materials to use for building walls are wood, foam core, or Styrofoam sheets. If your room will have windows, these can be cut out and framed with handcrafted balsa wood. Real pieces of glass or Plexiglas can be used for windows, as long as they do not cause unwanted reflections. You might be able to find ready-made windows at any store that sells crafts or model supplies for doll houses. The same applies to furniture, clocks, or other miniature household objects. Let your imagination flow when exploring model shops or craft stores, and look for elements that might look good in your set. The overall design scheme you are going after will ultimately determine whether you can get away with ready-made props or the need to create everything from scratch. Basically, with all stop-motion sets, your job is to create a miniature world. You can create the same things with which you would normally dress up a life-size room, just in a much smaller scale. Wallpaper designs can be scanned into the computer, scaled down and reprinted, as can paintings or portraits to be placed into miniature picture frames. You can even create interior sets and props entirely out of clay (see Figure 11.3) if your characters are made of clay and you want to achieve a unified design style throughout. In going this route, make doubly sure that you don't nudge parts of the set when you go to animate your puppets; otherwise you may create unwanted smudges and jitters in the background.

Figure 11.3 *The Slipper Cycle,* a short film. (Courtesy of Anthony Silverston.)

When lighting an interior set, consider where your main light source is, whether it comes from outside the windows or from within the room itself. Any light source that is literally shown in the shot, such as a lamp (see Figure 11.4), is referred to as a *practical light*. Miniature practical lights can be created with Christmas lights or tiny keychain-sized flashlight bulbs, and any wires leading to them need to be concealed somehow, unless they are battery operated. Battery-powered lights must be watched closely with the frame grabber and replaced if they start to dim or burn out. In many cases, the practical light will not be bright enough to illuminate the set by itself, so additional light must be projected onto the set from outside the frame. The light can be shaped with barn doors or gobo masks to make it appear as if it is coming from the practical light. This technique is common in live-action film and theater and must be synchronized properly for moments when a character turns a practical set light on or off.

Exterior Sets

An exterior set is for any scene that takes place outdoors. Common objects that must be created for exterior sets range from buildings and vehicles (for neighborhoods or cityscapes) to trees, rocks, or sand (for forests, deserts, or countrysides). Wood and Styrofoam, again, are useful materials for creating buildings, which can be painted or covered with a thin layer of clay to give them the right texture. Buildings might sometimes be created as an exterior set unto themselves, for close-up shots of a castle tower, for instance. Figures 11.5 and 11.6 show "before and after" shots of the Gargoyle Tower set from *Twisteeria*.

Miniature trees or foliage can be found ready-made at model shops. Since many people are enthusiasts for building model train sets, that is a good area to look into. They may also have fake grass surfaces or kits for building hills or road signs. If you build trees from scratch, they can be built with armature wire and covered with paper bark and leaves. Or you can make them out of real twigs and branches from outside. When going for a realistic approach, real materials will obviously work best whenever possible, so long as they do not deteriorate when removed from their natural elements. A useful material for making leaves or large fern plants is copper foil or Cinefoil covered with paper, so they can hold their shape if they need to be animated. Rocks and hills can be shaped with chicken wire or a wire mesh and covered with painted papier-mâché or Rigid Wrap for a textured rock appearance. Another material that is easy to find in most art or craft supply stores is Celluclay, a paper pulp that you mix with water, sculpt to any shape, and air dry for a rock-like appearance. Behind your exterior set, you will need a backdrop, particularly for the widest shots in your project. The backdrop may be only a painted sky, or it could also have a horizon or extra background elements painted into it, to give it a sense of depth to blend into the physical set.

The lighting for an exterior set will depend on the time of day in your scene. The main light source is the sun or the moon, so for a bright sunny day, you want to bathe the set in light to achieve that illusion. An overcast day will require a more diffused lighting overall, with no harsh shadows. Atmospheric lighting for a moonlight shot can be achieved with colored gels and emphasis on rim lighting. Night shots are tricky, in that you usually need a good deal of light to expose the image on camera, but the shot is intended to be dark. If you have extensive means for post-production effects, you could shoot your set as a day shot and color-correct it afterward to make it appear like night. Again, the whole point behind your set is to create a miniature world, so exterior shots tend to require more space to get the right lighting and feel for the great outdoors (see Figure 11.7), as opposed to an interior space, which is more enclosed to begin with.

Figure 11.4 *Room 710* set designed by Karethe Linaae and built by George Grove. (Courtesy of Ann-Marie Fleming, Sleepy Dog Films.)

229

Figure 11.5
Gargoyle Tower—
Before. (Copyright
1998 Bowes
Productions.)

Figure 11.6
Gargoyle Tower—
After. (Copyright
1998 Bowes
Productions.)

The Art of Stop-Motion Animation

Figure 11.7 An exterior set from MTV/Insight Films *Monster Island*. (Copyright 2004 Bowes Productions.)

Alternative Set Methods

In some cases, depending on your project, an elaborate set with walls or foliage may not be necessary. Some stop-motion shorts, such as Tim Hittle's *Potato Hunter* and *Canhead*, take place on an abstract or stylized tabletop with very little in the way of props or a recognizable environment. The effect is one of a miniature world that calls attention to the fact that it's stop-motion on a tabletop, while at the same time creating an alternate universe that we accept the characters interacting in. A film like Aardman's *Pib and Pog* simply uses a plain white background, so to the audience it could be interior or exterior, and the focus is just on the animation.

My student film *Snot Living* involved a clay character that interacted with a live-action character, so my apartment simply acted as the set itself. The funny thing about that film was that I only lived in the apartment where I shot all of the live-action shots with Brandon (my friend who played the main character) for the summer, and when I had to move out, I still had some close-up animation shots to create. I planned ahead so that any wider animation shots that obviously took place in the same apartment were done first. I still had a few close-up shots to do where my puppet was on the floor, and luckily after I moved out, the landlords ripped up the carpet to replace it, so I snatched a piece of it and animated the remaining floor shots at my parents' house. So although the film was shot in a few different locations, it appears to be shot all in one place. (The magic of guerilla filmmaking!) So basically, in a situation like this for a film that has several different shots, you want to maintain the continuity of the film in any way possible. Films that feature tiny stop-motion puppets on actual-size sets are somewhat of a rarity, but they have a great look to them. Historically, some of the noted animators who have made films this way include Charley Bowers and Jan Svankmeyer (see Chapter 1, "Appeal and History of Stop-Motion Animation").

Another simple method for putting your puppets into an actual environment is to just use a backdrop, such as a photograph or painting, by itself (see Figure 11.8). You will not be able to do much in terms of changing camera angles or achieving the same level of depth in the shot, but for some purposes it can be very effective. At the very least your character will have some kind of context to his scene, rather than just a plain background. For a dialogue exercise, which was the purpose behind the penguin scene in Figure 11.8, it's a good "quick and dirty" option that still looks good on-camera.

Figure 11.8 Penguin puppet and set by Andy Simpson.

Chroma-Key Compositing

Another very popular option for creating backgrounds in stop-motion is to shoot puppets or partial sets in front of a blue screen (for film) or green screen (for video). By lighting the screen evenly, everything that is blue or green in the frame surrounding the puppet can be replaced with separately shot background footage in a process called *chroma-keying*. The same process is used for everything from live-action films to television weather reports. The chroma-key process can be used for many different purposes in stop-motion, such as if CG elements such as water or sky are needed to surround part of a set (see Figure 11.9) or if puppets are suspended in midair with rigs for jumping or falling shots (see Figure 11.10). In the falling rig case, the background composited in later would be a moving live-action shot, to give the illusion that the camera is following the puppets as they fall, when in fact the puppets and camera are stationary.

For large studio shots like these, a lot of space is required, as you can see, but the process is also rather simple to do yourself for smaller productions. Keep in mind that this method will not allow you to have your puppets throw shadows onto your set, if that is the effect you want. Its use depends on the type of film you are making.

If you are shooting your stop-motion on video with a capture card and software package, you will want a green backdrop to go behind your puppets. The backdrop can be a sheet of fabric, an actual screen, or even a flat piece of foam core. As long as the backdrop is one universal color and lit evenly with no shadows, any green color can be used with a coat of paint or ready-made died cloth. To get the best results, you can look into acquiring a green screen material manufactured specifically with the right color for chroma-key compositing. This might come in a ready-made chroma green screen or sheet, or you can buy a gallon of Rosko video paint and spread an even coat onto a sheet of foam core. An important factor in using the

Figure 11.9 Russell Papp on set from MTV/Insight Films' *Monster Island*. (Copyright 2004 Bowes Productions.)

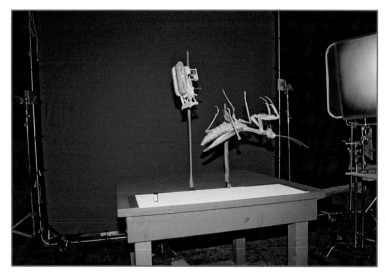

Figure 11.10 MTV/Insight Films' *Monster Island*. (Copyright 2004 Bowes Productions.)

green screen is to make sure your puppets do not have any of the same bright green in them, or else the background will show through in these parts where you may not want it to. Also make sure your background is far enough away behind your puppets so that the green color does not reflect too much onto them. You want the puppets to be as distinct from the green as possible to ensure a crisp composite.

I used this method for my student film *Bad News*, where my puppets were supposed to be shown "live on location" in a sheep field. The video of the field was shot separately, and the animation was done in front of my homemade green screen (see Figure 11.11). Then I used AfterEffects to composite the two together and adjust the color so that it looked like my puppets were outside on an overcast day (see Figures 11.12–11.16).

In After Effects, import your animation file into the timeline with your background video file behind it

Figure 11.11 A simple setup for puppets in front of a green screen.

(see Figure 11.12). Under Effects & Presets, select Color Key, drag the icon onto the monitor's image, and the Effect Controls dialog box will open. Select the Eyedropper tool, and click on the green color in the monitor (see Figure 11.13). In the Effect Controls dialog box, move the slider for Color Tolerance until all of the green color is gone. There may still be a slight rim of green around your puppet if there was any color spill reflected onto it (see Figure 11.14). Use the Edge Thin slider to decrease the green rim around the puppet, and the Edge Feather slider to soften the edges if needed (see Figure 11.15). If you need to adjust the colors of your puppet to match the background better, find the Hue/Saturation Effect controls and use the sliders to adjust the color. In Figure 11.16, the colors are adjusted to make Hamish look more like he is outside on an overcast day.

If you are using Adobe Premiere as your editing software, you can also create your final composite within the software. Import your animation and background files and place your background into the Video 1A track. Place your animation file into the Video 2 track, and right-click the file to select Video Options > Transparency (see Figure 11.17). Under Key Type, select Green Screen, and the green color will automatically be keyed out (see Figure 11.18). Select the Mask Only box (see Figure 11.19) so that your sample image appears as a black-and-white matte. Use the Threshold slider to adjust the black outside your puppet, and use the Cutoff slider to adjust the gray inside your puppet, making the matte as straight black-and-white as possible.

Figure 11.12 Import the animation and background files into the timeline.

Figure 11.13 Select the green-screen color with the Eyedropper tool.

Figure 11.14 Adjust the color tolerance to get rid of the green color.

Figure 11.15 Thin and feather the edges to smooth out the edge of the puppet.

Figure 11.16 Adjust the hue and saturation to make your puppet match the background.

11. Sets and Props

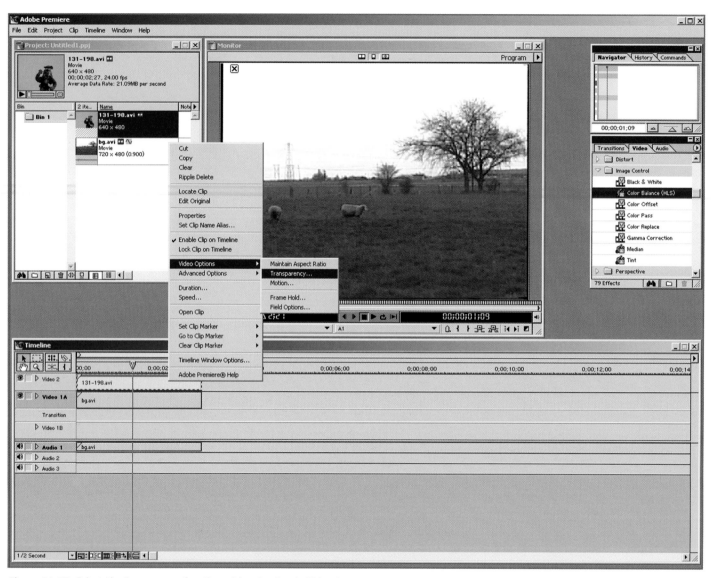

Figure 11.17 Select the Transparency function with animation in Video 2.

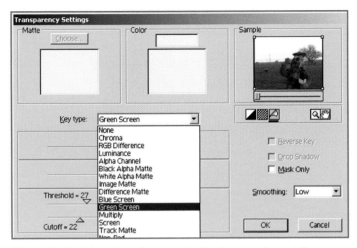

Figure 11.18 Select Green Screen under Key Type to wipe out the green color.

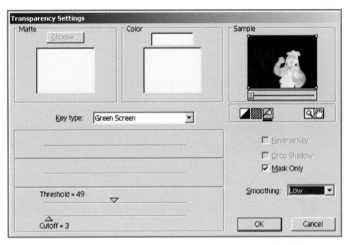

Figure 11.19 Select Mask Only to provide a crisp black-and-white matte.

The Smoothing drop-down menu can be used to smooth out the edges of your puppet if necessary. The Color Balance effect controls can be used to adjust the hue, saturation, and lightness of the puppet to match the background (see Figure 11.20).

Once all of these steps for compositing are done, the final version can be edited with sound, etc., and rendered out. For this shot, the animation was created at 24 frames per second and was exported as such, especially so it would sync with the dialogue. The background, however, had been shot with an analog video camera and captured at 29.97 frames per second, which is the standard NTSC video frame rate. Compositing the two together and exporting at 24 (or 23.98) frames per second would cause the background footage to move slightly faster than its original speed. Since the background did not have much movement in it, other than some grazing sheep, the differences in frame rate really didn't matter to me. It was more important to have the animation at the proper speed. If you are doing a composite where the background and animation must be at the same frame rate—for instance, if the puppets are interacting with the live action in a Ray Harryhausen-type fashion—you should look into shooting your background footage with a DV camera that will shoot at 24 frames per second. These are becoming more readily available and are marketed as 24p cameras. By using compositing software further, you can create more detailed effects in regard to layering foreground elements and developing more elaborate shots. By studying the rear projection and matting methods of the past, used by the likes of Willis O'Brien and Ray Harryhausen, you can get some inspiration for the kinds of effects that are possible with today's digital technology.

11. Sets and Props

Figure 11.20 Adjust the hue and saturation with the Color Balance tools.

Props

Just like sets, any props that exist in the background or for being handled by your puppets (see Figure 11.21) can either be built from scratch or sometimes found already made. Craft stores and model shops often sell miniature props that can be used for your stop-motion project. Props built from scratch are built based on the design of the overall piece and for the scale to which they relate to the set and puppets. The most important element of any prop used by a character is that it be as lightweight as possible. A prop that is too heavy will put too much weight on your puppet, making it hard to keep the puppet's arm in position or difficult to fasten the puppet's grip around the prop. If your puppet's hand has strong wires inside, everything should be designed so that the fingers themselves can actually keep the prop in place without slipping. If this proves too difficult, you can try applying tiny drops of hot glue or putty where the fingers grip the prop and are hidden from the camera's view. Most props are built from balsa wood, foam, or a polymer clay (such as Sculpey or Fimo) that can be baked and painted (see Figures 11.22–11.23). Paper items such as magazines or newspapers can be created with actual words and images on the computer and shrunken down for printing. They can then be cut out and glued to copper foil or thin metal Cinefoil, which can be found in photography shops. Oftentimes, the amount of detail put into props such as these may not fully register on camera, but the point is more about authenticity to the miniature world you are creating. Props are the unsung heroes of stop-motion that add that extra bit of realism for the audience. Attention to detail is very important and can make for some fantastic pieces to complement your stop-motion project.

The final point I want to emphasize about sets and props for stop-motion films is how important they can be in helping you tell your story and develop your characters. When a character is shown in his natural habitat, such as his bedroom or kitchen, the surroundings can communicate a lot to the audience about who he is. A messy set with lots of clutter and different kinds of props may indicate to the audience that the character who inhabits it is lazy, disorganized, or perhaps just likes to collect things. The missing pieces will be answered by the movements or

Figure 11.21 "Trooper of Xon" puppet with gun prop. (Courtesy of Michael Stennick, Space Monster Pictures.)

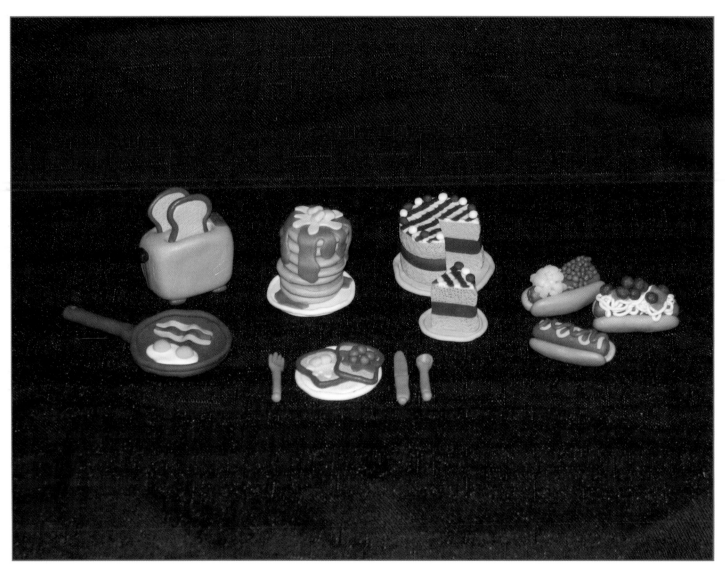

Figure 11.22 Polymer clay props designed and sculpted by Katie Nielsen.

Chapter 12
An Interview with
Nick Hilligoss

Figure 12.1
Nick Hilligoss.

Nick Hilligoss (see Figure 12.1) is an independent filmmaker living in Australia. He designs and builds his latex puppets and the three-dimensional sets they move around in and painstakingly animates them frame by frame in a makeshift studio. He has worked at the Australian Broadcasting Corporation for about 19 years, first as a model maker, then scenic artist and designer. His film credits include *Once Upon Australia* (1995), *A Bunch of Fives* (1998), and *Good Riddance* (2003). Nick is a regular visitor to www.stopmotionanimation.com, and images of his work can be found on his Web site, www.picturetrail.com/hilligossnic. His animation shorts and tutorials are on www.stopmoshorts.com. After seeing so much of his work all over the Internet, I knew he would have much wisdom to contribute to this book.

KEN: *Please give me a brief bio of yourself and how you got started in stop-motion.*

NICK: I got interested in stop-motion as a kid after seeing *The Seventh Voyage of Sinbad*, with Ray Harryhausen's Cyclops and other creatures, at a local cinema in St. Louis, Missouri. After saving for many months for a used 8mm movie camera, I attempted to do something similar with plasticine dinosaurs, only to see my carefully made scaly skin dissolve into a mass of thumbprints after a few frames. I tried a few other things but was dissatisfied with the results. I had never heard of clay animation and didn't realize its possibilities; I only knew it didn't work for what I wanted to do. I did keep an interest in art, and after some delay did graphic design at art school in New Zealand. The breakthrough for me was getting a job as a property maker with the New Zealand Ballet & Opera workshop. I found that making things in three dimensions really suited me. It was years later, working as a props maker and scenic artist for ABC [Australian Broadcasting Corporation] television, when I realized I knew about working with all the materials, including foam latex, that were needed to make stop-motion puppets. I saved up and bought a 16mm Bolex and started doing animation tests. While working on a comedy program as an assistant designer, I showed some of my tests to the producer and ended up doing little animated insert shots of cockroaches and rats, on top of my other duties. While designing sets for various shows, I built some dinosaurs at home and started doing tests of those. By chance, I had my can of film in my hand when I got into a conversation about Australian dinosaurs with the head of the Natural History Unit. I was loaned to Natural History to make a documentary on prehistoric Australia (see Figure 12.2) and have stayed on with them as a producer ever since. During the making of my stop-motion dinosaur epic, the film *Jurassic Park* came out and rendered what I was doing obsolete overnight. After that, I was never going to impress anyone with my low-budget efforts, so I did the only thing I could, which was try to make mine funnier. Since then, my productions have moved more into puppet film rather than special effects.

KEN: *I think it's great that you are able to make these intricate short films on your own! How large is your studio space, and what kind of equipment do you use?*

NICK: For a while, I worked in a room 8 meters (26 feet) long by 4 meters (13 feet) wide. There was a workbench and sink along one short side and half a long side. Opposite that was my backdrop frame, 4.8 meters (15 feet) wide, going up to the ceiling at 2.7 meters (8 feet) high. This worked fine for interior sets, where a room is about 3 feet wide and up to 2 feet deep. For big outdoor scenes, the 13-foot depth was very restricting. You need at least 3 feet [of] space between the back of the set and the backcloth, so you don't get the shadows of trees or buildings cast onto the sky. The set might be 2 meters (6.5 feet) deep or more. To get a wide shot, the camera was often right up

Figure 12.2 A scene from *Once Upon Australia*. (Courtesy Nick Hilligoss/Australian Broadcasting Corporation.)

against the back wall, so I couldn't get my head behind to look through the viewfinder. Often I could only get in or out of the room by crawling under the set. During the production of *Good Riddance,* I moved to a space that was 6 meters (20 feet) deep, which works much better (see Figure 12.3). The only problem now is space to store sets. At the opposite end of the scale, I've done a simple setup with one puppet in a small room where the set was 1.5 feet wide and sat on a desk, with the camera about 2.5 feet away.

I shot *Once Upon Australia* blind with a 16mm Bolex, and for the *Bunch of Fives* shorts, I had a VHS camcorder bolted to the side so I could capture each frame on video, then shoot on film. For *Good Riddance*, I moved up to 35mm film. I used a Mitchell S35R, with reflex viewing and a built-in black-and-white video tape. Recently I've been setting up a system for my own low-budget independent productions. I wanted to eliminate the costs of film, processing, and telecine transfer and do as much as possible myself. I bought a Nikon D70 digital SLR camera as soon as they became available. This gives me a better than high-def image that I can save direct to the computer, with the same quality and steadiness I got from 35mm film. I chose the Nikon because they kept the same lens mount they had for decades, so I could use the older manual lenses. I use a little security video camera looking through the Nikon

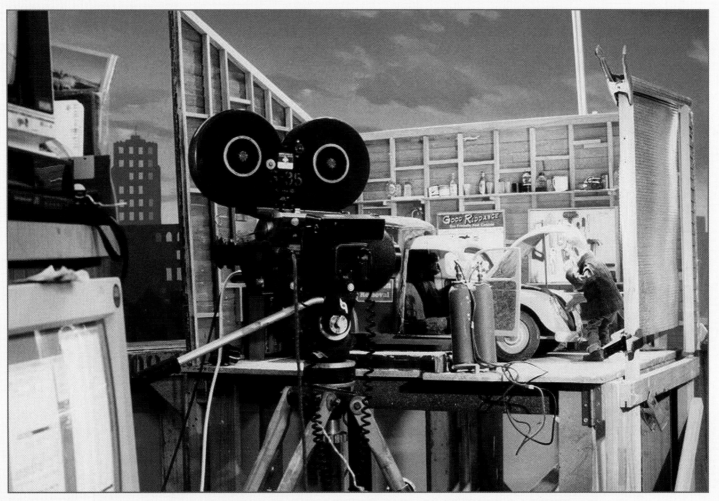

Figure 12.3 A set from *Good Riddance*. (Courtesy Nick Hilligoss/Australian Broadcasting Corporation.)

viewfinder so I can capture a video preview image at the same time. So the workflow is similar to using film, except that I can review the high-def footage immediately instead of waiting to finish a roll of film and process it. I use a tripod with a geared center column, with an added disc marked off in tiny increments, which lets me raise and lower the camera in measured amounts each frame. I've also built a dolly track unit to track the camera along. A geared tripod head lets me do pan and tilt moves a frame at a time as well.

My lighting is a mixture—old TV studio lights like a 2000-watt Fresnel that I use for the sun in the outdoor sets, and a 500-watt minuette. Most are home-made with a 12-volt, 50-watt domestic downlight kit for about $12 (AUS) each. I make up a platform to hold the light and transformer, with a bent strip of steel or aluminum to swivel it from, and homemade barn doors from sheet metal so I have something to clip lighting gels to. I also use 6-volt, 30-watt Pinspots from disco lighting suppliers, because they cast a bright but very narrow beam, ideal for backlighting a puppet without spreading light all over the set. I light the sky with a pair of Iris lights, long halogen tubes with an asymmetric reflector so it can hang from above the set, and throw more light down to the lower part of the backdrop, which is further away. At a pinch, I use two 500-watt domestic floodlights. I also have fluorescent tubes mounted on a piece of timber end-to-end, which I can place just behind the set to add an extra glow on the horizon.

For puppet and set building, I have various tools such as a band saw, jigsaw, circular saw, belt sander, drill press, cordless drill, gas torch, plus triple beam balance, Sunbeam Mixmaster, and oven for foam latex.

KEN: *How long does it usually take to produce your films?*

NICK: A 5-minute film for broadcast TV takes about 6 months all up, building sets and puppets, shooting, and post production. The half-hour documentary *Once Upon Australia* took 2 1/2 years, the five *Bunch of Fives* shorts about the same. The 40- or 50-second mini-films for the Web are done over four or five evenings and maybe a Saturday, plus one more day for sound.

KEN: *How do you typically plan your animation, in terms of the posing and timing?*

NICK: If I have dialogue or music to synch to, that pretty well determines the timing. But mostly I try to tell the story with actions rather than words, which gives me a lot more freedom to move. I will know what I need to happen in a shot, but not exactly what frame it happens on. My storyboard gives me only a basic outline. As I work on a sequence of shots, I usually come up with a few ideas to get a bit more fun out of it. I like to leave a little room for improvisation—it helps to keep the animation from getting too tedious if I haven't planned it down to the last detail. Usually I cut on the action, like going from a close-up of the character turning to a wide shot where we can see what he is turning to look at, and I will know what happens in that wide shot, and that I will probably need around 200 to 250 frames before I cut back to the close-up for the character's reaction. I probably have a few poses in mind, but I'm not really thinking in terms of key poses and in-betweens. I'm more of a straight-ahead animator, focusing on each frame as it comes, easing in and out of the moves, and thinking just a few frames ahead. I don't think, "This walk should have 14 frames for each step," and divide the distance to see how far I move the foot; I move the foot what feels like the right amount each frame, and it works out to about 14 frames. I know where the foot has to land, because I've predrilled the tie-down hole, and I know about where the puppet will get to before I want to move the camera, but I don't know how many frames that will take. I cut to the next shot when I've got to the point where I need to draw the audiences' attention to something else, or where it feels like they would naturally want to see what the puppet is thinking, or what it is seeing, whatever frame number it turns out to be.

When there is dialogue or prerecorded music, I have to do it the other way, I know that on frame 73, the frog starts to sing, so I've got to pace the moves so I am ready at that frame. Everything becomes more planned. I will have marked out on my dope sheet that I will cut from the close-up of the green frog to the mid-shot of the three banjo frogs on frame 225 (see Figure 12.4).

Figure 12.4 A scene from *A Bunch of Fives: Banjo Frogs*. (Courtesy Nick Hilligoss/Australian Broadcasting Corporation.)

KEN: *Do you ever use video reference or any other methods?*

NICK: I occasionally act out something in front of a video camera, like doing a little jig so I can animate a dancing possum at the right rhythm if I don't already have music to work to. With actions that are pure physics, like the way a tree falls or a pendulum swings, I might do a quick video test to check the speed, without all the character animation. For character stuff, I often perform the action, just to get a feel for the balance—which leg you put your weight on when your arm swings around—but without accurately measuring the timing. I don't have a stopwatch, but I might count elephants—one elephant, two elephants, for a very rough idea of how many seconds it might take. Usually my animation compresses time anyway, reducing or removing many of the pauses and repetitions of live action, so absolute realism isn't really the aim.

KEN: *What do you see in the future of the stop-motion medium?*

NICK: The computer technology that killed stop-motion as a special effects medium is now giving us tools to make it easier and better than ever before. It is becoming more accessible to beginners with the use of video and computer frame grabbers than when it could only be shot on film. Other tools like compositing programs and nonlinear editors now allow an individual artist to do virtually all aspects of film production on [his] own computer. I'm hoping to see a lot of very individual work emerging from independent animators. Most of this will be short films; animation is ideally suited to short-form works, and because it still takes a very long time to do, few would have the resources for longer projects. But I would hope to see the occasional feature film like *Corpse Bride* that makes full use of the handcrafted look of stop-motion. I do see computer animation getting better at imitating other animation media and as a medium in its own right, and becoming more cost effective, so I don't see a boom in stop-motion ever happening.

KEN: *Do you have any plans for future projects more ambitious than what you've already done? Any untapped areas you would like to explore?*

NICK: I definitely have ambitions to do better work, but not necessarily longer films. It would be nice to make films that are the best I can do, rather than the best I can do by the deadline with inadequate facilities and a very low budget. It would be good to make a short film that is just the length it needs to be to tell the story, rather than having to fit a predetermined timeslot.

My work for the ABC has been based around natural history and environment themes, and mostly with an identifiable Australian content. I have a number of ideas in mind that explore mythological themes, stories drawn from European folktales, things I haven't been able to do at the ABC. I'm planning to build my own studio soon and have already used several mini-short films as a way of working out a production workflow that relies less on expensive post-production facilities (see Figure 12.5).

KEN: *What advice would you have for someone who wants to be a stop-motion animator?*

NICK: If [that person is] in Australia or North America, I'd probably say, forget it, and get a real job. There just isn't any continuity of work. Of course, the real animator is going to ignore that advice, and any obstacles, and just do it. So I'd say, get a real job to support you and pay for your materials so you can animate. Even a top animator like Anthony Scott (see Chapter 8), who is likely to be offered work on any major stop-motion project, needs to be a good CGI animator for those long periods when there just aren't any stop-motion films being made.

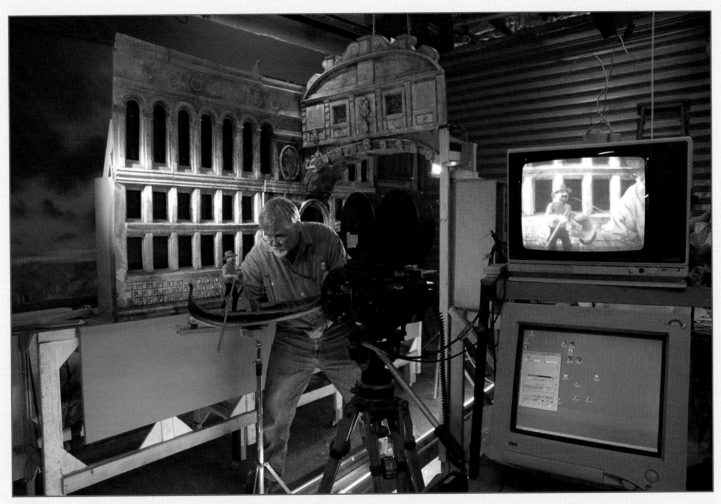

Figure 12.5 Nick Hilligoss at work on a short film. (Courtesy Nick Hilligoss.)

PART III

Showing Your Stuff

Chapter 13
Making a Film

O nce you have learned the history of stop-motion animation and the expectations of the industry, and you have become proficient at building puppets and animating them successfully, you should have a good idea as to whether you want to take your skills to the next level and attempt to make your own film. When I say *film*, I am referring to a piece of animation that is at least one to two minutes or longer, and which perhaps tells a story. Anything less is more like a *scene* or an *exercise* or could possibly fall under the category of being used as a bumper (a short interstitial for television or the Web) or commercial. The semantics behind this are quite debatable, but basically, a *film* is in a different league from the exercises in previous chapters.

At this point, I want to emphasize a few important things. In my own experience as a filmmaker and in being around animation students for several years, I have seen some common bad habits that are not easy to break. Most people get into animation because of a particular film they saw that "changed their life." For many stop-motion animators, this was *King Kong* or any of Ray Harryhausen's films. For the newer generation, it may be *Wallace & Gromit*, or countless others. I'm sure this has been the case for you as it has for me. When we start creating our own animation, those films are always in the back of our minds as the Holy Grail for which we strive to emulate and achieve the same level of greatness. There is nothing wrong with this, as it is always important to aim high in any art form. The danger is in thinking that you can do it alone, and quickly. Often we forget that most feature films are made by hundreds of people with millions of dollars at their fingertips, and it still takes 3 to 5 years. And so, too many people try to make an epic film that they think will be the *Citizen Kane* of stop-motion, only to end up losing interest, going broke, or ultimately abandoning it for a variety of reasons. I am guilty of this myself. I think this is why it's important not only to look to big-budget productions for inspiration, but to attend film festivals or go online to see what others are creating with smaller budgets and resources. If more of us strove to create simpler, shorter films, there would be more stop-motion out there because more of us would actually finish what we started. Short films created on your own can lead to becoming noticed by other artists who may end up helping you create your more elaborate dream projects down the road. There have been a few "overnight success" stories in stop-motion film history, but they are few and far between compared with the artists who have invested decades of hard work before finally getting noticed by the public. Anything worth doing takes time, and animation is one of the most time-consuming trades ever discovered, so making a film independently will *always* take longer than you think it will. If you make a film in stop-motion, your motivation should ultimately come from a love for the art form and your desire to share a piece of yourself with the world. If your motivation is fame, fortune, and a hot tub, or if you think it can be done quickly and easily with no mistakes made, forget about moving puppets around and do something else.

Since stop-motion is a very individualized craft where one animator creates a performance through a puppet (as opposed to key and in-between animators), it is very common for films to be made by one person only. However, the point I'm trying to make is that most of the films that actually get made still receive support from a team. At their best, films are made possible with the collaboration of others, whether it be financial or artistic assistance. So think big and never lose sight of your vision, but be open to the input of others to make your stop-motion dreams a reality. My experience has been that whenever you embark on a personal project and find yourself faced with dilemmas or things you don't know how to do, the right people show up out of nowhere with the right solutions. You might be scratching your head wondering how you are going to light your set, and then you randomly get introduced to someone with theater lighting experience. It's the universe's way of letting you know you're on the right path. Having a support team like this also keeps you accountable for finishing your film. If you have enough people who support what you're doing, they will keep up your enthusiasm for getting it done so they can all see it and celebrate your efforts. It's easy to get stubborn at times and want to do absolutely everything on your own so that you have complete control over it. But I find, again and again, that contributions made by others make the whole process of filmmaking much easier, more fun, and in the end, more rewarding. There are so many elements that must be created: story, sets, lights, puppets, animation, music, editing, sound, distribution. You can't expect to be a pro at all of them, so ask for help when you need it. It will still be your film and vision in the end, only made better by input from people who may have ideas you never would have thought of yourself. Often, it's the advice or contribution of a friend that saves a film from disaster.

If you are a student, see if there is opportunity in your school to make a film as a class project or an independent study. The advantages to student films are mainly access to equipment and a specific time frame. Deadlines are much harder to set for yourself, so if you have one given to you, it teaches you discipline, time management, and how to "let go" of your film. If you have a specific time frame to work in for having it completed, in most cases it *will* get finished. There will be *tons* of things you will wish you had time to go back and change, but that is the reality of filmmaking. A student film will seldom be perfect, but it should be the closest thing possible to the vision in your head, given the time and money allotted to you. All you can do is the best you can, and in most cases you may be pleasantly surprised by the results.

There are many disciplines and layers to making a short film, and plenty of books and courses that focus only on filmmaking, so I would recommend using them to complement this book. Experience, as always, is the best teacher, so in this chapter I will share a little bit of my experience and cover briefly some general points to think about while making a film, specifically in stop-motion animation.

Ideas and Film Types

What kind of film do you want to make? Will it be funny or more dramatic? Will it be for adults only or for children? Will it have a story or be more lyrical or abstract? Will there be dialogue or pantomime acting? Is there a specific message you want the viewer to take from it? You may be interested in all of these ideas, and if you keep things short and simple, there will be time to explore many different genres of filmmaking. Ideas for films can come from anywhere, inspired by all sorts of situations or other art forms. The most obvious place to look for ideas is your own life. Think back to experiences you had as a child or people who were influential to you. Is there a favorite funny story that always gets brought up at family gatherings? Do you have a relative or a friend you could record and then animate a short dialogue? Do you have any sad or scary memories that would make a good film? A strong basis for many film stories is the idea of "What if…" because it gets our brains thinking about how things would be if they were different. Think of experiences you've had or places you've been, ask yourself "What if…" and let your imagination fill in the blanks. Keep a sketchbook and take notes, writing down ideas as they come to you, and drawing character designs that could later be turned into puppets. In the beginning, don't think too much about the practical side of *how am I going to do this?* Just let your imagination go wild, come up with a good story, and then edit things down later. It's always better to take an idea to its extreme and scale it back, rather than not take it far enough.

It's inevitable that your final film will differ a great deal from your original idea, and that is perfectly OK. The best stories are usually the ones that have been rewritten hundreds of times, until every possible approach and angle has been explored. It can be difficult making changes to precious story ideas or characters you grow attached to, but ideas are evolutionary things that keep developing as you work on them. Especially in stop-motion, you will find yourself making changes to your story or character designs once you get into the practical nuts and bolts of how to build everything in three dimensions. My original sketches and ideas for my student film *Snot Living* involved a tiny clay character that was mostly humanoid in appearance, with arms and legs. But at the time, I had no idea how to build an armature, so I made the character into a blob with arms that would just slide across the floor. I think this decision helped the film a great deal, as I could put the focus more on facial expressions and timing, rather than get bogged down with too many technical details like making the character walk. The initial concept for *Snot Living* (see Figure 13.1) was inspired by the fact that many other student films I saw featured depressed, whiny people just hanging out in their apartments. So naturally I thought, wouldn't it be neat if a pesky clay booger tried to get them to cheer up and go outside for a change?

If you abandon an idea, that doesn't mean it will never see the light of day. It will often resurrect itself in a different way for another project. One of my 2D characters, a baby elephant in my current film-in-progress, *Storytime with Nigel*, was originally developed for another film idea but was brought back once I had a better story to use him for. The stop-motion narrator Nigel was originally going to be a newscaster in my *Bad News* film but was made into a children's storyteller instead. Any concepts that are not developed fully can still be changed to suit better purposes, as your ideas ebb and flow to an actual green-lit film project. The most important thing for keeping ideas going is to keep yourself inspired. Explore antique shops and museums, go to film festivals and open screenings, meet interesting people and talk to them. See as many short films as possible (AtomFilms and other Web sites are good to visit) and read as much as possible. Read short stories, history, mythology, fairy tales, and ancient legends. This material lends itself extremely well to stop-motion animation due to the fantasy element created by the medium itself. That is another key thing to remember: *Think of an idea that takes advantage of the medium*. Stories about toys coming to life are an obvious choice, as are myths and fairy tales, because these kinds of stories have been told by live puppets for centuries. Think of an idea that will be easy to do in stop-motion, especially for your first short project; something that takes place on a simple interior set or plain background would be best. Making a film with epic battle scenes, pyrotechnics, or giant sets is best left to the professionals with sound-stages and a big budget, and not ideal for the fledgling puppet film.

Figure 13.1 The clay nemesis plots in *Snot Living*. (Copyright Ken Priebe 1998.)

Narrative Films

Filmmakers of today are coming up with many unique ways to tell stories through the short film medium. Your ultimate goal as a storyteller must be to identify with your audience, make them empathize with your characters, and be able to relate to them. To make a film that tells a story, it's good to know a little bit about story structure and common themes. My goal in this section of the book is not to elaborate too much on how to write a good story, but simply to provide some good starting points and things to watch for when you analyze other short films.

The most basic structure for any story, whether it be one minute or 90 minutes long, is like a three-act play:

Act One: Establish the location and introduce the character(s).

Act Two: Present a conflict or challenge for the character(s) to overcome.

Act Three: Resolve the conflict.

If you think of any movie trilogy or single film, this is the most common pattern you will find. Look for it when watching films, and try to identify where these transitions between acts occur. It may be more obvious in longer films, but try to think in terms of a short film as well. In my film *Snot Living*, which is 13 minutes long, I started Act One by introducing the unnamed live-action character (played by my friend Brandon, so I will name him as such) by showing him fall out of bed, fail at eating breakfast, and head straight to the television. He is obviously hung over, his apartment is a complete disaster, and his food is rotten, so the location and props are used to tell the audience about who he is. He picks his nose and wipes a booger underneath a table. (I had a sick sense of humor back then.) Act Two begins when the booger, brought to life through clay animation, begins terrorizing Brandon by unplugging the television and enticing Brandon to chase him around the apartment. Eventually, Brandon catches the booger, throws him into the microwave, and kills him, thereby resolving the conflict and segueing into Act Three. Brandon feels remorse and decides to finally go outside, where the film changes from black-and-white to color. He is transformed by what he realizes he has been missing (the beauty of nature) and starts walking down the street, when the booger resurrects to remind him he forgot his pants.

In another example, Tim Hittle's Oscar-nominated short film *Canhead* (viewable at AtomFilms.com), the Jay Clay character and his dog Blue are introduced as they take a rest after a long walk. The conflict is presented when Blue disappears on the other side of a canyon, and a giant comes out of the ground to chase Jay Clay. To resolve the conflict, Jay duels with the giant, defeats him, and makes it to the other side of the canyon to be reunited with Blue. The audience empathizes with Jay because his relationship with Blue is evident from the first act. Having a close relationship with a dog is something many of us can relate to, as well as the desire to be reunited with a loved one. Therefore, we root for the hero and hope he can defeat the giant.

Variations on this three-act pattern can even be implemented into one minute. In Aardman Animation's short film *Comfy*, directed by Seth Watkins (also on AtomFilms), the audience is introduced to a character with incredibly long limbs in a tiny bed. The conflict arises when the character cannot sleep comfortably, so he proceeds to remove his limbs one by one. At the end, he has no arms or legs and seems to be finally falling asleep, but then he falls out of the bed. The film is funny, because we can all relate to being uncomfortable and having trouble sleeping, and I'm sure most of us secretly wish we could remove our limbs at times.

Even though there is a lot that happens in these films, they are simple enough that their story can be summarized into one sentence. When you are pitching your film for funding or distribution, it helps if your story can be told in one simple sentence—for example:

A young slacker is disturbed by a booger that comes to life.

A man battles a giant so he can be reunited with his dog.

A character who can't fit into his bed tries to get a good night's sleep.

The other important fact about all three of these films is that none of them has any dialogue, so they can be understood by anyone all over the world, with no language barriers. Automatically, silent films have a broader appeal for distribution in film festivals. Today, so many animated films and television series are primarily dialogue-driven that it's becoming difficult to find inspiration for films that simply tell their story through acting and characterization. It is a true testament of acting ability for an animator to be able to communicate to his audience what a character is thinking without dialogue. It is a challenge, but at the same time, it's easier to tell a story shortly and simply if you don't need to have your characters speak. Study silent films by Charlie Chaplin, Buster Keaton, and also more modern characters like Mr. Bean, for inspiration.

Some films may not have much dialogue but will instead have a narrator who tells the story. A couple examples are the short films *Uncle, Brother, Cousin* and the Oscar-winning *Harvie Krumpet* by Adam Elliot. All of Elliot's films follow a similar biographical pattern, telling us about the lives of misfit Plasticine characters. The humor in them comes mostly from the writing and the character design, and although they are rather tragic at times, they are also very touching. Through the medium of the narrative short film, animators can make very personal films that connect with audiences.

As a starting point for a short narrative film, perhaps try animating a character who finds something that sparks his curiosity. Many great stories start this way, going all the way back to the Greek myth of Pandora's Box, or Alice finding the rabbit hole in *Alice in Wonderland*, or Bilbo Baggins finding the ring in *The Hobbit*. This is the moment that calls them to adventure. Even in a short film, a character could come across a box, for instance, and whatever is in the box either leads the character on a journey or starts a conflict that must be resolved. Plan ahead and keep it simple!

Objects with Personality

When I was studying filmmaking at the University of Michigan, my film professor Frank Beaver showed us a stop-motion film called *Crosspaths* made by a former student, James Pinard (see Figure 13.2). The film had no dialogue or camera movement, just eggs moving around on a tabletop set to music. Through this very limited spectrum of materials, the eggs told a spiritual allegory that moved me to tears the first time I saw it. And yet, there were no sets or puppets, just eggs. One of the most unique things about stop-motion, compared to other mediums, is that you can take ordinary objects and bring them to life this way. You don't always need fancy wire armatures, foam latex, clay, or detailed sets; as long as you have a good story, you can make a film out of absolutely anything.

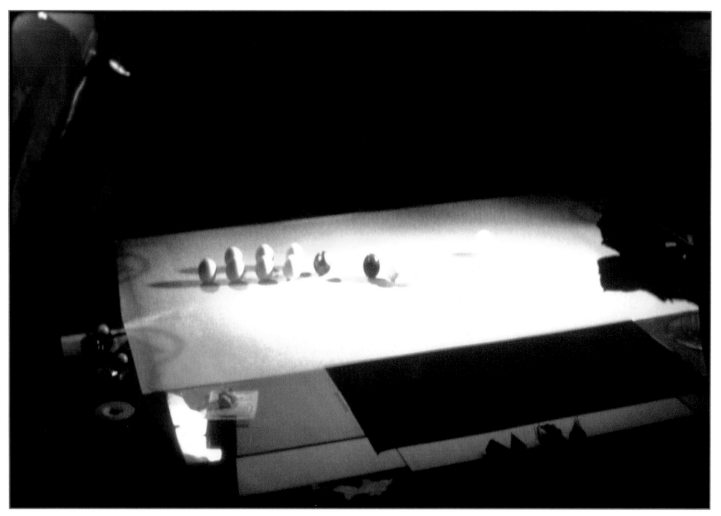

Figure 13.2 Behind the scenes on *Crosspaths*. (Courtesy of Jim Pinard.)

Take the desk lamp exercise from Chapter 5, "Basic Animation," and expand on it to tell a short story. Perhaps the lamp could travel around your house and get into an adventure with other household objects. Giving your objects personality and making them appear to think will be expressed through the timing, in terms of how fast or slow you move them and how long you hold them. Remember how important holds are to the rhythm of your animation and the pacing of your story. (Some strange and creative examples of object animation can be viewed at www.eatpes.com.)

Not that human beings are objects, but they can also be animated through a process called *pixelation*, which is a term used for animating real people frame by frame to achieve impossible feats. Have a friend sit in a chair in front of your camera, take a frame, and then have him scoot up a few inches, and take another frame. Repeating this process will result in your friend sliding across the room in the chair. Or have him jump into the air and try to capture a frame during that split second before he lands, and he will appear to fly across the room. Pixelation has been used to great effect in films like Norm McLaren's *Neighbors* (1952) and the Bolex Brothers' *The Secret Adventures of Tom Thumb* (1993). Experiment with the technique, and then think of a story you can tell using it.

Characterization Films

Some films do not necessarily tell a story with three acts or a beginning, middle, and end, but instead focus on dialogue or character animation. The best example of this genre would be the *Conversation Piece* series from Aardman Animations. Their earliest films by Peter Lord usually focused on one character being interviewed or telling some kind of story, all improvised from interview recordings. Years later, Nick Park tried a different approach in his Oscar-winning *Creature Comforts* (1989) by having a "vox pops" montage of different interviews with animals in the zoo. The entertainment in *Creature Comforts*, both the short film and the television series inspired by it, comes not from a linear story, but through the mannerisms of the characters. It is a brilliant concept combined with amazing character animation, where these animals really seem to be thinking, speaking, and living. Any short monologue, improvised piece of dialogue, or song can be animated in stop-motion and result in a short film. Avoid using copyrighted material for a film like this; instead, record your own dialogue or music. Record your crazy uncle who tells funny stories and animate it, or make a music video for your local garage band.

Abstract Films

If telling a linear story or animating characters is not really your thing, or if you want to try something completely different, you could experiment with making an abstract film. Through stop-motion, you can explore the possibilities of light, color, sound, or patterns of imagery with shapes or found objects. Many filmmakers have used stop-motion to create films that defy the typical narrative story structure and instead revel in the miracle of the moving image. Art Clokey's film *Gumbasia* (1955) is a classic example of using clay to create patterns of movement set to music. Will Vinton had a brief segment exploring the same concept in his film *Closed Mondays* (1975), and even Jim Henson animated colored pieces of paper to music in his experimental short film *TimePiece* (1965). Other abstract stop-motion effects have been explored by filmmakers Carmen D'Avino, Oskar Fishinger, and the Brothers Quay.

Storyboarding and Editing

Storyboarding and editing for stop-motion differs from other animation mediums. In a 2D or CG film, the camera is almost an abstract entity that can swoop, glide, and be positioned absolutely anywhere, due to the fact that the environment it is capturing is either flat or virtual. There is a greater level of control over the animation and how the camera relates to it. In 2D animation, things can simply be redrawn, and in CG animation, cameras can literally go through walls. Stop-motion, however, is much closer to live-action filmmaking, in that the camera is a physical object that exists in a physical space. So there are more challenges and limitations placed on where the camera can go. Plus, once the set is built, it is much harder for the director to change his mind on a camera angle. A wall, unless it is removed, may not allow for that much flexibility. The story direction for stop-motion usually relies more on simple camera angles, which must be planned in advance through careful storyboarding, which serves as the blueprint for any show.

The art of planning your film with storyboards is a vast topic which is best learned through studying live-action or stop-motion films and paying attention to how they are structured. How and when do camera angles change? What is the camera drawing your attention to, and why? As a filmmaker, what you are essentially doing, through editing, is being selective about what you are showing your audience to tell your story. There may be only one action, like a conversation, taking place in one location, but to keep it interesting, that action may be broken up into different angles, cutting back and forth. It's important to think cinematically and visually, so you can manipulate the audience's reaction by how you set up your shots. There are entire books and courses to refer to for fully mastering the art of storyboarding, but following are some basic principles to get you started.

Shots

Films are made up of different kinds of shots, angles, and camera movements, which differ in how much they show of the actors or locations, based on how close or far away the camera is. They can also have different psychological effects on the audience. Here are some basic kinds of shots and what they mean in the language of filmmaking:

- An **establishing shot** will usually open up a film and is typically a wide view of the location where the action takes place. This could be a house, a room, or an entire city. After briefly establishing the location, you can take your viewer into the story by cutting to any of the following shots, demonstrated with stills from *Snot Living*.

- A **long shot** (see Figure 13.3) shows a character from a distance, far enough away so that you can see the whole body. It is a kind of establishing shot that can still communicate to the audience the character's surroundings.

Figure 13.3 Long shot.

13. Making a Film

263

◆ A **medium shot** (see Figure 13.4) takes the camera closer to the character, usually from the waist up. It puts the audience's focus on the character, and may be used for a dialogue, pantomime, or action scene.

Figure 13.4 Medium shot.

◆ A **close-up shot** (see Figure 13.5) goes even closer, revealing a character's facial expression or an object in a very intimate way. In between these different shots might be variations such as medium-long or medium close-up.

Figure 13.5 Close-up.

◆ An **extreme close-up** (see Figure 13.6) focuses on a character or object so tightly that he takes up almost the entire frame, and zeros in on the one important aspect you want the audience to see.

◆ A **POV shot** (see Figure 13.7) stands for point-of-view, where the camera becomes the eye of one of the characters, seeing exactly what that character sees from its perspective. It is usually preceded by a medium or close-up shot of a character looking at something, so that the audience understands that it's from the character's point of view.

Figure 13.6 Extreme close-up.

Figure 13.7 POV shot (on right).

◆ An **over-the-shoulder shot** (see Figure 13.8) is similar to a POV shot, except that we see what or who the character is looking at over his shoulder, or close to it. This shot is often used for dialogue between two characters. Shots described as a one-shot, two-shot, or three-shot refer to how many characters are in the same shot at once. A group shot would feature several different characters on-screen at once.

Figure 13.8 Over-the-shoulder "two-shot" (also typically behind the character's shoulder).

Angles

Certain shots are dictated by the angle at which the camera is positioned in relation to the subject, which also have various psychological effects on the audience.

◆ **Low angle shots** (or up shots) can serve two purposes. In one aspect, they are essentially POV shots of small characters looking up at big characters or objects, like an ant looking up at a tree, or a tiny clay character looking up at a human (see Figure 13.9). They are also used to make characters look powerful or threatening. **High angle shots**, or down shots, are also POV shots of characters looking down, as if they are in a tree or on top of a building, but they can also be used to make characters look alone, insignificant, or in danger.

Figure 13.9 Low angle shot (on right).

◆ A **Dutch angle** (see Figure 13.10) is when the camera is titled slightly, close to a 45-degree angle. It is an artistic statement by the director to imply that something mysterious or wrong is about to happen.

Figure 13.10 Dutch angle.

Camera Moves

Any of these previous shots and angles can be combined with a camera move to further enhance the action or bring the viewer into the story. Following are some basic terms for different camera movements.

- ◆ **Panning** refers to the camera moving on an axis, rooted to its tripod, from left to right, or right to left.
- ◆ **Tilting** refers to the camera moving up or down on a tripod axis.
- ◆ **Tracking** refers to the camera actually moving left/right or right/left on a dolly.
- ◆ **Trucking** refers to the camera moving on a dolly either into the scene or away from it.
- ◆ A **zoom** is a trucking move that is achieved with the zoom lens of the camera, which is stationary.

Composition

Look for ways to make your shots interesting. Think of each shot in your film as a painting that tells part of your story on its own, and uses angles, lines, and shapes to create appealing shapes for the viewer (see Figures 13.11–13.12). Each shot should be thought of this way, and in relation to the other shots that move through the film. If too many of the shots in your storyboard start looking the same, always from a straight-on angle, try changing the camera angle slightly so that the horizon line, or perhaps the edge of a wall, goes diagonally across the frame. Each shot should have a central area of focus. What is the most important thing for the audience to see in the shot? Make this the most important element of your shot, and frame your background around it. It's important that your characters have room to breathe and move around. Think of the negative space around your character, and keep that interesting as well. One thing that makes for good composition is having characters or objects bleed outside of the frame slightly. Do not feel like you need to cram a whole bunch of objects into the frame in full view. Instead, have a vehicle, piece of furniture, or a window showing partly on the side, to frame in the action and give the sense that the world you are showing the audience extends beyond the frame. Also, foreground elements add depth to a shot and make your audience feel they are looking at a real environment (see Figures 13.13–13.14).

While all of these elements are important in individual shots, it's important to keep the continuity going from one shot to the next, in terms of the story pacing and also in terms of movement. If your character is walking from left to right in a long shot, then cut to a medium shot of him still walking, and keep him moving in the same direction. You would not want the camera suddenly on the other side and show him moving from right to left, as this would be disrupting to the viewer. Your set is like a stage with a proscenium arch, and the camera can be positioned anywhere, high or low, within one side of the stage, but never beyond it (see Figure 13.15).

13. Making a Film

Figure 13.11 Shooting at an angle makes for a more interesting composition. (Courtesy of Nick Hilligoss/Australian Broadcasting Corporation.)

Figure 13.12 Placement and posing of the rats, combined with lighting from an open kitchen area, tells the story and draws in the audience within one shot. (Courtesy of Nick Hilligoss/Australian Broadcasting Corporation.)

Figure 13.13 Composition of the character off to the side draws the viewer in to enter into the background with him. (Courtesy of Nick Hilligoss/Australian Broadcasting Corporation.)

Figure 13.14 Foreground and background elements of the bed and window suggest a larger world outside the frame. (Courtesy of Nick Hilligoss/Australian Broadcasting Corporation.)

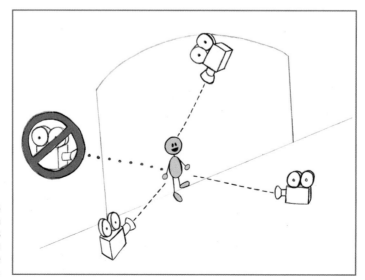

Figure 13.15
The camera should never cross the axis line in the middle of the stage.

Lighting

Lighting is not usually something that is planned very specifically in the storyboard stage, but it helps to have a good sense of what kind of lighting your shots will have. For stop-motion production, this might have an effect on the placement of your camera, so it never hurts to be prepared. Lighting can add some great moods and effects to your film, and it can help to tell the story or tell the audience something about the characters or the atmosphere you want to create (see Figures 13.16–13.18).

Figure 13.16 Exterior moonlight creates a gentle evening atmosphere. (Courtesy of Nick Hilligoss/Australian Broadcasting Corporation.)

Figure 13.17 A long shot from *Snot Living*. German Expressionist-inspired lighting creates angular shadows closing in and suggests isolation and depression, adding to the mood of this particular scene.

13. Making a Film

273

Figure 13.18 Lighting from below with one strong key light will make your character look sinister. (Clay puppet by Ken Priebe.)

Editing

In live action, quite often a scene will be shot several times from different angles, including a master long shot that shows the whole scene, and then again with medium shots and close-ups. Later on, the way all of these shots cut and relate to each other will be decided in the editing room. In animation, the editing is determined before shooting begins, all planned out in the storyboard stage. Occasionally, there may be some changes or last-minute ideas worked out in editing, but an animated film is essentially already edited from the beginning, and then it's just a matter of putting the shots together in proper sequence. Each shot should have a few extra frames at the beginning and end so that there is more breathing room for changing the pacing during the editing stage.

Cuts between shots are essentially in two kinds: jump cuts and match cuts. A *jump cut* is a transition between two shots that are basically independent of each other in terms of the action taking place. It may be simply a change in camera position, as from an establishing shot to a medium shot, or from one character to another in two different locations, possibly at different times, jumping between them. A *match cut* is an edit that happens in the middle of an action. For example, by starting with a close-up of a prop and having a character's hand reach into the frame to grab it and start to pick it up, you would then cut to a medium or long shot of the character continuing the action. The last frame of the long shot and the first frame of the medium shot would have to line up with each other in sequence. In stop-motion, this would involve animating the character up to a certain point of his action, changing the camera position, and then continuing the animation. It would be very important for the puppet to remain still without sagging or falling over during the camera change.

Figures 13.19–13.32 show a brief sequence from *Snot Living* with comparison storyboards, showing how many of these shots and camera angles work together when edited. Separate panels show different actions in the same shot, unless indicated by a cut. This sequence from the film is also featured on the CD.

Figure 13.19

Figure 13.20

Figure 13.21

Figure 13.22

Figure 13.23

Figure 13.24

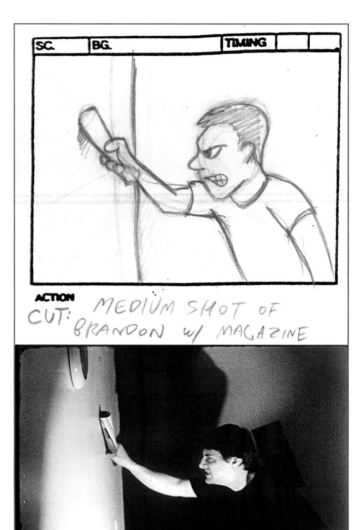

Figure 13.25

Figure 13.26

Figure 13.27

Figure 13.28

Figure 13.29

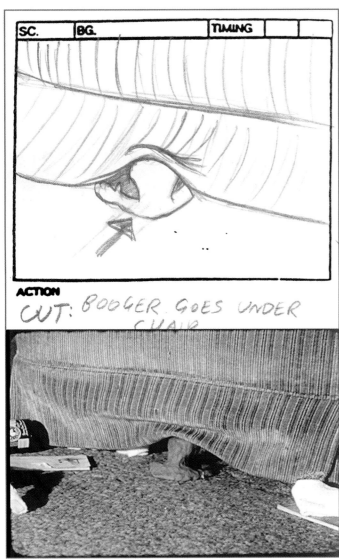

SC. | BG. | TIMING

ACTION

CUT: BOOGER GOES UNDER
CHAIR

Figure 13.30

SC. | BG. | TIMING

ACTION CUT: BRANDON EXITS FRAME.

Figure 13.31

Figure 13.32

The Art of Stop-Motion Animation

Getting It Made

Once your artistic decisions have been made for the story and look of the film, the technical issues (besides building puppets and sets) need to be addressed before shooting begins. Following are some basic principles to consider.

Format

Before shooting your film, and even as early as the preproduction stages, you should have an idea of what the final distribution format of your film will be if you're shooting it digitally. Are you making it for Web broadcasting or video transfer only? Will you ultimately have it transferred to film? These factors may determine what kind of equipment you will need to shoot it, whether you can get away with just a regular video camera or need something with better resolution, like a digital still camera. If you plan on outputting your digital frames to film, you may want to capture your frames at Hi-Definition resolution, which is 1920×1080 pixels. Standard definition is 720×480, which will work fine for output to video or DVD. You also need to decide if you will shoot it in an aspect ratio of standard 4:3 format or widescreen 16:9 format. Once you have decided, make sure your camera, capturing software, and editing output are all set to the same format all the way through. Programs such as Adobe Premiere or Final Cut Pro can be used to import your animation and edit it with sound, titles, and effects.

Animation is typically shot at 24 frames per second, but NTSC video and DVD play back at 29.97 frames per second, duplicating every fourth frame to keep an even playback rate. If outputting directly to videotape, you may need to perform a 3:2 pull down to your film, using a program like Virtual Dub or Adobe Premiere. For DVD, most players will now play back files at their original frame rate of 24 frames per second (technically 23.98) and automatically update while playing. Audio, which includes sound effects, music, and dialogue, should all be recorded, if possible, at a sampling rate of 48kHz, which is standard playback speed for DVD. If your sound is at a lower sampling rate, use a program like

Sound Forge to convert it to 48kHz for editing, and ensure that the length of your audio clips does not change. These steps will ensure your sound and picture stayes in sync when playing back on DVD.

Sound

For purposes of story reels or simple independent projects, sound can be recorded in the comfort of your own home with a good microphone fed into the sound card on your computer. For a higher profile production, I would recommend spending the money to have dialogue, sound effects, and music recorded professionally at a real sound studio. Budget for as many hours as you need to record, and plan ahead so that you don't waste precious recording time and money making changes or fiddling with details. Create your own original sound effects and music, or get someone to compose an original score for you. Royalty-free sounds and music can be found at your local library or purchased from the Internet. Never use copyrighted material for your film unless you have obtained permission to do so.

Titles

Titles can be created with almost any editing software, and credits can be placed either at the beginning of your film (like in the old days) or at the end, or a little of both. Title formats vary depending on whether the film is independent or being commissioned by a studio or broadcaster. If any credits appear at the beginning for a professional studio film, they are typically only for the key members of production: major voice actors, screenwriters, editors, composers, art directors, cinematographers, producers, and the director(s), always credited last. All other crew members and special thanks are mentioned in the end credits. Opening credits are usually most interesting during an opening sequence of the film, so that the audience can get right into the story and not need to sit through a title sequence by itself. The amount of time it takes you to say each title out loud is long enough for each title to remain on-screen.

For an independent short you produced mostly by yourself, you don't need to have this many titles at the start. In this case, try to avoid long, drawn-out, or overly dramatic title sequences. You don't want to bore the audience before your film even starts. Start with an invented studio name or logo, include a title with your name or studio, and then the title of your film, and get right into it. White letters on a black background may sound boring, but they suit their purpose well and are easy to read, so they are typically the best bet to stick with. You want your audience to remember your animation, not your flashy titles. As with everything, watch as many short films as possible to get an idea of how titles work.

Schedules

Give yourself a realistic budget and deadline schedule so that you can actually finish your film. It may take you weeks, months, or even years, but don't let the years drag on too long, or you may run the risk of never finishing, going over budget, or losing interest in the project altogether. If you want to submit your film to a contest or a specific film festival, find out what their submission deadline is and plan your schedule around that date. It's easy to get burned out on a film after spending so much time making it, but it takes just as much full-time effort to promote and distribute it, so keep the momentum going!

Above all, have fun, enjoy the process, keep it short and simple, and save your big ambitious feature film for the day when you have millions of dollars and a major studio crew to help you.

Chapter 14
An Interview with Lynne Pritchard

Figure 14.1
Lynne
Pritchard.

Lynne Pritchard (see Figure 14.1) is a stop-motion animation artist from London, England. Coming from a theater background, she has worked on several stop-motion studio productions as an animator, set builder, and model maker. She also teaches workshops and lectures on animation for several different colleges around London. I first met Lynne in 2005 when she came to VanArts to take a one-month summer intensive course in computer animation. Her Web site is www.gingermog.com.

KEN: *Lynne, which stop-motion programs inspired you, growing up in the UK?*

LYNNE: I was a small child in the late '70s, and this was a great time for stop-motion in the UK, and my mother had no problem in letting the TV entertain me for a few hours at a time, which I greatly thank her for. I have no doubt in my mind that the animation I watched as a child helped feed my imagination and sew the seeds for my future career.

A big favorite with me and many other people of my age is *Bagpuss*, created by Oliver Postgate and Peter Firmin of Smallfilms. Bagpuss is a "saggy, fat, cloth cat" who lives in a strange, forgotten shop with his friends, Madeline the rag doll, Professor Yaffle (a woodpecker bookend), a toy frog, and many enthusiastic mice. In every episode, a strange, forgotten object is brought into the shop, and Bagpuss and friends always find out the story behind the object through charming, funny songs and inventive cutout animation. Although I suppose not much actually happens from an adult's point of view, and the characters are simple, there is a quality of magic about this animation, something really beautiful and gentle.

Next I would choose *The Wombles* as an inspiring stop-motion series, created by Elizabeth Beresford. It was centered around the antics of a group of amiable creatures called "Wombles," who live in a newspapered borough underneath Wimbledon Common, collecting the left-behind rubbish and creating labor-saving gadgets that always end up creating chaos. There is a strong theme of recycling and mend-and-make-do, which appeals to most UK residents of a certain age, and I imagine all stop-motion animators hoard old tins of paint, lolly sticks, cardboard, bits of old plastic toys, etc., "just in case they come in handy one day," which I'm really guilty of.

Finally, I would choose Cosgrove Hall's *Charlton and the Wheelies* as a superb, slightly surreal animation aimed at younger kids (I think) but also a little bit scary due to a cackling witch, who lived in a black tea kettle and had spies who were mushrooms who would pop up in unlikely places and had staring eyes. Chorlton, the main character, was friendly enough, and most of the characters whizzed about on wheels (an excellent way of avoiding difficult walk cycles!).

At the time, I greatly enjoyed other children's stop-motion series such as *Cockleshell Bay* and *Portland Bill*, but they were forerunners of "sensible" children's stop-motion series like *Postman Pat* and *Fireman Sam*, which although engaging and lovely, the characters and environments are drawn from real life situations and have "safe, believable adventures." Personally, I like to be transported to another place—you get enough of the real world around you every day; animation gives you a chance to push the boundaries, to live in that world you find through the wardrobe...but maybe that says more about me.

KEN: *Were most of the shows that inspired you British productions, or were there any from other countries that stand out in your memory?*

LYNNE: As a young child, although most of the animation I watched was made in the UK or imported American cartoons, I did have exposure to some Russian and East European animation dubbed in English, which was much darker with odd, stylized puppets. These films would be shown at odd times during the day and looked totally different from British animation. I probably watched Lotte Reiniger's fairy tale adaptations, as I remember many of them consisted of cutout animation. Also, as an older child around eleven, I saw *Harpya* by Raoul Servais, a nightmarish tale of a man followed home by an evil mythical creature who is half-woman half-bird and proceeded to torment him, possibly eating him alive, if I remember correctly. The film has very haunting imagery, which made me realize that stop-motion was not just a medium for warmhearted children's entertainment but could be a medium for darker, expressive, more intense storytelling. From the U.S., there was the fantastic partnership of Rankin-Bass, who created one of my all-time favorite stop-motion films, *Mad Monster Party*.

KEN: *On the surface, from a North American perspective, many people get the impression that the UK is one of the biggest havens for stop-motion production, perhaps more so than over here. How is the scene over there from your perspective?*

LYNNE: I never thought of stop-motion being quintessentially British before, as I would have said Russia and East Europe were the biggest producers of stop-motion animation. Certainly, in the UK, we have some hit companies such as Aardman Animation and Hit Entertainment, whose work is known internationally and who have been great commercial successes, but my students from India have grown up watching *Gumby*, which I have never seen.

As a stop-motion animator who also works in 2D, I would say one of my biggest frustrations is that stop-motion is frequently dismissed by producers as being just for small children up to the age of five or six, and after that children want something with more action, faster, not so soft and cutesy. I would really disagree with this; a lot of 2D animation is produced because it is fast and cheap in comparison to making a stop-motion alternative, and I think companies such as Aardman with their films and adverts have been pushing the boundaries of what can be achieved with stop-motion animation, altering people's perception of the medium. Tim Burton's *Corpse Bride* (an American/Anglo production) certainly wasn't a small children's film; this film wasn't about cute little puppets existing in a safe, colorful world. *Corpse Bride* is a melancholy, gothic tale with glorious detailed sets and puppets, appealing to a much older audience, again opening the medium to a wider market. A few years ago in the UK, we had a stop-motion series called *Crapston Villas*, produced by Spitting Image, which went on air very late in the evening, as the antics of the puppet residence of a decrepit group of flats was far too risqué for small children's eyes.

I think stop-motion is still seen as a novelty in the UK, often overlooked by the massive 2D market, but things are changing, and as so many animators now work in CGI, which a few years ago looked like would take over stop-motion (but hasn't), there is a quiet respect for those who still work in a medium that you can actually touch with your hands.

KEN: *So how did you get started working with stop-motion animation?*

LYNNE: As a child, I was an avid model maker, making entire small-scale towns inside my room made out of any materials that came to hand. I drew all the time, mostly characters I invented and the imaginary worlds they lived in. I wanted to be a comic book artist until a visit to the Pantomime when I was 11, where I became transfixed with the beautiful sets and decided to be a theatre designer. It was at Theatre College seven years later, where we designed scaled-down theatre sets and I had access to a model lighting studio, that I really became drawn into animation. I found myself happily spending eight hours at a time in the darkness of the model lighting studio, experimenting with the scaled lights and my model set designs, reproducing different lighting effects. I used to record them with a stills camera, and it wasn't long until I started moving the model actors around and fell heavily in love with the idea of becoming an animator. So I decided to gather what resources I had, bought myself a secondhand Super 8 camera out of the local paper, and watched all the stop-motion animation I could, with a stopwatch in my hand trying to work out the timing. The only book I could lay my hands on about animation was Tony White's *The Animator's Workbook*, which is for drawn animation, but I could adapt some of the basic animation principles to stop-motion. I later spent some time doing work experience at his studio Animus and at Griffilms. Both studios created 2D animation, but I was desperate to get any animation experience that I could.

In my final year at college, although I was actually on a theatre design degree course, I somehow convinced my tutors to let me specialize in animation for my final-year project. This led to [my] making a series of very badly animated but imaginative stop-motion films where I experimented with lots of mediums, colored glass, sand, paint, Plasticine, latex and wire-frame armatures, even ice. Thankfully, my roommates were very patient about the saucepans of sand I dyed on the stove and having little Plasticine models encased in ice blocks nestling among the frozen peas.

After college, I put together a portfolio and a show reel of my work and approached around 20 animation studios, eventually receiving an interview at Ealing Animation, a studio which specialized in stop-motion and 2D graphics, where I was appointed production assistant. I'm sure originally they intended me to stay in the production team, but I had other ideas. My real ambition was to work in the stop-motion studio, which was in the basement, several floors below the 2D studio. As production assistant I was lucky enough to work with both departments and got to know the animators well. The team director, Kevin Griffiths, knew I was very keen and gave me jobs such as prop and material-buying and often requested me to do photocopying and other organizational work for the stop-motion department. After six to nine months I became a full-time assistant model maker, and with the kindness and generosity of the other stop-motion animators, I learnt all I could about stop-motion animation, and within two years had worked my way up to being the assistant to the director, who was at that time Liz Whitaker. Since then I have just kept on going.

KEN: *Which projects that you've worked on are you the most proud of, or were the most challenging?*

LYNNE: My most recent challenging project was eight minutes of animation for a new BBC Digital Web site. I only had eight weeks to devise a character, build the puppet and sets, animate, and edit it. It was extremely tough to get it finished for the deadline, and in the final weeks, I was working 14 to 16 hours a day. Crazy hours are all part and parcel of an animator's job, but my non-animator friends do think it's a bit insane how much time and effort I put into my work. Fortunately, my husband works as a computer programmer, a similar time-consuming occupation, so we can appreciate why we spend so much of our time working and how important it is to get things to be the best they possibly can be.

Some of my favorite projects to work on were for kids TV. *Shrinking Violet* (see Figure 14.2) was a pilot produced by Elephant Productions, and this still stands out as one of my favorite projects I worked on. There were only two model makers working on the sets, myself and Graeme Owen, so I had the opportunity to design and make a lot of the set. Also, it was a bigger scale than I had been used to working on since leaving theatre. The tree we carved was taller than I am (5' 6"). I was able to use my set-painting skills for the background, and to create all the different greens of the grasses and leaves, I got inventive and spent hours mixing standard dye colors into these glorious colors (which luckily didn't stain my bath permanently).

El Nombre (see Figure 14.3), one of the first series I worked on, is a favorite, too; Christopher Lillicrap is such a clever screenwriter, and although we had a low budget, we created a great set. The original set was modified out of cardboard boxes, but you would never guess! I like that alchemy part of stop-motion: the world you re-create for the camera becomes totally real. It was a hit with kids and students who were skipping lectures and later became a bigger series in its own right with a more elaborate set. I liked working on *Numbercrew*, too; by the end of the second series, I had churned out literally hundreds of props. It was hard work, and I had to learn on my feet, but I am grateful to the director Liz Whitaker for allowing me to have so much responsibility, which enabled me to learn a lot. I had the opportunity to design my first sets on this series, which was a step up from doing all the little props no one else wanted to do.

I am always trying to improve my animation technique, and on almost every project I take on, I learn something new, be it a different solution to creating an effect, a better way of animating a character, or a new software program in post-production. Animation is changing so fast there is no time to stagnate; I hope I always continue to keep on going forward. I would be worried if I felt I wasn't learning anything new.

KEN: *What kinds of projects are you currently working on?*

LYNNE: The project I am presently working on is for Golden Cage Films, where I've designed the puppet (see Figure 14.4) and made the set for the film they have written and will help out with the animation. After this project is finished, I'm designing some characters for a pilot.

What I am really excited about at the moment is that I have joined forces with my creative partner Ellen Kleiven to form Ellefolk (www.ellefolk.com). The name Ellefolk derives from the Norwegian word for light elves, a group of mischievous little people derived from Elfish folk who live in the woods and lowlands of Norway, who can change form, foretell the future, sing, and compose fascinating and enraptured music. We both share a love of mythology and fairy tales and are extremely enthusiastic about animation, especially about mixing up different technologies and experimenting with techniques.

Figure 14.2 Set design from *Shrinking Violet* by Lynne Pritchard. (Copyright Elephant Productions.)

Figure 14.3 Set design from *El Nombre* by Lynne Pritchard. (Copyright 1999, The Santa Flamingo Corporation Limited.)

Figure 14.4 Stop-motion puppet built by Lynne Pritchard, with cat for scale.

We are presently working on a few projects, fitting the time to work on ideas around commercial jobs. (After all, a girl has to eat, and there are bills to be paid.) I've got a lot of ideas buzzing around my head at the moment, which is great. My main problem at the moment is finding the time to do everything, but I'd much rather be frantically busy than uninspired. It's a good time creatively for me right now.

KEN: *What challenges do you find in teaching stop-motion to students?*

LYNNE: I think one of my biggest challenges was actually starting to teach stop-motion animation. I was asked the very day after finishing my post-grad in character animation to step in and bridge an emergency gap in an established computer animation course, where the students needed to learn more about animation. The thought of standing in front of a class and actually teaching petrified me! I had one voice in my head saying, "But you don't know anything!" Luckily, the freelancer part of my brain, which never says no to a job, kicked in and I heard myself say, "Sure, I'll give it a go."

Although I had worked consistently in animation for about six years before my post-grad, I still felt very wet behind the ears with a lot to learn. I had mostly worked with guys with over 20 years experience in the industry, so I have a standard that it takes years to become a good animator. However, a wise animator friend, Paul Stone, advised me that I probably knew a lot more than I thought I did, so armed with a tool box of materials and a hastily devised handout on how to make a balsa and wireframe puppet (I felt I had to have a handout to be a proper teacher, and it also helped organize my thoughts), I faced my first class of CGI animators. And they loved it! And surprisingly, I could help them; I could see their animation getting better week by week…it was working! So after my first six sessions were up, to my surprise I was asked back to teach the next term, and since then I've been developing the course, pushing it further and further each term. I didn't realize before that teaching was such a two-way thing: You give out a lot, but you get so much back in return. It's stimulating but exhausting; the students are so inventive; they make me think of things in a different light. I also continue to work in the industry, and I think that helps the students, as I am honest that it's not an easy industry to survive in, but if I am making it, so can they.

In the past, I have been worried that one day I would have a die-hard CGI student who only wanted to work on software packages and give me a lot of attitude about doing girly puppet stuff (sorry guys, no offense; I know most stop-motion animators are men), but so far it hasn't happened. Most of my students are male and want to work in CGI animation and can be initially surprised when they find themselves in my class and I bring out the wire and glue. However, I convince them that animating with a puppet is very similar to animating a rigged character in a CGI and if you can animate well in stop-motion, using straight-ahead acting, then you can animate anything. (Well, that's a line I give them anyway.)

I've studied CGI packages, and I understand how frustrating it is to most of us (whiz kids aside) that we can't get the computer to do what we want. We have an idea in our heads what we want to create, but somehow we just can't re-create it, and our attempts are a poor imitation, until we get to grips with the software, which takes a while. I feel that my stop-motion class gives the students who feel like this a break. In a session, or two they can create a puppet and get straight to experimenting with moving it around in space. Yes, their first attempts are usually way too quick and a bit wobbly, but I ask them to analyze their animation and see how they could improve it. Often students try to be a bit too ambitious with their first scenes, but it does give them the opportunity to be creative without being intimidated by the software. I point out that what they learn in stop-motion class, they can bring back to their exercises they are working on in CGI. Frequently, students are disappointed that the stop-motion software won't add in animation between key frames and that they have to go back and reshoot that scene again, but it does give them a chance to think about what they are animating.

My classes give students an opportunity to be openly creative; some of them haven't used their hands to make things since they were small children, and they often surprise themselves. Making things is part of unlocking the creative process. We talk a lot in class, ideas bounce back and forth, and we experiment with new ideas. I want my students to enjoy my class, but I don't want their work to be sloppy. I'm serious about the students producing good work; it takes time to be a good stop-motion animator, too. Depending on the college I'm working at, I usually teach between 7 to 14 students. It's less hectic when there are fewer students, as there are more computers and other equipment to go round. When 14 people are straightening and twisting aluminum wire all at the same time, things can get a bit crazy, especially if the classroom isn't very large. You need some space to lay out the materials and tools, for students to work on their models and to animate in an area where hopefully you can control the light, and the tripod isn't in danger of being knocked.

KEN: *I can certainly relate to much of that! What kind of equipment do you use in your classes?*

LYNNE: The materials I use are aluminum wire, balsa wood, foam, foam board, cork board (shower mats from B & Q), Plastizote foam (one of the hardest materials to acquire since it's used for packaging really expensive medical equipment, but the manufacturing factory gave me a few free sheets a few years ago), polystyrene balls, air-drying clay, lots of different glues, material scraps, wool and embroidery thread, beads for eyes, and so on; just lots of bits and bobs I find and hoard until the right occasion appears to use them.

At the moment, I tend to start the class off by showing the students how to make a puppet based on a balsa and aluminum wire frame and using foam and material to build up the body (see Figure 14.5) Aluminum wire is by no means as precise and easy to use as ball-and-socket puppets, but they would be too costly and time consuming for a regular class to make. Also, I've worked on lower-budget children's series such as *El Nombre*, where aluminum wire frame puppets worked really well. By building their puppet first, students are encouraged to think about the character they are going to develop. Who are they? What sort of person will they be? How will they move? Later they will develop a simple narrative around their puppet through which they can practice character animation. If I'm teaching a shorter workshop, I will encourage students to use Plasticine or cardboard cutouts, as you can produce animation more immediately.

To capture the animation, I use StopMotionPro. It works on practically every PC computer I have ever installed it on and is easy to use. The onion skin facility is great when you're first learning and getting a feel for stop-motion, and you can play back your work immediately. Normally, I edit the footage and add sound in Premiere; some of my students use Final Cut Pro. In recent years, we've used After Effects to do some post-production for some small special effects and green screen. I started out using digital cameras to shoot the footage, but you couldn't use the onion skin with some of the cameras, and I really wanted my students to have access to that, so I changed to using some old Sony Video cameras we already had at college, and for my own projects, I have a Sony Handycam.

Lighting is a bit more hit and miss. Eventually, I would like to have a proper scaled-down lighting studio in the college with a set of Redhead and Dedo lights and gels, but to get enough lights for several setups would be expensive, so for the time being, I use an assortment of scaled-down and adjustable-angle poise lights bought from furniture stores such as Ikea and Habitat. It works after a fashion, but for green screening, I am working on my college to allow me a space to set up a designated stop-motion studio [that] can be used by stop-motion students who want to work on their projects outside of class. I know how invaluable it was to me as a student to have a space where I could work uninterrupted for several hours at a time. Space in any college is at a premium, but luckily my head of department is very supportive, so we should have our stop-motion studio soon.

Figure 14.5 Maria Kuzmicheva from Lynne's class works on her stop-motion puppet.

KEN: *What advice do you have for aspiring stop-motion animators?*

LYNNE: My advice to anyone who has aspirations of becoming a stop-motion animator is just grab some Plasticine, or whatever material you can get your hands on, and create a character of your own. It's never been easier to make your own stop-motion films; most people have access to a computer, if not at home, at school. You don't need a fancy camera; even a webcam will do if you don't have anything else. You can download free software to capture and edit from the Net, even add your own sound effects or compose your own soundtrack if you're musically minded. There is so much information available out there on animation forums and Web sites. If you're stuck, you can ask for advice; you don't have to wait a week anymore for Kodak to send back your developed roll of Super 8 film only to find out you shot it all out of focus. You can also use the Web as a platform to show your work (YouTube), get feedback, and to look at other animators' work (such as Atom Films).

Although I think you learn the most from getting your hands dirty and working out your own problems that occur when you're animating in stop-motion, I would encourage people to look at other animators' work. I think it's important to stop being a passive consumer of animation and really start analyzing what it is about a certain piece of animation that makes it tick. Is it the design of the characters? The story? What makes it funny or interesting? Is it the timing of that gag that makes it funny? Who's the animator or character designer? What else have they done? On most DVDs of recent animation films, there are documentaries and commentaries about the making of the film. Often, these are fantastic sources of information to learn from. Study other animators' techniques; ask yourself, how do they make their characters come alive?

By all means, be influenced by other animators, but I wouldn't recommend you rip their characters off directly. If you're trying to re-create a famous character with a lot less resources, it is doubtful your version will be a favorable comparison. *The Matrix* has two sequels; do we really need to see another version of someone trying to re-create a fantastical martial art movement with a fixed camera? By all means have a go—a challenge is always a good thing—but what I am trying to say is be original, experiment, push boundaries, let your imagination go wild. When making your own animation film, it's your very own environment you're re-creating. Don't worry about making an animation you think other people want to see. Create a film you, yourself, want to see.

Chapter 15
Distribution

Once you have a short film or some completed animation exercises, for anyone besides your mom to appreciate you, you must get your work seen! Luckily, there are many opportunities for stop-motion animation to be shown and embraced by the general public. This chapter highlights ways to let your work be shown and get noticed, leading to inevitable fame, fortune, and that coveted little golden statue everyone dreams of.

Demo Reels

A demo reel, sometimes referred to as a "show reel," is not generally intended for distribution to be seen by an audience, but rather more as a showcase for your talents. It is like a visual résumé of your animation skills, and it's sent to studio recruiters who are looking for employees. Studios receive dozens of demo reels every week from artists wanting to break into the animation business. The best ones will likely be called in for an interview, which is what really gets them the job. Your demo reel is just a way of knocking on studios' doors and letting them know you exist. First impressions are extremely important, especially in an industry as competitive as animation. It is amazing how many animation hopefuls shoot themselves in the foot by neglecting to follow some simple guidelines for making and submitting a demo reel, so following are some tips to help you.

First of all, when it comes to approaching studios, *do your research!* Do not just compile a list of every studio that does stop-motion and blindly send reels out. Find out who they are and what kind of work they do. Most studios have Web sites that should tell you something about their size, work history, staff, and current projects. Many of them will have a list of job postings, indicating if they are looking for animators, puppet builders, or other personnel. When you send your reel to a studio, you should be able to say, "I hear you are looking for animators," rather than "I need a job." They might need someone to empty their trash, but that won't help you much if you want to animate. Researching the company and showing them you know their history shows them you are interested in working for *them*, and that you're not just in it for yourself. You are offering your talents to serve the studio team. Approach them with the attitude of a humble servant, and let your work reflect this. You may want to have several different versions of your reel, if you have different skills. If one studio is looking for animators while another is looking for set builders, and you can do both, create specific reels that emphasize these respective fields.

Demo reels can be submitted on VHS, as they traditionally have been for many years, and there are some studios that still prefer this format. However, it is becoming more common for DVDs to be submitted, as VHS slips further into extinction with every passing year. This is another good thing to find out while researching the companies to which you apply, in terms of what format they prefer. If you send your reel on VHS, do *not* use the same standard 2-hour tape you use to record your soaps. It is a serious waste of tape, as your reel should be no longer than 1 to 3 minutes. Using a 2-hour tape will also be heavier, making it more expensive for mailing, and it looks extremely unprofessional. Shorter tapes are not sold in most convenience stores, so search for a supplier or warehouse in your area that will sell you blank videotapes of 5 to 10 minutes only. They will usually sell them in bundles of 10 tapes and will also sell paper sleeves to put them in.

Do not start your reel with a test pattern. This is a major turn-off for studio recruiters who have to sit through dozens of reels every day. Start with about 3 to 5 seconds of black, and then create a simple black-and-white title card with your name. Leave it there for about 3 seconds, and then go into your animation. Do not make a flashy title with little movie-premiere floodlights or moving graphics, as this will come across as cheesy. Also, avoid fancy wipe effects to lead into your animation scene; a simple cut will do fine. Your work should speak for itself, and that is what people want to see, so cut to the chase, or the studio might eject your reel before it even starts.

Keep your reel short—like I said, down to only a few minutes. Your reel should not consist of every piece of animation you have ever done, but instead only your absolute best work, which should be the first thing the recruiters see. If your animation does not pique their interest from the very first frame, the reaction will be "Next!," and your reel will end up in the trash. When looking for animators, studios like to see things like dialogue, pantomime acting, or personality walks—basically anything that shows you understand the basic principles of animation and know how to deliver a performance. If your reel grabs them right away, they will continue to watch it until the end. Avoid putting offensive subject matter on your reel, unless you know that is the kind of work the studio produces.

If you have a short film, pick the best animated scenes from the film and start your reel with a montage of sequences. You can put your entire film on afterward, so that if the recruiters like your animation, they may be enticed to actually sit through the whole thing. Starting your reel with the film itself may try a recruiters' patience if they actually have to sit through a title sequence or exposition to get to the best parts.

Keep music to a minimum, if you use any at all. Most studios watch reels with the sound off, unless they are watching a dialogue piece. If you put music on your reel, make sure it is not loud or obnoxious, as this may also send it to the reject pile. Royalty-free music is the best way to go, because it does not infringe on any copyrights and is usually subdued and generic. Music's only purpose should be to enhance the visuals, not compete with them.

Label your reel with a typed label, not a handwritten one. Use a font that is easy to read, and make sure to include your name, phone number, and e-mail address.

Accompany your reel with a cover letter, résumé, and possibly a portfolio. Your cover letter should reflect your interest in the studio and why you feel your skills would be useful to them. Your résumé should be simple and demonstrate your educational background, work experience, and personal interests. Do not make these documents gaudy or artistic—just plain text on good quality bond paper will suffice. Present yourself as willing to learn and work as a team player, and do not come across as arrogant, desperate, or timid. Be yourself!

Once you send your demo reel to a few studios, do not be alarmed if it takes a long time to hear back from them. This will be the case 9 times out of 10. If a studio likes your reel and has an immediate opening, it will contact you. The important thing is to keep developing your skills and send a studio updated reels every 6 months or so. Being called in for an interview is all about timing. To reiterate what I said in Chapter 2, "The Stop-Motion Industry," your reel is typically only half the battle. Networking and nurturing relationships with other artists in the animation field is the best way to stay connected and ultimately get your foot in the door. When studios are looking to hire people, they often do internal referencing among their own connections first, to see if they know anyone good who is looking for work. Your name may be referred by a friend or colleague, and if they have your reel on file already, that is when they will contact you, so make sure you are easily accessible by phone or e-mail.

Personal Web Sites

Another way to showcase your animation is to create your own personal Web site. The same rules about your demo reel apply here: To keep it simple, not too flashy, and not too self-indulgent. Make it fun and creative, but keep it professional and relevant to your artwork. Most personal Web sites consist of links to a personal bio, résumé, portfolio, and a QuickTime movie of your demo reel. You can also include an online filmmaking journal or blog with behind-the-scenes clips or pictures of how your animation was created. There are free Web servers you can use to create simple Web sites, but it looks more professional if you pay for your own domain name. If you do not know HTML coding, then learn a program such as Dreamweaver to create your site.

Internet

In addition to hosting your own site, there are many other opportunities online for showcasing your animation. The Internet is an amazing revolutionary achievement, and few things have contributed more to the global community of animators all over the world. Here are just a few of the most popular sites for submitting and showcasing your stop-motion short films.

www.stopmoshorts.com

The excellent StopMoShorts site was started by a group of regulars from the stopmotionanimation.com message board for the exclusive purpose of showcasing experiments and short films created in stop-motion. Every few months there's a call for submissions called a Visual Haiku, where a series of words are presented that act as inspiration for combining story elements and themes for short animation pieces. You will find many innovative short films on this site, including several excellent tutorials by Mike Brent, Nick Hilligoss, and others. To submit your work to this site, you must encode your film as QuickTime in Sorenson 3 with a file size limit of 20MB.

www.atomfilms.com

Atom Films is a huge site devoted to showcasing short films, music videos, and games. It has have entire sections devoted to animation, including a showcase of stop-motion. Most of Aardman's shorts are available for viewing there, as well as Tim Hittle's shorts, *The Potato Hunter* and *Canhead*, and much more. Atom Films is connected with many festivals and film producers, and it is dedicated to helping independent filmmakers get noticed. It accepts films on tape, disc, or through a Web link, and it requires that your film is 100% original with registered copyright.

www.ifilm.com

Ifilm is one of the leading online media networks, which showcases a vast array of independent films, animation, parodies, music videos, and more. It is affiliated with major networks Viacom and MTV and has a broad spectrum of broadcasting partners. You can find links to practically every major film festival through this site. It has stop-motion films that can be found by clicking the "Shorts" link in the bottom-right corner of the home page, and then clicking the categories for *Animation, Claymation,* and *Lego.* It accepts films on Beta SP or DV tape, or QuickTime files with specific technical specifications, and also requires you to own all the rights to your work.

If you can get your animation seen on any of these Web sites, a great variety of opportunities could open up for you. At the very least, your work will be seen by millions of people around the world. Currently, Web services such as YouTube and PutFile are popular ways to post animation to the Internet. There are often more sites like this popping up, so do a Google search for other opportunities to get your work seen online. It is important to make sure that any Web site or festival you submit work to lets you retain your own copyright.

Festivals

Film festivals are a prime location for submitting your film, networking with other filmmakers, and getting noticed. They range from very small independent events in tiny theaters to large-scale events in giant halls. Many festivals will have workshops, master classes with famous filmmakers, panel discussions, and lots of parties. Most film festivals focus mainly on live-action features, shorts, and documentaries but will still accept animation or have their own category for it. It is best to seek out their Web sites or phone numbers to get details on how to submit a film, as they all have different specifications. Most festivals will have an entry fee ranging from $30 to $50, but some smaller ones might have no fees. Filling out applications and saving up for all of their various fees can turn into a very laborious process, so it's important to do your research and make sure you are sending your work to good-quality festivals. Start out by seeing if there are any festivals in your hometown or anywhere else close by, as these will be the easiest ones to attend. It's always a nice bonus if you are able to attend a festival where your film is showing! If your film is not selected, don't be discouraged, as the competition is very stiff, and there are many others in the same boat. Just keep animating and looking for ways to get your work seen.

For animation exclusively, the biggest opportunities are in several event festivals that are held regularly at a specific location, and also some touring festivals that travel to cities throughout North America. Some of the most popular animation event festivals include these:

◆ Annecy International Animated Film Festival (France), www.annecy.org

◆ Zagreb World Festival of Animated Films (Croatia), www.animafest.hr

◆ Anima Mundi International Animation Festival (Brazil), www.animamundi.com.br

◆ Ottawa International Animation Festival (Canada), www.awn.com/ottawa

There are many other festivals to be found, and the best place to look is the Animation Industry Database at www.awn.com, which lists every festival throughout the world.

Of the touring festival variety, there are many new options as well, and in the U.S. specifically, there are at least two that stand out as prime options for submitting your film with the hopes of having it picked for distribution.

Spike and Mike's Animation Festival (www.spikeandmike.com)

Craig "Spike" Decker and the late Mike Gribble started their underground animation festival in the 1970s, and it quickly grew into a phenomenal cult following, consisting mainly of college kids with an enthusiasm for bizarre independent animation. Since then, two different festivals from Spike and Mike have toured theaters and college campuses all over North America: the Sick & Twisted Festival (for adults only) and the Classic Festival (for all ages). For the stop-motion medium, these festivals have done much to boost the popularity of artists such as Will Vinton, Nick Park, Corky Quackenbush, and even Matt Stone and Trey Parker, who made their first *South Park* short as paper cut-out animation. Attending a Spike and Mike show in your hometown is a rare treat for animation fans, and if you can get your film shown with them, you are bound to see great things happen for you. If they like your film, they are willing to pay you for it and transfer it to 35mm film for distribution. They prefer films submitted on VHS or DVD for prescreening.

The Animation Show (www.animationshow.com)

Following in the footsteps of their mentors Spike and Mike, Mike Judge (creator of *Beavis & Butthead* and *King of the Hill*) and Don Hertzfeldt (creator of short films such as *Rejected* and *The Meaning of Life*) launched their own touring Animation Show in 2001. They have shown all kinds of mediums from all over the world, including stop-motion pieces by Adam Elliot, Peter Cornwell, Pjotr Sapegin, and others. This show is definitely one to watch for as it tours the country, and it's another great place to send your work by submitting it on VHS or DVD.

By getting your work seen through any one of these venues, if you're lucky, a door could be opened for you to either work for a studio or get the opportunity to have your short turned into a series. Make sure to protect yourself from bad business deals, and try at all costs to maintain the integrity and legal rights to your work. The more creative control you can continue to have over your precious animated creations, the better off you will be. Even if your work does not get noticed to this degree, at the very least relish the rare privilege to have your work seen and appreciated by other people who love animation as much as you do.

Of course, you can also organize your own film premiere by renting a movie theater for an hour or so and inviting your friends and family to see your opus on the big screen. I premiered *Snot Living* at the Michigan Theater in Ann Arbor (see Figure 15.1), which was originally a silent movie house built in the 1920s, so it was appropriately screened with live organ accompaniment. It was a great way to celebrate the efforts of everyone involved. Remember, in these CG-saturated times, the world needs more stop-motion, so get it out there!

15. Distribution

Figure 15.1 The marquee at the Michigan Theater for my film's premiere.

Chapter 16
Conclusion

I once did a live puppet performance for kids at a church service, lip syncing a Kermit the Frog puppet to the song *Rainbow Connection*. Afterward, I found out that some of the kids were asking their parents which button I pushed to make him move. I was amazed by this comment, in that what I was doing was so simple; I was only using my hand. My puppet didn't require batteries or a memory chip to entertain them. It made me wonder, is the practice of using our hands to create art or movement going to die out? It seems to me that some children learn how to click a mouse before ever picking up a pencil or sculpting out of clay. The fascination that comes from the tactile experience of physically holding something in your hand and creating the illusion of life, in one way or another, has been around as long as we have inhabited the planet. Thus, I think it's a vital part of what makes us human. What happens if we lose that?

This sci-fi vision of the future may sound a bit bleak, but I do think that computer technology is certainly a wonderful thing in many ways. Without it, the art of stop-motion animation might be in a very different state. The point I'm trying to make is that I hope that the concept of getting one's hands dirty to create traditional art continues to be nurtured from the earliest age. I've noticed that when adults who use computers all day long have the opportunity to move a puppet around, there is a childlike vitality that returns to them for that moment in time, as if they are taken back to the simpler days of Play-Doh and action figures. I only hope that today's younger generation can have enough of their own memories like this to retreat to, along with their electronic blips and bleeps. To me, this is a big part of the reason why stop-motion animation should always be alive and well as an art form. It keeps us connected to something bigger than ourselves, and to our past.

Whether you make stop-motion animation into a lifelong passion or just a brief curiosity, the important thing is that having done it yourself, you have contributed to the history and future of something special—the art of making physical things come to life. It is a creative privilege; even if your puppet falls apart or jitters too much, you are still adding your own pebble to the same road paved by the likes of Ladislas Starewitch, Ray Harryhausen, Will Vinton, and the other professionals interviewed in this book. If you dare to take this creative challenge into your own hands, I hope this book has been useful for you in getting started building puppets and animating, and I hope it serves as a good launching pad for possibly making your own film, starting a new hobby, or being lucky enough to eventually land a job in animation. Today there is more information available about stop-motion than ever before, through books, DVDs, Web sites, and online forums, but experience is always the best teacher. Remember, it's inevitable that you will make mistakes, get frustrated, pull your hair out, and find things that don't work. When this happens, take a deep breath, slow down, do your research, ask for help, and get back into it. It's all part of the process. Enjoy it!

I personally thank you for your interest in keeping this wonderful art form alive, and sincerely wish you the best in all of your projects.

See you in the movies!

Appendix A
Suggested Supplies for Stop-Motion Animation

Basic Animation and Simple Puppet, Set, or Prop Building

The following materials can be found in most hardware stores, art supply stores, craft stores, dollar stores, and hobby shops (Home Depot, Lowe's, True Value, Michael's, Lewiscraft, Opus, or your local neighborhood "mom-and-pop" shops).

Oil-Based Modeling Clay (Plasticine or Van Aken Plastalina)

Sculpey or Fimo Polymer Clay

Sculpting Tool Set (typically made of wood, plastic or metal) or Dental Tools

Mineral Spirits (good for smoothing out clay)

Beads (for eyes, typically made of wood, plastic or glass)

Pasta Machine (for flattening clay)

Styrofoam Balls (round or egg-shaped, in various sizes)

Wire Mesh

Balsa Wood Pieces

Aluminum Wire (comes in various thicknesses)

Alumaloy Sculpture Wire

Steel Wire

Floral Wire

Craft Wire

Wire Cutters

Pipe Cleaners (good poseable alternative to wire)

Needle-Nose Pliers

2B and Blue Col-Erase Pencils (for sketching character designs and thumbnailing)

Dry-Erase Markers

Power Drill

Epoxy Putty (or ProPoxy)

Latex Gloves

K&S Tubing

Small Hand Saw

Miter Box

Hot Glue Gun and Glue Sticks

Spray Adhesive Glue

Super Glue or Two-Part Epoxy Glue

Duct Tape

Miniature Flower Pots

Foam (comes in sheets or ready-made shapes such as hands/fingers for sporting events)

Mattress Foam (rolls in different thicknesses can be bought at the Foam Shop)

Doll Stand

Helping Hand Ball-and-Socket Rig

Climpex System (for building rigs)

Surface Gauge

Toaster Oven

Acrylic Paint

Brushes

X-acto Knife

Sticky Tack (or Fun Tak, Poster Putty)

Tweezers

Cinefoil, Copper or Aluminum Foil

Corkboard

Thumbtacks

Plexiglas

Thin Fishing Line or Monofilament Wire

KY Jelly (for motion blur effects on glass)

Nuts, Bolts, Washers and/or Wing Nuts (for tie-downs)

Scissors

Felt and Fabric Scraps

Sewing Equipment (needles, thread, etc.)

Doll Clothes, Shoes, Wigs, Eyeglasses, Hands, Tights, Accessories

Plastic Doll Armatures

Cotton Pads and Sheeting

Liquid Latex Rubber (mold builder)

Celluclay

Rigid Wrap

Doll House Furniture

Model Foliage, Trees, Grass

Lumber and Tools (saws, screwdrivers, hammers, nails, tape measure, etc.)

C-Clamps

Christmas Lights or Small Bulbs (for practical lights)

Cardboard

Foam Core

Foam Scrapers, Knives, and Cutting Tools

Rosko Video Paint (for chroma-key green or blue backdrop)

Halogen Flood Lights/Spotlights

Junk, Various Odds and Ends

Ball-and-Socket Armature Construction

Ball Bearings

Thread Screws

Cold-Roll Steel Flats

Punch Tools

Pliers

Hand File

Drill

Drill Press Vice

Carbon Steel Rods (for brazing onto balls)

Brazing Flux

Silver Brazing Alloy

Hammer

Allen Key (for tightening tension of joints)

Blowtorch

Suppliers for Ball-and-Socket Armature Kits

Armaverse Armatures (www.armaverse.com)

Tom Brierton Armatures (tombrierton.com/briertonanimation.html)

Clay-Mate (www.clay-mate.com)

Animate Clay (www.animateclay.com: Stop Motion Store Link)

Foam Latex Puppet Building Supplies

Oil-Based Clay (for sculpting)

Ultracal 30 (for mold making)

Potter's Clay (water based and air-hardening)

Potter's Turntable

Loose Weave Burlap

Craft Sticks and Sculpting Tools

Water Spray Bottle

Chisels

Sandpaper and Scraping Tools

Vaseline

Foam Kit (includes latex base, foaming agent, curing agent, and gelling agent)

Mold Release

Apron, Gloves, and Oven Mitts

Electric Mixer (with three speeds)

Safety Goggles

Mixing Bowl

Brushes (for painting and dusting)

Plastic Cups (for measuring foam agents)

Rubber Spatula

Triple Beam Scale

Gauge (for measuring humidity and temperature)

Electric Fan

Mold Straps

Convection Oven

Stopwatch or Timer

Woodburning Tool or Soldering Gun

Cuticle Scissors

Q-tips

Cabosil Powder

Hair Dryer

Balloon Rubber

Foam Latex Paint (or Acrylic Paint with Pros-Aide)

Suppliers

GM Foam, Inc. (www.gmfoam.com)

Burman Industries, Inc. (www.burmanfoam.com)

The Monster Makers (www.monstermakers.com)

Gypsum Solutions (www.gypsumsolutions.com/distributor/map.asp to find a distributor near you for Ultracal 30)

Appendix B
Stop-Motion Animation Studios

USA

Bent Image Lab, Portland, OR
www.bentimagelab.com

Bix Pix Entertainment, Chicago, IL
www.bixpix.com

Chiodo Brothers Productions, Inc, Burbank, CA
www.chiodobros.com

Clokey Productions/Premavision Studios, CA
www.premavision.com

Freak Show Films, New York, NY
www.freakshowfilms.net

FreeWill Entertainment, Portland, OR
www.freewill.tv

John Lemmon Films, Charlotte, NC
www.jlf.com

LAIKA Entertainment, Portland, OR
www.laika.com

Panic Button Pictures, Seattle, WA
www.panicbuttonpictures.com

Screen Novelties, Los Angeles, CA
www.screen-novelties.com

Space Bass Films, Hollywood, CA
www.spacebassfilms.com

Wholesome Products, Beverly Hills, CA
www.wholesomeproducts.com

Canada

Bowes Productions, Inc, Vancouver, BC
www.bowesproductions.com

The Clayman's 3D Cartoon Communications, Vancouver, BC
www.theclayman.com

Cuppa Coffee Studios, Toronto, ON
www.cuppacoffee.com

Global Mechanic/Sleepy Dog Films, Vancouver, BC
www.globalmechanic.com / www.sleepydogfilms.com

The Halifax Film Company, Halifax, NS
www.halifaxfilm.com

Head Gear Animation, Toronto, ON
www.headgearanimation.com

National Film Board of Canada, QC
www.onf.ca

UK

3 Bear Animation, Cumbria
www.3bears.co.uk

Aardman Animations, Bristol
www.aardman.com

Banana Park Animation, London
www.bananapark.co.uk

Cosgrove Hall Films, Manchester
www.chf.co.uk

HIT Entertainment, London
www.hitentertainment.com

Loose Moose Animation, London
www.loosemoose.net

MacKinnon and Saunders, London (puppet building)
www.mackinnonandsaunders.com

Scary Cat Studio, Bristol (puppet building)
www.scarycatstudio.com

Elsewhere

3D Films, Australia
www.plasto-scene.com.au

Animacijas Brigade, Latvia
www.latfilma.lv/ABoom/

Juergen Kling, Germany
www.juergenkling.de/

Kinopravda, Norway
www.kinopravda.no

Pedri Animation, Holland
www.pedri.com

XYZOO Animation, South Africa
www.xyzooanimation.com

Appendix C
Stop-Motion Animation Courses

H ere is a list of some schools that offer courses or workshops in stop-motion animation.

USA

The Art Institute of Pittsburgh
420 Boulevard of the Allies
Pittsburgh, PA 15219
1-800-275-2470
Entertainment Design Program
www.artinstitutes.edu/pittsburgh/index2.asp

Brooks Institute of Photography
801 Alston Road
Santa Barbara, CA 93108
805-966-3888
Specialty Courses: Stop-Motion Animation
www.brooks.edu/programs/mpvideo_sanim.asp

CalArts (California Institute of the Arts)
24700 McBean Parkway
Valencia, CA 91355-2397
661-255-1050
BFA, MFA Programs in Experimental Animation
www.calarts.edu/schools/film/programs/programs-anim-exp.html

Center for Puppetry Arts
1404 Spring Street, NW at 18th
Atlanta, GA 30309-2820
404-873-3089
Puppet Workshops
www.puppet.org/edu/workshops.shtml

College for Creative Studies

201 East Kirby

Detroit, MI 48202-4034

313-664-7698

Animation and Digital Media: Experimental and Stop-Motion Animation

www.ccscad.edu/study/majors/animation

DeAnza College

21250 Stevens Creek Blvd.

Cupertino, CA 95014

408-864-5678

Junior College two-year curriculum. General Animation but can include Stop-Motion at student's option.

http://www.deanza.edu/animation/fac_index.html

Rochester Institute of Technology

One Lomb Memorial Drive

Rochester, NY 14623-5603

585-475-2411

School of Film and Animation, 2065-372 Introduction to Stop-Motion Animation

www.rit.edu/~animate/filmandanimation.htm

Savannah College of Art and Design

PO Box 3146

Savannah, GA 31402-3146

912-525-5100

ANIM 218/318 Stop Motion Courses

www.scad.edu/academic/majors/anim/courses.cfm

School of the Museum of Fine Arts

230 The Fenway

Boston, MA 02115

617-267-6100

Stop-Motion Animation: FLM 1012 C1/N1

www.smfa.edu/Continuing_Education/Fall_Studio_Art_Courses/Film_Animation.asp

School of Visual Arts

209 East 23rd St.

New York, NY 10010-3994

212-592-2000

Stop-Motion Animation: ANC-3020-A

www.schoolofvisualarts.edu/ceCourseFinder/app?sCourse=ANC-3020-A

Canada

Arts Umbrella (clay animation courses for kids)

1286 Cartwright St., Granville Island

Vancouver, BC V6H 3R8

604-681-5268

www.artsumbrella.com/programs-visual-arts-classes.html

Max the Mutt Animation School

952 Queen Street West

Toronto, ON M6J 1G8

416-703-6877

Stop-Motion Workshops

www.maxthemutt.com/StopMotionAnimation.htm

Reel Youth Claymation Workshops
1529 Frances Street
Vancouver, BC V5L 1Z2
604-676-9779
www.reelyouth.ca/clay.html

VanArts (Vancouver Institute of Media Arts)
910-626 W. Pender St.
Vancouver, BC V6B 1V9
604-682-2787
Intro to Stop-Motion Animation, Part-Time Course
www.vanarts.com

UK

Canterbury College
New Dover Road, Canterbury, Kent CT1 3AJ
10-week courses
www.cant-col.ac.uk/courses/art/pt/animation.htm

Cavendish College
35-37 Alfred Place
London WC1E 7DP
www.cavendish.ac.uk/creative/creativehome.htm

Staffordshire University
College Road
Stoke on Trent, Staffordshire ST4 2DE
Stop Motion Animation and Puppetmaking Levels 1 and 2
www.staffs.ac.uk/schools/art_and_design/underinfo/stop_motion.htm

University of the West of England
Bristol School of Animation
Bower Ashton Campus
Kennel Lodge Road, Bristol BS3 2JT
The 3-Month Bristol Animation Course
amd.uwe.ac.uk/index3.asp?pageid=285

Elsewhere

Juergen Kling
Muhlenstrasse 8A
Gelnhausen, Germany
Stop-Motion Workshops
www.juergenkling.de

The Animation Workshop
ETNA (European Training Network for Animation)
Kasernevej 5, 8800 Viborg, Denmark
Partners with animation training centers all throughout Europe.
www.animwork.dk

Appendix D
Timeline of Important Events in the History of Stop-Motion Animation

circa 800 B.C: Potehinos, the first known puppeteer, performs at the theatre of Dionysus in Athens, Greece.

A.D. 130: Principle of persistence of vision proven by Greek astronomer Ptolemy.

1872: Edward Muybridge begins studying motion with strategically placed cameras.

1882: Ladislas Starewitch is born in Moscow; Etienne Jules Marey develops an early prototype for a compact movie camera.

1886: Willis O'Brien is born in California, USA.

1889: Charley Bowers is born in Iowa, USA.

1890: Thomas Edison develops the Kinetoscope, a private viewing station with one long film strip.

1893: Edison opens the first movie studio in New Jersey.

1895: The Lumiere Brothers create the Cinematograph, a combination movie camera and projector; Edison makes trick film *Execution of Mary Queen of Scots*.

1898: Albert E. Smith and J. Stuart Blackton create *The Humpty Dumpty Circus*, the first animated puppet film.

1902: George Melies makes *A Trip to the Moon*.

1906: Blackton makes *Humorous Phases of Funny Faces*, the first sequentially drawn animated film; Emile Cohl makes *Bewitched Matches* on a table top.

1908: George Pal is born in Hungary.

1912: Starewitch makes *Revenge of the Cameraman*, the first narrative puppet film; Jiri Trnka is born in the Czech Republic.

1915: Willis O'Brien starts experimenting with animation.

1918: Starewitch leaves Russia.

1919: O'Brien creates dinosaur animation for *Ghost of Slumber Mountain*.

1920: Starewitch moves to Paris; Ray Harryhausen is born in Los Angeles.

1921: Art Clokey is born in Detroit Michigan, USA.

1923: Experimentation with sound film begins in New York City.

1925: *The Lost World* is released, featuring animation effects by Willis O'Brien.

1926: Lotte Reiniger releases the first animated feature, *The Adventures of Prince Achmed*; Charley Bowers makes his first known live-action/stop-motion short, *Egged On*.

1927: Warner Brothers releases first sound film, *The Jazz Singer*.

1928: The first female Czech animator, Hermina Tyrlova, begins making films.

1930: Charley Bowers makes his first sound film, *It's a Bird*.

1933: Starewitch releases *The Mascot*; RKO releases *King Kong*; George Pal sets up studio in Prague.

1934: Jan Svankmeyer is born in the Czech Republic.

1939: World War II breaks out in Europe; Pal moves to Hollywood and sets up Puppetoon studio; Walt Disney's *Snow White and the Seven Dwarfs* becomes the first widely successful animated feature.

1941: Starewitch's first feature-length puppet film *The Tale of the Fox* is released in France.

1946: Jiri Trnka opens his studio in Czechoslovakia.

1948: Will Vinton is born in Oregon, USA; the first televisions begin making their way into people's homes.

1949: Harryhausen works as O'Brien's protégé on *Mighty Joe Young*.

1950: Pal moves on to start directing live-action sci-fi features, starting with *Destination Moon*.

1951: Phil Tippett is born in Illinois, USA.

1952: Henry Selick is born in New Jersey, USA.

1953: Harryhausen's first Dynamation film, *Beast from 20,000 Fathoms*.

1954: The first American stop-motion feature, *Hansel and Gretel*, is released.

1955: Art Clokey creates *Gumbasia* and the *Gumby* series for television.

1958: Harryhausen ventures into color with his animation for *The Seventh Voyage of Sinbad*; Nick Park is born in the UK, and Tim Burton is born in Burbank, California.

1959: Art Clokey's *Davey and Goliath* is commissioned by the Lutheran Church.

1960: Rankin/Bass begins producing their first *Animagic* series in Japan.

1961: Bob Godfrey brings cutout animation into popularity in the UK with his film *Do-It-Yourself Cartoon Kit*.

1963: *Jason and the Argonauts* is released.

1964: Rankin/Bass' *Rudolph the Red-Nosed Reindeer* debuts on television, as does Serge Danot's *Magic Roundabout* series; Svankmeyer begins making films.

1965: Trnka's last film, *The Hand,* is released.

1969: Terry Gilliam's animation for *Monty Python's Flying Circus* continues the popularity of the cutout technique.

1975: Will Vinton and Bob Gardiner's *Closed Mondays* becomes the first stop-motion film to win an Academy Award for Best Animated Short.

1976: Peter Lord and David Sproxton found Aardman Animation Studios in Bristol, and create the *Morph* character for the BBC.

1977: Co Hoedeman's National Film Board of Canada film *The Sandcastle* wins the Academy Award for Best Animated Short; *Star Wars* is released, featuring stop-motion by Phil Tippett and revolutionizing special effects; Spike and Mike's Animation Festival is born.

1979: The Brothers Quay make their first films; Nickelodeon debuts on cable TV.

1980: *The Empire Strikes Back* is released, featuring first uses of go-motion technique by Tippett at ILM.

1981: *Dragonslayer* and Harryhausen's last film, *Clash of the Titans,* are released; MTV begins broadcasting on cable TV.

1982: Tim Burton directs his first stop-motion short *Vincent* at Walt Disney Studios, with animation by Stephen Chiodo, and develops art for *The Nightmare Before Christmas.*

1984: Clay animation short *Sundae in New York* by Jimmy Picker wins an Academy Award.

1985: Burton leaves Disney and directs his first feature, *Pee-Wee's Big Adventure*; Vinton makes his first feature, *The Adventures of Mark Twain*.

1986: Peter Gabriel's video *Sledgehammer* is released.

1987: *The New Adventures of Gumby* and *Pee-Wee's Playhouse* provide a training ground for a new generation of stop-motion animators.

1988: Vinton's *A Claymation Christmas Celebration* wins an Emmy for Outstanding Animated Program.

1989: Nick Park's *A Grand Day Out* and *Creature Comforts* are released; Video Lunchbox frame-grabbing systems begin making their way into stop-motion production.

1990: Production begins on *The Nightmare Before Christmas* and *Jurassic Park*; Cristoph and Wolfgang Lauenstein's film *Balance* wins an Academy Award.

1991: *Creature Comforts* wins an Academy Award.

1993: *Jurassic Park, The Nightmare Before Christmas,* and Nick Park's *The Wrong Trousers* are all released.

1994: *Bump in the Night* debuts on television; *Wrong Trousers* wins an Academy Award.

1995: Pixar's *Toy Story* is released, ushering in a new medium for feature animation; Nick Park's *A Close Shave* is released.

1996: Henry Selick's *James and the Giant Peach* is released; *Close Shave* wins an Academy Award.

1998: *Celebrity Deathmatch* debuts on MTV; software such as Stop Motion Pro and Framethief become available for use on personal computers.

1999: Vinton's *The PJs* debuts as the first stop-motion prime-time series; Anthony Scott creates StopMotionAnimation.com.

2000: *Chicken Run* is released, the first feature produced by Aardman and Dreamworks.

2001: Henry Selick's *MonkeyBone* is released.

2002: Will Vinton Studios is taken over by Phil Knight and eventually becomes Laika Entertainment; Vinton goes on to start his own company Freewill Entertainment.

2004: Adam Eliott's *Harvie Krumpet* wins an Academy Award.

2005: *Wallace & Gromit: Curse of the Were-Rabbit* and *Corpse Bride* are released within two weeks of each other; *Corpse Bride* is the first stop-motion film to be shot digitally; Aardman's entire studio archive burns down.

2006: *Curse of the Were-Rabbit* becomes the first stop-motion film to win an Academy Award for Best Animated Feature; production begins on Henry Selick's next feature *Coraline*.

Glossary

2D Animation. Two-dimensional animation created by photographing a series of individual drawings in sequence.

A

Academy Award. See *Oscar.*

Analog. Recording format that captures images magnetically rather than digitally.

Anima. The root word for animation, meaning soul, breath or life.

Animagic. Trademarked term for the animated stop-motion films of Rankin-Bass Studios.

Animatic/Story Reel. A reel that syncs storyboard drawings or 3D models to a soundtrack to provide a blueprint for the final appearance and pacing of a show.

Anticipation. The act of an object moving in the opposite direction before executing any action.

Armature. A structure made of plastic, wood, balls-and-sockets, or wire that provides a poseable skeleton for a stop-motion puppet.

Asymmetry. The opposite of symmetry, having variations between the left and right halves of a character.

B

Block Booking. A contractual obligation for movie studios to distribute film packages to theaters in a specific format, mainly implemented in the US in the early 20th century.

Bolex. A brand of 16mm film camera.

C

Cable Release. Manual trigger device that can be attached to a film camera for capturing frames without touching the camera itself.

Celluclay. Trademarked brand of papier-mâché craft material.

CG/CGI. Abbreviations for "Computer Generated" or "Computer Generated Imagery."

Chroma-Key. Video technique that replaces a universal background color with another image for compositing.

Claymation. Term coined by Will Vinton for his brand of stop-motion films animated in clay.

Composition. The manner in which objects, lights, and background are arranged in the frame.

Concept Art. Production artwork used to develop the design of a show.

Cushion. Animation term for a slow-out or slow-in, a gradual deceleration or acceleration of spacing between positions.

D

Dailies. Studio procedure where employees gather in a screening room to review, analyze, and discuss shots in a show as they are completed or in progress.

Demo Reel. A short video or DVD showcase of an animator's work, used for applying at a studio.

D.I.D. "(Dinosaur) Digital Input Device" armature developed by Phil Tippett and his colleagues with electronic encoding for translation into 3D computer models.

Digital SLR Camera. "Single Lens Reflex" camera with manual settings for capturing images digitally.

Dope Sheet. A vernacular term for exposure sheet.

DV/Mini DV. Digital Video, term for brand of camera or tape that captures images digitally.

Dynamation. Trademarked term for animation and film compositing techniques used in the films of Ray Harryhausen.

E

Emmy. Award for excellence in television given out annually to winning nominees by the Academy of Television Arts and Sciences at the Emmy Awards.

Epoxy Putty. A two-part compound material used for plumbing, masonry, and concrete repair, which is also often used for adhering puppet pieces together.

Exposure Sheet. A chart that serves as a guide for an animator to plan movements, break down dialogue, and establish timing for an animation sequence.

F

Film. Strip of celluloid used to capture sequential still images with a movie camera, available in widths measured by millimeters: 8mm, 16mm, 35mm, and 70mm.

Fimo. A brand of polymer clay.

Firewire (IEEE 1394 or I-Link). A serial bus interface connection that provides real-time speed and communication between a computer and video device or hard drive.

Foam Latex/Foam Kit. Material used to create puppets out of molds, consisting of a base and different agents for foaming, curing, and gelling.

Foley Artist. A person who uses various items in a sound studio to create sound effects for film.

Follow-Through. An animation principle used when an object causes another part of that object to trail behind it and overlap its motion.

Frame. An animation/film term for each individual image captured and projected.

Frame Grabber. A video device or software feature that allows an animator to store captured frames and compare them with their current live frame.

Front Projection. Compositing technique that involves projecting foreground elements or other images onto a screen to combine with an actor or puppet set.

G

Go-Motion. Term coined by Phil Tippett and his colleagues at Industrial Light and Magic to describe their stop-motion technique with motion blur effects to achieve greater realism.

H

Hi-8. Brand of analog or digital camera or tape that captures high-resolution images on 8mm video tape.

Hold. An animation term for when a character or object pauses for more than one or two frames, which should generally be a minimum of six frames.

J

Jump Cut. A transition between two shots independent of each other in location, time, or action.

K

K&S Tubing. Brass tubes bought in hobby shops.

L

Life Drawing. The art of drawing from real-life observation.

Light Meter. A device that measures the amount of light reflected by an object so that the correct exposure setting can be adjusted for filming.

M

MacGyver-ing. Slang term based on the popular television personality, involving the creative use of found objects to solve problems or to build pieces for film sets or puppets.

Markers. Computerized dots or marks in a software application that provide reference points for the animator.

Masonite. Trademarked term for brand of fiberboard.

Match Cut. A transition between two shots in the middle of an action.

Matte. A black card that obscures part of an image for compositing effects in film.

Mock-Up. A preliminary version of a puppet or set created for scale or experimentation purposes.

Modeling Clay. Oil-based non-hardening clay commonly used for clay animation.

Mold. A hollow two-part form for shaping plastic or latex material into an exact duplicate of a sculpt.

Morph. Vernacular term for the transition of one form into another.

Motion Blur. A blurring effect given to an object in motion.

Motion Control. Computerized device that programs camera movements.

O

Onion Skinning. Digital feature allowing a stored video image to be superimposed behind a transparency of a live video image.

Oscar. Award for excellence in film given out annually to winning nominees by the Academy of Motion Picture Arts and Sciences at the Academy Awards.

Overlapping Action. An animation principle that involves the staggering of different parts of an object in motion.

P

Persistence of Vision. The scientific principle of the illusion of continuous motion caused by rapid succession of still images.

Pixelation. A stop-motion technique involving the animation of live actors posing for each individual frame.

Plasticine. A specific brand of oil-based clay originating from the UK, also used as a generic term for all modeling clay.

Plexiglas. Trademarked brand of transparent plastic sheeting.

Plussing. An animation term for adding extra exaggeration or emphasis to a pose or action.

Polymer Clay. Moldable clay that can be baked in an oven for hardening.

Post-Production. Final stages that follow principal photography for a show, typically including sound effects, scoring, editing, rendering, duplication, and distribution.

Pre-Production. Preliminary stages that precede the actual shooting of a show, typically including scripting, storyboarding, concept art, puppet-building, sound recording, and animatics.

Prop. A static object that either serves as a background object or for a character to interact with.

ProPoxy. See *Epoxy Putty*.

Puppet. A special kind of doll or sculpture manipulated by a puppeteer or animator to create the illusion of life.

Puppetoons. Film series directed by George Pal at Paramount Studios in the 1930s-40s.

R

Rear Projection. Compositing technique that involves projecting background elements on a screen behind an actor or puppet.

Replacement Animation. Technique made famous mostly by George Pal, involving several different puppets or puppet appendages being replaced in front of the camera for each frame.

Replacement Mouths. Different individual mouths created for changing syllables in character dialogue.

Rig. Device used for holding up an object, often painted out in post-production in each frame.

Rigid Wrap. Trademarked brand of craft material consisting of gauze caked with plaster.

Rotoscoping. A film technique that involves using live-action for reference and drawing or positioning an animated character directly over it for an exact duplication of the movement.

S

Sculpey or Super Sculpey. A brand of polymer clay.

Sculpt. A sculpture made of polymer or modeling clay created to shape a mold around.

Set. A miniature background and environment surroundings for a show.

Shot. A single uninterrupted sequence or image within a film.

Show. Vernacular term used by industry professionals to describe a production.

Show Reel. See *Demo Reel*.

Squash and Stretch. Animation technique involving the squashing and stretching of objects to give the illusion of elasticity, texture, or weight.

Storyboard. A series of static drawings in individual panels that visually describe the action, camera angles, and pacing of a show.

Surface Gauge. A metal pointer on a stand that is used by stop-motion animators to keep track of their movements in each frame.

S-Video. Video connection format that divides a video signal into luminance and chrominance channels.

T

Take. Acting term used to describe characters reacting to or changing their mind about something.

Thumbnailing. The practice of creating tiny sketches to explore a particular movement of animation.

Time-Lapse Photography. The act of taking a series frames in long intervals over an extended period of time to condense time into a shorter span on screen.

Toggling. Flipping back and forth between stored frames and live frames with a frame-grabbing device.

Tripod. A three-legged stand used for keeping a camera steady and positioned into any angle.

U

USB. A universal serial bus interface connection for computer devices and video units.

V

Video Assist. Method of placing a video camera either alongside or looking into the viewfinder of a film camera or still camera in order to feed into a video monitor.

Video Lunchbox. Hardware used for capturing video images.

W

Wacom Tablet. Alternative to a computer mouse that uses a pen and an electronic tablet.

Webcam. A brand of camera used for broadcasting live images directly into a computer.

Z

Zoetrope. An early device used to demonstrate the illusion of moving drawings inside a rotating drum.

Bibliography and Further Reading

Books and Publications on Stop-Motion Animation

Brierton, Tom, *Stop-Motion Armature Machining: A Construction Manual*, MacFarland & Company, 2002

Brierton, Tom, *Stop-Motion Puppet Sculpting: A Manual of Foam Injection, Build-Up and Finishing Techniques*, MacFarland & Company, 2004

Brierton, Tom, *Stop-Motion Filming and Performance: A Guide to Cameras, Lighting and Dramatic Techniques*, MacFarland & Company, 2006

Goldschmidt, Rick, *The Enchanted World of Rankin-Bass*, Miser Bros. Press, 2001

Goldschmidt, Rick, *Rudolph the Red-Nosed Reindeer-The Making of an Animated Classic*, Miser Bros. Press, 2001

Harryhausen, Ray and Dalton, Tony, *Ray Harryhausen—An Animated Life*, Billboard Books, 2004

Harryhausen, Ray and Dalton, Tony, *The Art of Ray Harryhausen*, Billboard Books, 2006

Lane, Andy and Simpson, Paul, *The Art of Wallace & Gromit: The Curse of the Were-Rabbit*, Titan Books, 2005

Lane, Andy, *Creating Creature Comforts*, Pan McMillan, 2003

Lord, Peter and Sibley, Brian, *Creating 3D Animation: The Aardman Book of Filmmaking*, Harry N Abrams, 1998

Salisbury, Mark, *Corpse Bride: An Invitation to the Wedding*, Newmarket, 2005

Shaw, Susannah, *Stop-Motion: Craft Skills for Model Animation*, Focal Press, 2003

Sibley, Brian, *Chicken Run-Hatching the Movie*, Harry N Abrams, 2000

Spess, Marc, *Secrets of Clay Animation Revealed* (e-book available at www.animateclay.com), Animate Clay, 2000

Thompson, Frank, *Tim Burton's Nightmare Before Christmas: The Film, The Art, The Vision*, Disney Editions, 1994/2002

Turner, George E., *Spawn of Skull Island:The Making of King Kong*, Luminary Press, 2002

Webber, Roy P., *The Dinosaur Films of Ray Harryhausen*, McFarland & Company, 2004

Cinefantastique Volume 31, Issue 1 & 2 (Celebrating 100 Years of Stop-Motion Pioneers), 1999

Other Useful Books About Animation and Puppets

Beck, Jerry, *Outlaw Animation: Cutting-Edge Cartoons from the Spike and Mike Festivals*, Harry N Abrams, 2003

Beck, Jerry, *The Animated Movie Guide*, Chicago Review Press, 2005

Blair, Preston, *Cartoon Animation*, Walter Foster, 1994

Curell, David, *The Complete Book of Puppetry*, Plays, 1975

Finch, Christopher, *Jim Henson: The Works-The Art, The Magic, The Imagination*, Random House, 1993

Johnston, Ollie and Thomas, Frank, *Disney Animation: The Illusion of Life*, Disney Editions, revised 1995

Laybourne, Kit, *The Animation Book*, Three Rivers Press, revised edition 1998 (includes chapters on cut-out, object, and puppet animation)

Mazurkewich, Karen, *Cartoon Capers: The History of Canadian Animators*, McArthur & Company, 1999

Simon, Mark, *Producing Independent 2D Character Animation: Making and Selling a Short Film*, Focal Press, 2003

Solomon, Charles, *The History of Animation: Enchanted Drawings*, Random House Value Publishing, Revised edition 1994

Taylor, Richard, *The Encyclopedia of Animation Techniques*, Book Sales, 2004 (includes chapters on stop-motion puppets and sets)

White, Tony, *The Animator's Workbook*, Watson-Guptill, revised 1988

Williams, Richard, *The Animator's Survival Kit*, Faber & Faber, 2002

DVDs with Behind-the-Scenes Features on Stop-Motion Animation

Chicken Run, Dir: Peter Lord, Nick Park, Dreamworks/Aardman, 2000

Corpse Bride, Dir: Tim Burton, Mike Johnson, Warner Brothers, 2005

Creature Comforts: Seasons 1 and 2, Dir: Richard Goleszowski, Sony Pictures, 2003-2006

Davey and Goliath, Volume 1-3, Starlight Home Entertainment

Do-It-Yourself Foam Latex Puppetmaking 101 (with Kathi Zung, available at www.angelfire.com/anime4/zungstudio/)

James and the Giant Peach, Dir: Henry Selick, Touchstone/Disney, 1996

Jurassic Park, Dir: Steven Spielberg, Universal Studios, 1994

King Kong (1933, 2-disc Special Edition), Dir: Merian C. Cooper, Ernest B. Schoedsack, Turner Home Entertainment

The Miracle Maker: The Story of Jesus, Dir: Derek W. Hayes, Stanislov Sokolov, Family Home Entertainment, 2000

MonkeyBone, Dir: Henry Selick, 20th Century Fox, 2001

Monster Island (featuring David Bowes of Bowes Productions, Inc), Dir: Jack Perez, MTV/Insight Films, 2004

The Nightmare Before Christmas, Dir: Henry Selick, Touchstone/Disney, 1993

Wallace and Gromit in Three Amazing Adventures, Dir: Nick Park, Universal, 1996

Wallace and Gromit: The Curse of the Were-Rabbit, Dir: Steve Box, Nick Park, Dreamworks/Aardman, 2005

Other DVDs Worth Viewing

The Brothers Quay Collection: Ten Astonishing Short Films 1984-1993, Kino Video, 2000

The Cameraman's Revenge and Other Fantastic Tales by Ladislas Starewitch, Image Entertainment, 2005

Cartoons for Victory (includes Hermina Tyrlova's *Revolt of the Toys* and Lou Bunin's *Bury the Axis*, available through www.thunderbeananimation.com)

Charley Bowers-The Rediscovery of an American Comic Genius, Lobster Films/Image Entertainment, 2004

The Collected Shorts of Jan Svankmeyer, Kino Video, 2005

George Pal: Flights of Fantasy, Dir: Arnold Leibovit, Image Entertainment, 2005

Monster Road (available from www.brighteyepictures.com), Dir: Brett Ingram, Bright Eye Pictures, 2005

The Puppet Films of Jiri Trnka, Image Entertainment, 1951

The Puppetoon Movie, Dir: Arnold Leibovit, Image Entertainment, 1987

Ray Harryhausen: The Early Years Collection, Sparkhill, 2005

Stop-Motion Madness (coming soon from Thunderbean Animation)

Web Sites for Stop-Motion Animation

www.stopmotionanimation.com (Web Master: Anthony Scott. Message Board, Picture Gallery, Shop, Tons of Links and the very helpful Stop-Motion Handbook.)

www.stopmotionworks.com (Web Master: Lionel Ivan Orozco. News, Galleries, Tutorials, and Links)

www.stopmoshorts.com (Web Master: Eric Scott. Short Films, Contests, Links and Tutorials)

www.picturetrail.com/hilligossnic (Web Master: Nick Hilligoss. Photos and Tutorials.)

www.darkstrider.net (Web Master: Mike Brent. News, Links, Tutorials, and Extensive Video Gallery of Rare European Animation and other Stop-Motion Treasures)

www.animateclay.com (Web Master: Marc Spess. News, Links, Tutorials, Online Shop)

www.loneanimator.com (Web Master: Richard Svensson. Puppet Gallery and Links.)

www.willvinton.net (Will Vinton's Web Site, with studio history and links to current projects.)

www.rankinbass.com (Rick Goldschmidt's Enchanted World of Rankin-Bass Studios)

www.geocities.com/topspeed_jmv/jeremy/ (Jason Vanderhill's tribute to Jeremy "Colargol" the Bear)

perso.wanadoo.fr/ls/tsommair (Informative Site about Ladislas Starewitch by his own grand-daughter, L.B. Martin-Starewitch)

laserblast.multiply.com (Michael Stennick and Space Monster Pictures)

en.wikipedia.org/wiki/Stop_motion_animation (with links to other Wikipedia entries)

Other Web Sites

www.awn.com (Animation World Network)

www.cartoonbrew.com (Cartoon Brew, Amid Amidi, and Jerry Beck's daily reports on the animation world.)

www.imdb.com (The Internet Movie Database)

www.atomfilms.com (Atom Films)

www.ifilm.com (Ifilm)

www.spikeandmike.com (Spike and Mike's Festival of Animation)

www.theanimationshow.com (The Animation Show)

www.sagecraft.com (The Puppetry Home Page)

www.muppetcentral.com (Ultimate Fan Site for Jim Henson's Muppets)

www.rock_afire.tripod.com (Ultimate Fan Site for Chuck E Cheese and Showbiz Pizza Place, Animatronic Characters of the 1980s)

www.kodak.com/US/en/motion/super8/history (History of Super8mm Film)

www.filmsite.org/milestonespre1900s (Timeline of Important Milestones in Film History)

Index

A

Aardman Animation Studios, 26, 33, 57, 286
  Conversation Piece, 262
  foam latex puppets, 159
  Sledgehammer animation, 29
abstract films, 262
The Abyss, 18
Academy Awards, 25
ACM SIGGRAPH (Association for Computing
    Machinery's Special Interest Group on
    Graphics and Interactive Techniques),
    48
acting skills, 46
action shots. *See also* anticipation-action-
    reaction
  character design for, 133
Adobe Photoshop, 48
  rig, removal of, 89–91
Adobe Premiere, 48
  final composite, creating, 234–240
  importing with, 282
The Adventures of Prince Achmed, 31
After Effects, 48
  chroma-keys, adjusting, 234

age of character, 131
Alice, 22
Alice in Wonderland, 32, 215, 260
Allen, Dave, 18
Almaloy, 149
alternate universe sets, 232
aluminum alloy wire, 149
The Amazing Mr. Bickford, 173
analog RCA cable, 67
angles, 270
  for shots, 267–268
Anima Mundi International Animation
    Festival, 300
animagic specials, 28
animateclay.com, 149
"Animated Motion," 59
animating through method, 205
animation. *See also* puppet animation
  basics, 83–84
  cycle, 99
  phase, 40–43
Animation Show, 301
Animation World Network (www.awn.com),
    50

The Animator's Workbook (White), 287
anime, 3
Annecy International Animated Film Festival,
    11, 48, 300
anticipation-action-reaction, 108
  jumping sack animation, 108–113
  for puppet animation, 197–199
Antz, 33
arc of bouncing ball, 92
Archangel Gabriel and the Lady Goose, 21
armatures, 14, 130. *See also* ball-and-socket
    armatures
  ball-and-socket armatures, 146–149
  for clay puppets, 173–174
  designs, 39
  doll armatures, 141–146
  for foam latex molds, 162
  for go-motion technique, 18
  for Hamish McFlea, 137
  Internet resources, 146
  for latex build-up puppets, 166–168
  Starewitch using, 20
  wire armatures, 149
Army of Darkness, 19

art concept, 36
art of the film, 46
ASIFA (International Animated Film
    Association), 48
asymmetrical poses, 189
At Half Past Midnight, 51–63
Atom Films, 257, 295, 299
audio sync, 73
Aupperle, Jim, 18
Australian Broadcasting Corporation, 245
Automatic Moving Company, 9
Avery, Tex, 3, 4, 11
Avi format, 73

B

Baby Snakes, 31, 173
backdrops for sets, 232
backgrounds, 78. *See also* chroma-keys
    composition and, 272
    rig removal and, 89–91
backlights, 78
Bad News, 135, 142
    chroma-keys for, 234
Bagpuss, 285
Baird, Bil, 27
ball-and-socket armatures, 146–149
    Harryhausen, Ray and, 219
balls. *See* bouncing balls
Barrington Bunny, 215, 217, 218
Barta, Jiri, 21
Bartlett, Craig, 29
Bass, Jules, 28
BBC, 29
Beast from 20,000 Fathoms, 16
Beauty and the Beast, 32
Beavis & Butthead, 59, 301

Beetlejuice, 32
Beresford, Elizabeth, 285
Bewitched Matches, 9, 10, 19
Bickford, Bruce, 31, 173
bidding process, 55–56
Big Time, 29
The Big Story, 74
Bitmap format, 73
black characters, 25
Blackton, J. Stuart, 9, 10
blinks, 200, 204
Bob the Builder, 29
body shapes, 131
    for Hamish McFlea, 138
Bolex Brothers, 262
Bolex cameras, 65
Borthwick, Dave, 33
bouncing balls, 92–96
    with pigtails, 104–107
Bowers, Charley, 11–12, 232
Bowes, David, 51–60, 137
breathing sounds, 213
Brent, Mike, 299
Brothers Quay, 22
    abstract films, 262
    Sledgehammer animation, 29
Bruce, Barry, 26
A Bug's Life, 181
building puppets, 129–180. *See also*
    armatures
    character design, 130–135
    clay puppets, 173–176
    cut-out animation, 177
    foam latex methods, 158–165
    latex build-up puppets, 166–172
    molds for, 158–165
    simple wire puppet, building, 150–157

Bump in the Night, 29
Bunch of Fives, 245–246
    Banjo Frogs scene, 249
Bunin, Lou, 25, 32, 215
bunny morph animation, 113–118
Burton, John, 26
Burton, Tim, 19, 32, 34, 181, 286
Bury the Axis, 25

C

California Raisins, 29–30
Calvi, Chris, 40
cameras, 63–64. *See also* shots
    angles, 267–268, 270
    axis line and, 272
    Bolex cameras, 65
    digital SLR cameras, 68–69
    Hilligoss, Nick on, 246, 248
    moves by, 269
    shots, 270
    tripods for, 69–70
    video cameras, 66–68
    webcams, 69
Cameron, James, 18
Canhead, 182, 232, 299
    narrative in, 259
Canon Powershots, 68
capital, raising, 57
capture cards, 70
careers in field, 43–50
The Carrier, 218
Carroll, Lewis, 22
Castin' Craft's Mold Builder, 170
Catizone, Rick, 218
Caveman, 18

Celebrity Deathmatch, 29
Cellular One, 55
Center for Creative Studies (CCS), 215
CG (computer-generated) animation, 3–4
   Larson, Larry on, 220
   Pritchard, Lynne on, 292–293
   steps in, 7–8
Chaplin, Charlie, 260
character design, 130–135
   evolution of character, 135–140
   and gravity, 132–133
characterization films, 262
Charlton and the Wheelies, 286
children, head proportions of, 131
A Christmas Gift, 26
Christmas Dream, 21
chroma-keys, 75
   rig removal and, 89
   working with, 233–240
Chuck E. Cheese's, 129
Clash of the Titans, 16, 17
Classic Festival, 301
classical animation, 3
clay animation, 26
   full feature films, 32
clay puppets, 173–176
Claydreaming, 121
A Claymation Christmas Celebration, 29
clays, 80–81
   for clay puppets, 174
   potter's clay, 160
   for props, 241
   Thomas, Dave on, 126–127
ClayToons, 80–81
cleaning, 81
   clay puppets, 173

A Clockwork Orange, 143
Clockwork Monkey, 142–143
Clokey, Art, 27, 131, 183, 262
Clokey Productions, 27–28
A Close Shave, 26
close-up shots, 264–265
Closed Mondays, 25–26, 262
clothing for Hamish McFlea, 138
Cocklesheel Bay, 286
Cohl, Emile, 10, 12, 19
colors
   chroma-keys, 75
   for clay puppets, 173
   for clays, 80
Colossal Pictures, 183
Combustion, 48
Comfy, 259
commercials, 218
competition in field, 44
composition of shots, 269–272
computers, 70. *See also* software
   knowledge about, 48
continuity of shots, 269
Conversation Pieces, 26, 262
Cook, Randall William, 18
Cooper, Merian C., 14–15
Coragol, 29
Cornwell, Peter, 301
Corpse Bride, 34, 70, 181, 286
   shooting on ones in, 84
cotton strips, working with, 168–169
cover letters with demo reels, 298
Crashbox, 121, 124
crawforddesigns.net, 146
Creation, 14
Creature Comforts, 26, 39, 132, 262

creature effects, 13
Crosspaths, 260–261
Cuppa Coffee Studios, 71, 124–128
Curse of the Were-Rabbit, 34
cushioning holds, 85–86
   for jumping sack animation, 109
cut-out animation, 12, 177
Czechoslovakia, stop-motion in, 20–22

D

Danforth, Jim, 16–17
Danger Productions, 29
Daniels, David, 29
Danot, Serge, 29
Dark Town, 32
The Dark Crystal, 129
Davey and Goliath, 16, 27, 121
   head proportions in, 131
Davey and Goliath's Snowboard Christmas, 181
D'Avino, Carmen, 262
Decker, Craig "Spike," 301
Dedo lights, 77, 293
demo reels, 297–299
designs
   character design, 130–135
   concepts, 36
   for interior sets, 226
   puppet designs, 38–40
   set designs, 38–40, 223
desk lamps, 119
Destination Moon, 25
The Devil Went Down to Georgia, 182
diagram of set, 224

dialogue
character design and, 133
mouth shapes and, 205–207
props and, 244
in puppet animation, 205–213
rhythm for, 208
tips on animating, 213
digital animation, 3
digital SLR cameras, 68–69
digital video cameras, 66–67
dinosaur effects, 14
Disney Studios, 3, 9, 20, 31, 108
The Nightmare Before Christmas, 32–33
Scott, Anthony on, 186
distribution, 297–301
demo reels, 297–299
format for, 282–283
of silent films, 260
***Do-It-Yourself Cartoon Kit,* 12**
Do-It-Yourself Puppetmaking 101 (Zung),
159
doll armatures, 141–146
donut mouths, 205
***The Doodlebug's Circus,* 27**
dope sheets, 37–38, 113–114
blinks. planning for, 204
key poses, recording, 199
Scott, Anthony on, 183
for walking, 192
double takes, 203
Dr. Seuss, 11
***Dragonslayer,* 18**
drawing, 46–47
DreamWorks, 33
***Dumbo,* 20**
Dutch angle shots, 268
DVD format, 282

E

Eastman Kodak company, 26, 63
Edison, Thomas, 9, 130
editing, 263, 275–282
frame editing, 71
Harryhausen, Ray and, 16
education in field, 44–46
effects, 4
in *A Trip to the Moon,* 9
creature effects, 13
80-frame morph, 113–118
***El Nombre,* 288, 290**
Elephant Productions, 288
Ellefolk, 288
Elliot, Adam, 260, 301
***The Emperor's Nightingale,* 31**
***The Empire Strikes Back,* 18**
Engel, Sam, 27
***Epic of Gilgamesh,* 215**
epoxy putty, 168–169
establishing shot, 263
***Evil Dead II,* 18, 218**
***Evolution,* 181**
evolution of character, 135–140
***Execution of Mary, Queen of Scots,* 9**
***Experimental Animation 1933,* 205–206**
exporting to movie files, 73
exposure sheets. *See* dope sheets
exterior sets, 228–231
extreme close-up shots, 265
eyes
blinks, 200, 204
designing, 132
and facial expressions, 200–201
for Hamish McFlea, 139

F

***The Fabulous World of Jules Verne,* 21**
face symbols, 131
facial expressions, 132
for Hamish McFlea, 136
puppet animation and, 199–204
***Family Guy,* 3**
fat characters, 132
feature films, 31–34
Scott, Anthony on, 183
feet. *See also* tie-downs
walking animation, 191–197
***Ferda the Ant,* 21**
***Fern Flowers,* 20**
festivals, 300–301
fill light, 77–78
film, 64–66
film festivals, 300–301
film production, 46
film theory, 46
filmmaking, 255–283
abstract films, 262
characterization films, 262
composition of shots, 269–272
editing, 275–282
ideas for films, 256–257
narrative films, 259–260
personality, objects with, 260–262
pixelation, 262
schedules, creating, 283
sound, recording, 283
storyboarding, 263
titles, creating, 283
types of films, 256–262
Fimo clay, 81
for props, 241

final composites, 234–240
Final Cut Pro, 48
  importing with, 282
Fireman Sam, 286
Firewire connections, 67, 71
  computers with, 70
Firmin, Peter, 285
Fishinger, Oskar, 262
Flame, 48
Flash animation, 12
Flatworld, 177
Fleischer brothers, 9
Flesh Gordon 2, 218
flipping, 87
floral wire, 155
flying illusion, 92
foam latex methods, 158–165
foamation, 29
  full feature films, 32
follow-through, 97–113
  bouncing ball with pigtails animation, 104–107
  vine animation, 98–103
  in walking, 193
foregrounds in composition, 272
formats
  for demo reels, 297–298
  of film, 282–283
  Jpeg format, 73
  Mini DV format, 66
  Mpeg format, 73
The Fox and the Hound, 32
frame averaging, 73
frame editing, 71
frame grabbing/toggling, 42–43, 71, 87, 183–184
FrameThief, 71

Freewill Entertainment, 29
front-projection, 13
Fun in a Bakery Shop, 9

G

Gabriel, Peter, 29
Gardiner, Bob, 25–26
Gargoyle Tower, 228, 230
Gary & Mike, 29
The Gate, 18
Ghost of Slumber Mountain, 14
Ghostbusters, 18
Gilliam, Terry, 12
glare, reducing, 89
glass
  for jumping sack animation, 109
  motion animation with, 91–92
  for motion blur, 214
go-motion technique, 18
Godfrey, Bob, 12, 145
Golden Cage Films, 288
The Golden Voyage of Sinbad, 17
Goldner, Orville, 26
Good Riddance, 245–247
goose-neck desk lamps, 119
A Grand Day Out, 26, 244
gravity, 89–92
  character design and, 132–133
  posing and, 189
The Great Cognito, 26
Greaves, Daniel, 177
Gribble, Mike, 301
Griffiths, Kevin, 287
Grove, George, 229
Gumbasia, 27, 262
Gumby, 27, 39, 121, 185, 286
gypsum, 160–161

H

Hall, Cosgrove, 32, 286
Hall Train Moving Pictures, 124
halogen flood lights, 77
Hamish McFlea, 135–140
  dialogue of, 208–212
  facial expressions of, 199–204
The Hand, 21
hands
  designing, 132
  for Hamish McFlea, 139
Hansel and Gretal: An Opera Fantasy, 32
Harpya, 286
Harris, Megan, 221
Harryhausen, Ray, 15–16, 17, 219, 226, 239, 245, 255, 303
Harvie Krumpet, 260
The Haunted Hotel, 9
HBO Family, 124
HD (High Definition) video, 70, 282
heads
  for Hamish McFlea, 139
  for latex build-up puppets, 166–167
  proportions for, 131
  replacement heads, 203
Henry's World, 121
Henson, Jim, 27, 129, 262
Here Comes Peter Cottontail, 28
Herman, Pee-Wee, 29
hero shots, 40–41
heroic characters, 132
Hertzfeldt, Don, 301
high stage of walk, 192
Hilligoss, Nick, 7, 85, 246–251, 270–273, 299
hip joints, 148

history of stop-motion, 8–11

Hit Entertainment, 286

Hittle, Tim, 182, 232, 259, 299

The Hobbit, 260

Hoedeman, Co, 22

holds, 85. *See also* cushioning holds; slow
    ins/outs
    in dialogue, 213

home movie cameras, 64

Hooker, Matt, 175

Hopkins, Willie, 10

Howdy Doody Show, 27

Hugo Rosenfield Prize, 20

human figure, 131
    and ball-and-socket armatures, 148

Humorous Phases of Funny Faces, 9

The Humpty Dumpty Circus, 9

Hurd, Earl, 9

I

ideas, 35–36, 256–257

ifilm.com, 300

importing animation, 235

in-betweens, 4–5

The Incredibles, 3

Industrial Light & Magic (ILM) studio, 18,
    185

Ingram, Bret, 173

inspiration, 36

instant real-time playback, 72

instructors in field, 44

Internet. *See also* Web sites
    armatures, resources for, 146
    showcasing work on, 299–300

It's a Bird, 11

J

Jackson, Michael, 32

James and the Giant Peach, 32, 128, 181

Japan
    anime, 3
    Rankin-Bass animation, 28–29

Jason and the Argonauts, 16, 17

jittery walks, 193

John Henry and the Inky Poo, 25

Johnson, Mike, 182

joints in ball-and-socket armatures, 148

JoJo's Circus, 29, 121, 124–128

Jones, Chuck, 3

Jpeg format, 73

Judge, Mike, 301

jump cuts, 275

jumping sack animation, 108–113

Jurassic Park, 18–19, 245

Justice Bill, 177

K

Katzenberg, Jeffrey, 32

Kawamoto, Kihachiro, 22

Keaton, Buster, 11, 260

Kelly, Walt, 32

key drawings, 4

key light, 77–78

key poses, 199

Khanzhonkov Studio, 19

kicker light, 77–78

Kinetograph movie cameras, 9

Kinex Studios, 26–27

King Kong, 14–15, 22, 181, 255
    ball-and-socket armatures, 148
    latex build-up puppets, 166

King of the Hill, 301

Kleiven, Ellen, 288

Knight, Phil, 29

The Koala Brothers, 29

Kodak Cinegraph company, 26, 63

Kohn, Justin, 182

Koko the Clown, 9

K&S tubing, 150

Kubrick, Stanley, 143

Kuzmicheva, Maria, 294

L

Laika Entertainment, 33

lamps, 119

Larson, Larry, 215–221

Lasseter, John, 3

The Last Starfighter, 3

latex build-up puppets, 166–172

learning in field, 44–46

Lewis, C. S., 35

life drawing, 46–47

The Life Aquatic with Steve Zissou, 33

Life with Loopy, 177

lights, 77–79
    below, lighting from, 274
    in composition, 273–274
    for exterior sets, 228
    glare from, 89
    Hilligoss, Nick on, 248
    for interior sets, 228
    Pritchard, Lynne on, 293

Lightwave, 48

Lillicrap, Christopher, 288

Linaae, Karethe, 229

line of action, 108
    for pose, 188

The Lion King, 7
The Lion, The Witch and The Wardrobe
    (Lewis), 35
lip smacks, 213
lip sync animation, 213
liquid latex rubber, 170
The Little Mermaid, 32
Little People, 121, 124
live-action posing, 190
Lloyd, Harold, 11
Lobster Films, 11
long shots, 263
looping, 71
Lord, Peter, 26, 29, 33, 262
Lord of the Rings, 3
Losey, Joseph, 11
The Lost World, 14, 18
low angle shots, 267
Lucas, George, 18, 32, 35
lumage, 32
Lunchbox systems, 64
Luxo Jr., 119
Lye, Len, 205–206

M

MacGyver method, 130
Macintosh computer software, 71
MacKinnon and Saunders, 147
Mad Monster Party, 32, 286
MAD TV comedy show, 29
Madagascar, 3
The Mad Potter, 53–54
The Magic Clock, 20
Magic Roundabout, 29
Magpie/Magpie Pro, 207–208

Mahoney, Stephanie, 142
Manipulation, 177
manual focus, 68
Marey, Etienne Jules, 9
markers, 71
    for spacing, 88
    for walking, 195–196
Martin the Cobbler, 26
The Mascot, 20
massage therapists, 41
match cuts, 275
materials, 80–81. *See also* clays
    discovering, 177
    for interior sets, 226
    Internet resources, 146
    Pritchard, Lynne on, 293
    for props, 241
    for puppets, 57
    Rigid Wrap, 145
The Matrix, 295
matte shots, 13
mattress/cushion foam, 153–156
May Street Productions, 54
Maya, 48, 218
McCay, Winsor, 3, 9
McLaren, Norman, 59, 262
The Meaning of Life, 301
medium shots, 264
Melies, George, 9
A Midsummer's Nights Dream, 31
Mighty Joe Young, 15
Mini DV format, 66
miniworlddolls.com, 146
The Miracle Maker, 34
Miracles in Mud, 9, 10
Miyazaki, Hayao, 3
mock ups of sets, 224–225

Modeling, 9
modeling clay, 80
modularhose.com, 146
Mold Builder, 170
Moldovanos, Paul, 163
molds, building puppets with, 158–165
MonkeyBone, 32, 181
Monster Island, 40, 57–58
    chroma-keys for, 233
    exterior set for, 231
Monster Road, 173
Monty Python's Flying Circus, 12
Moonwalker, 32
Morph, 29
morphs, 113–118
motion blur, 214
    Starewitch using, 20
    in walking, 195
motion control camera rigs, 70
mouths
    designing, 133–134
    dialog and, 205–207
    for Hamish McFlea, 139
    mouths, 133–134
movie files, exporting to, 73
Mpeg format, 73
Mr. Bean, 260
MTV, 300
Muppets, 27, 129
Muren, Dennis, 18
Murphy, Eddie, 29
music. *See* sound
music videos, 22, 29
Mutt and Jeff cartoons, 11
Muybridge, Edward, 9
Myerburg, Michael, 32

N

narrative films, 259–260
National Film and Television School, 26
National Film Board, Canada, 22
    "Animated Motion," 59
natural world, 177
negative film, 66
Neighbors, 262
The Neo-Impressionist Painter, 12
networking, 299
New Adventures of Gumby, 27, 181
New Adventures of Pinocchio, 28
Nickelodeon, 29
Nielsen, Katie, 174, 242–243
Nigel puppet, 145
The Nightmare Before Christmas, 19, 20,
    27, 32–33, 36, 181–182
    ball-and-socket armatures, 148
    character design and, 133
    shooting on ones in, 84
Nightmare on Elm Street, 18
Nine Inch Nails, 22
nitrate film, 11
Noah's Ark, 177
NTSC video, 282
Numbercrew, 288

O

Oakes, Steve, 29
objects with personality, 260–262
O'Brien, Willis, 14–15, 19, 239
Ogawa, Junko, 178
Once Upon Australia, 245–246
onion skinning, 71–72, 87
    for bouncing ball movement, 96

opportunities in field, 43–50
The Optimists of Nine Elms, 215
Orozco, Lionel Ivan, 149
Ottawa Film Board, 12
Ottawa International Animation Festival,
    48–49, 300
ovens for foam latex molds, 163
over-the-shoulder shots, 266
overexposed film, 64
overlapping action, 97–113
    for dialogue, 213
    head turns and, 199
    vine animation, 98–103
    in walking, 193
Owens, Graeme, 288
The Owl and the Lemming, 22
Oz, Frank, 129

P

Paddington Bear, 29
paints
    for foam latex puppets, 159
    for latex, 163
    for latex build-up puppets, 170
    Rosko video paint, 233
Pal, George, 15, 22–25, 29, 215
panning by camera, 269
Papp, Russell, 233
Paramount Studios, 24
Park, Nick, 19, 26, 34, 35, 81, 132, 262,
    301. *See also Wallace & Gromit*
Parker, Trey, 12, 301
pass stage of walk, 192
Patel, Dharmali, 179

Paul, John, 32
"The Peanut Vendor," 205–206
Pee-Wee's Big Adventure, 32
Pee-Wee's Playhouse, 29
Pepper kits, 77
Perception Video Recorders, 64
persistence of vision, 9
personality
    and facial expressions, 203
    of Hamish McFlea, 136–137
    objects with, 260–262
    posting and, 189
perspective, 96
Perzanowski, Tom, 148, 221
Pescitelli, Jim, 6
Pess, Marc, 149
Pete Roleum and his Cousins, 11
Phantom Investigators, 177, 181
Philips Radio, 24
photography, 46
Photoshop. *See* Adobe Photoshop
Pib and Pog, 232
pigtails, bouncing ball with, 104–107
Pinard, James, 260–261
pinspot disco lights, 77
Pinwheel, 29
pipe cleaners, 166
Pipes of Pan, 215–216, 218
Pixar Studios, 3, 182
    Luxo Jr., 119
    posing by, 190
    Toy Story 2, 181
pixelation, 262
The PJs, 29, 133
plants in sets, 226
plaster for foam latex puppets, 160

plastic doll armatures, 141–146
Plasticine, 80–81, 174
playing back animation, 88
Plexiglass sets, 75–76
plussing the pose, 188–189
Pogo for President, 32
Pojar, Bretislav, 21
poly resin material, 165
polymer clay props, 242
portfolios with demo reels, 298
Portland Bill, 286
posing, 187–190
    asymmetrical poses, 189
    and composition, 271
    dialog and, 109–210
    Hilligoss, Nick on, 248
    staging for, 187–188
Pospisilova, Vlasta, 21
post-production, 43
post-to-pose, 4
Postgate, Oliver, 285
Postman Pat, 29, 286
The Potato Hunter, 232, 299
potter's clay, 160
POV (point of view) shots, 265
The Primevals, 18
The Prince of Egypt, 33
Princess Nicotine, 9
Pritchard, Lynne, 285–295
production pipeline, 35–43
ProPoxy, 138
props, 241–244
    securing, 226
    for *Wallace & Gromit*, 244
Punch and Judy, 22

puppet animation, 187–214
    anticipation-action-reaction, 197–199
    dialogue, 205–213
    facial expressions, 199–204
    motion blur, 214
    posing, 187–190
    walking, 191–197
Puppetoons, 15, 24, 25, 29, 215

Q

Quackenbush, Corky, 29, 301
Quartz lights, 77
Quay, Stephen and Timothy. *See* Brothers
    Quay
QuickTime format, 73

R

racial stereotypes, 25
Raggedy Ann, 20
Rankin, Arthur, Jr., 28
Rankin-Bass, 28–29, 32, 286
real-time playback, 72
rear-projection, 13–14
recoil stage of walk, 192
Red Hot Riding Hood, 4
Redhead lights, 293
Reel of Knowledge, 9
reflections, 78
Reiniger, Lotte, 12, 31, 286
Rejected, 301
Ren & Stimpy, 4
replacement animation, 22, 24–25. *See also*
    mouths
    heads, 203

resculpting clay puppets, 173
researching studios, 297
résumés with demo reels, 298
Revenge of the Cameraman, 19
Revolt of the Toys, 21
Rigid Wrap, 145
    for exterior sets, 228
rigs, removal of, 89–91
risk-taking, 57
RKO, 14
Robot Chicken, 29, 177
Rodent Stew, 121–123
Room 710, 229
Rosko video paint, 233
rotoscoping, 74
RTV rubber material, 165
rubber balls. *See* bouncing balls
Rudolph and Frosty's Christmas, 32
Rudolph the Red-Nosed Reindeer, 28, 181
Rudolph's Shiny New Year, 28

S

S-video cable, 67
Sam and Friends, 27
The Sand Castle, 22–23
Sandmannchen (Little Sandman), 29
Santa Claus Is Coming to Town, 28
Sapegin, Pjotr, 301
schedules for film, 283
schooling in field, 44–46
Scott, Anthony, 27, 181
    Web site, 50
Sculpey, 39, 80–81, 174
    for props, 241

sculpture, 46
  for foam latex puppets, 159
  tools, 81
secondary drawings, 4
The Secret Adventures of Tom Thumb, 33, 262
Selick, Henry, 32–33, 181
Sellers, Peter, 215
Servais, Raoul, 286
sets, 75–76, 223–226
  alternative methods for, 232–240
  concepts for, 38–40
  designs for, 38–40, 223
  diagram of, 224
  exterior sets, 228–231
  Good Riddance, 247
  interior sets, 226–228
  mock ups of, 224–225
  securing, 226
  for *Wallace & Gromit,* 244
7 Faces of Dr. Lao, 16
The Seventh Voyage of Sinbad, 16, 215, 245
Shaheen, Adam, 124
Shake, 48
Shinde, Yatidranath, 179
shooting on ones, 84
shooting on twos, 84
  in vine animation, 99
short films, 25–26, 255
  demo reels for, 298
shots, 263–266
  angles for, 267–268, 270
  axis line and, 272
  close-up shots, 264–265
  composition of, 269–272
  continuity of, 269

Dutch angle shots, 268
  establishing shot, 263
  long shots, 263
  low angle shots, 267
  medium shots, 264
  over-the-shoulder shots, 266
  POV (point of view) shots, 265
show reels, 297–299
Showbiz Pizza Place, 129
Shrek, 3
Shrinking Violet, 288–289
shy actors, 46
Sick & Twisted Festival, 301
silent films, 260
silhouettes, 188
silicone rubber, 165
Silverston, Anthony, 227
The Simpsons, 3, 29
single-frame capability, 65
Skellington, Jack, 182
Skotak, Bob, 215
Skotak, Dennis, 215
Sledgehammer, 29
The Slipper Cycle, 227
slow ins/outs, 85–86
  in bunny morph animation, 114
  puppet animation and, 197
SLR cameras, 68–69
Smallfilms, 285
Smith, Albert E., 9
Snot Living, 176
  editing shots in, 275–282
  ideas for, 257
  motion blur in, 214
  narrative in, 259
  plotting in, 258
  premier of, 301–302
  sets for, 232

Snow Day, 55
Snow White and the Seven Dwarfs, 31
soft rubber molds, 165
Softimage XSI, 48
software, 71–75
  familiarity with, 48
sound. *See also* dialogue
  audio sync, 73
  in demo reels, 298
  recordings, 37–38, 283
  wave form, viewing as, 208
Sound Forge, 207
South Park, 12, 27, 300
Southworth, Ken, 148
spacing, 84–89
  for bouncing ball movement, 96
  markers for, 88
  for slow ins/outs, 86
  timing and, 84
speed
  spacing and, 85
  of walking, 192
Spielberg, Steven, 18
Spike and Mike's Animation Festival, 301
Spongebob Squarepants, 3
Sproxton, David, 26
squash and stretch, 92–96
  in facial animations, 202
  replacement heads for, 203
St. Amand, Tom, 185
staggering of actions, 97
staging, 187–188
Stanchfield, Steve, 215
Star Wars, 18, 25
Starewitch, Ladislas, 8, 19–20, 31, 303
Stennick, Michael, 225, 241

Stikfas, 109
Stone, Matt, 12, 301
Stop Motion Pro, 71
stopmoshorts.com, 299
stopmotionanimation.com, 184
story reels, 49
storyboards, 37, 263
    lighting in, 273–274
Storytime with Nigel, 145
    idea for, 257
Stoten, David, 74
straight-ahead animation, 4, 6
stride stage of walk, 192
Styrofoam, 173
Sullivan, Tom, 218
Super 8mm cameras, 63, 65
Super Sculpey, 174
supplies. *See* materials
surface gauges, 41
Svankmeyer, Jan, 8, 21–22, 232
swallow sounds, 213
symbols for characters, 130–131

T

Take Off, 54
The Tale of the Fox, 31
The Talking Rainforest, 53–54
Targa, 73
television
    cut-off area, 86
    in other countries, 29
    Scott, Anthony on, 183
    and stop-motion, 26–30
    Thomas, Dave on, 121–128

Terminator 2, 18
test patterns, 298
That Special Gift, 218
Thomas, Dave, 121–128
Thomas, Trey, 182
three-act pattern, 259
Three Blind Mice, 12
3:2 pull downs, 282
3D animation, 3
3D Studio Max, 48
thumbnailing, 97
    jumping sack animation, 108
    for pose, 188
tie-downs, 153–154
    for walking, 191
Tillstrom, Burr, 27
tilting camera, 269
time-lapse photography, 75
The Time Machine, 25
TimePiece, 262
Timespace, 218
timing, 84–89
    for facial expressions, 203
    Hilligoss, Nick on, 248
Tippett, Phil, 18, 185
Tippett Studios, 181
titles, creating, 283
Tom & Jerry, 24
Tool, 22
tough guy characters, 132
Toy Story, 3, 20
Toy Story 2, 181
tracking of camera, 269
traditional animation, 3
trees, constructing, 228
Tremblay, Nicole, 141

A Trip to the Moon, 9
tripods, 69–70
Trnka, Jiri, 21, 22, 31
Tron, 3
Trooper of Xon puppet, 241
trucking camera, 269
Tulips Shall Grow, 25
Twice Upon a Time, 32
Twisteeria, 6, 54, 228
2D animation, 3
    learning, 46
    order of drawings, 4
    rotoscoping, 74
    steps in, 7
Tyrlova, Hermina, 21

U

Ultracal-30, 160
Uncle, Brother, Cousin, 260
undercuts, 159
underexposed film, 64
United Kingdom
    clay animation films in, 26
    and Pritchard, Lynne, 285–295
USB connections, 67, 71

V

Van Aken's Plastalina, 80
VanArts, 71, 285
Vancouver Effects & Animation Festival, 16
varietydistributors.com, 146
Vermithrax, animation of, 18
VHS demo reels, 297–298

Viacom, 300
video-assist device, 42
video cameras, 64, 66–68
    Hilligoss, Nick on, 249
vine animation, 98–103
Vinton, Will, 25–26, 29, 30, 32, 133, 173,
    262, 301, 303
Virtual Dub, 282
voice of characters, 37–38
Voice of the Nightingale, 20
vox pops montage, 262

W

Wacom tablet, 92
walking, 191–197
    mechanics of, 191–192
    speed of, 192
Wallace & Gromit, 26, 33–34, 57, 255
    ball-and-socket armatures, 148–149
    clays for, 81
    set design for, 244
    shooting on twos in, 84
wallpaper designs, 226
War of the Worlds, 25
Wareing, Lucas, 78
Watkins, Seth, 259
Watts, Tim, 74
wave principle, 98–103

Web sites
    on animation careers, 48
    Animation World Network (www.awn.com), 50
    for film festivals, 300
    Scott, Anthony, 184
    showcasing work on, 299
webcams, 69
Welles, Orson, 63
When Dinosaurs Ruled the Earth, 16
Whitaker, Liz, 287–288
White, Tony, 287
white balance, 68
Who Framed Roger Rabbit, 32
Wholesome Productions, 177
Will Vinton Studios, 26, 29
Willy McBean and His Magic Machine, 32
Wind in the Willows, 32
windows, 223
wire armatures, 149
    simple wire puppet, building, 150–157
The Witch's Cat, 27
The Wombles, 285
Women in Animation, 48
Wood, Ivor, 29
wooden table top set, 75–76
work prints, 66
working in animation, 43–50
Worth, John, 76
The Wrong Coast, 29, 121
The Wrong Trousers, 19, 26

X

X-sheets. *See* dope sheets

Y

You Tube, 295

Z

Zagreb World Festival of Animated Films, 48,
    300
Zappa, Frank, 31, 173
Zeman, Karel, 21
zero pose, 197
zoetrope, 8
zoom lenses, 65
zooming camera, 269
Zung, Kathi, 159

License Agreement/Notice of Limited Warranty

By opening the sealed disc container in this book, you agree to the following terms and conditions. If, upon reading the following license agreement and notice of limited warranty, you cannot agree to the terms and conditions set forth, return the unused book with unopened disc to the place where you purchased it for a refund.

License:

The enclosed software is copyrighted by the copyright holder(s) indicated on the software disc. You are licensed to copy the software onto a single computer for use by a single user and to a backup disc. You may not reproduce, make copies, or distribute copies or rent or lease the software in whole or in part, except with written permission of the copyright holder(s). You may transfer the enclosed disc only together with this license, and only if you destroy all other copies of the software and the transferee agrees to the terms of the license. You may not decompile, reverse assemble, or reverse engineer the software.

Notice of Limited Warranty:

The enclosed disc is warranted by Course Technology to be free of physical defects in materials and workmanship for a period of sixty (60) days from end user's purchase of the book/disc combination. During the sixty-day term of the limited warranty, Course Technology will provide a replacement disc upon the return of a defective disc.

Limited Liability:

THE SOLE REMEDY FOR BREACH OF THIS LIMITED WARRANTY SHALL CONSIST ENTIRELY OF REPLACEMENT OF THE DEFECTIVE DISC. IN NO EVENT SHALL COURSE TECHNOLOGY OR THE AUTHOR BE LIABLE FOR ANY OTHER DAMAGES, INCLUDING LOSS OR CORRUPTION OF DATA, CHANGES IN THE FUNCTIONAL CHARACTERISTICS OF THE HARDWARE OR OPERATING SYSTEM, DELETERIOUS INTERACTION WITH OTHER SOFTWARE, OR ANY OTHER SPECIAL, INCIDENTAL, OR CONSEQUENTIAL DAMAGES THAT MAY ARISE, EVEN IF COURSE TECHNOLOGY AND/OR THE AUTHOR HAS PREVIOUSLY BEEN NOTIFIED THAT THE POSSIBILITY OF SUCH DAMAGES EXISTS.

Disclaimer of Warranties:

COURSE TECHNOLOGY AND THE AUTHOR SPECIFICALLY DISCLAIM ANY AND ALL OTHER WARRANTIES, EITHER EXPRESS OR IMPLIED, INCLUDING WARRANTIES OF MERCHANTABILITY, SUITABILITY TO A PARTICULAR TASK OR PURPOSE, OR FREEDOM FROM ERRORS. SOME STATES DO NOT ALLOW FOR EXCLUSION OF IMPLIED WARRANTIES OR LIMITATION OF INCIDENTAL OR CONSEQUENTIAL DAMAGES, SO THESE LIMITATIONS MIGHT NOT APPLY TO YOU.

Other:

This Agreement is governed by the laws of the State of Massachusetts without regard to choice of law principles. The United Convention of Contracts for the International Sale of Goods is specifically disclaimed. This Agreement constitutes the entire agreement between you and Course Technology regarding use of the software.